A Light In The Distance

A LIGHT IN THE THE DISTANCE

By

Stephen Veres

Veres Publishing Company
Burbank, CA

Library of Congress Catalog Card Number: 2002105939

ISBN: 0-9720241-0-7

Veres Publishing Company
E-mail: sveres@verespublishing.com
Website: verespublishing.com

Book Cover by Howard Goldstein

First Printing: June 2002

Manufactured, Typeset and Printed in the United States of America

With love to my kids, my wife, my grandchildren, my family, present and future, and my friends.

SURPRIIIZZE!

Preface

On November 1, 1995, I stood before my Kiwanis Club, ready to speak. I was not nervous; I had spoken to groups many times before, and I preferred to speak freely, without notes. But how could I compress my life into a ten-minute talk?

The Kiwanis president, Bob Gomez, who owned a Mexican restaurant in Burbank, had approached me about two weeks before while I was having dinner at his El Chiquito Restaurant with my wife Elaine. He told me he wanted to do something different at the weekly Kiwanis meetings. Each week he wanted one member to present an eight-to-ten minute "This is Your Life" kind of talk. So here I was – the second member to relate his life story.

I began my talk with some of the key moments in my life. I spoke about the war years, and the horrible conditions we lived under during the Communist rule in Hungary after World War II. I spoke of the revolt in Hungary, which changed our lives forever; and how we risked everything in our daring escape to Austria.

I expressed my gratitude for the generosity and help of strangers, who helped us immigrate to the United States and gave us the opportunity to start our lives over again in a new country. I stated how grateful I was to service organizations like the Kiwanis Club for giving tens of thousands of Hungarian refugees, including my family, the gift of a new life in a free country.

My short life story ended exactly at the ten-minute allotted time, to a standing ovation. The applause moved me, as did the dozens of heartwarming handshakes and comments of "Well done, Steve" from a great many members. Afterwards, several other members came up and told me how much they enjoyed my presentation. One of them, Harvey Branman, even suggested I write a book about my life. I told him that I had started to write one more than two years before, but I was too busy at that time to finish it. Now with more time on my hands, it was time to get back to it.

The writing of this book has been a struggle and at times very painful, but it's something I wanted to do for many years. I'm just glad that I was able to put it into book form. I'm not a writer but decided to write in spite of that! There was a lot more to tell, but it would have added endless pages to this manuscript. I wrote this book principally to tell my story to my children and my friends, and to share my experiences in the hope that this might help and inspire others.

In early 2001, my older brother Laszlo did a paper for his nephew Joshua Béla Veres (son of my brother George and his wife Tanis). Joshua had a school project to do about the Veres family's survival during the Nazi occupation and World War II. Zoltan, my eldest brother, also contributed to this. Much of the early history of the Veres family came from the paper Laszlo did. Thanks to his work and the input of Zoltan and my mom I learned much that I was not aware of. I want to thank my brother Laszlo for allowing me to use part of his paper in my book.

While very few people knew about my writing a book, those who did gave me the courage and strength to see it to the end. This book could never have been written without the enthusiastic support of my wife. A couple of friends read part or all of the manuscript and helped me correct the many spelling errors or use of words. I could not have done it without their help and encouragement.

Very special thanks to Erica Stux for her help in proofreading the entire book. To Bill and Diana Johnson for their encouragement and support. To Howard Goldstein for the book cover. To Craig Friedemann for reading and correcting some of the chapters in the book. Last but not least to the final editor of the book, Tina Farrell. Thanks Tina, for taking on this challenge.

This is a story of faith in my own ability and gratitude for so much, from the shining light of an Austrian border guard's flashlight which led us to freedom, to the countless number of caring people who helped my family and me in our time of need. They gave my family an opportunity that hundreds of millions will never have. This book is also a big thank you to the many more caring and wonderful people whose generosity, guidance, and encouragement helped enable a poor, young Hungarian refugee to be free and a successful citizen in this country — the greatest country on earth. My everlasting gratitude goes to the people who created and made this a great country and to those who gave their lives in the defense of freedom throughout the world.

This is a story of a dream come true. A life filled with hardship, uncertainty, joy, love, fear, and triumph.

Contents

A Light In The Distance

Part I

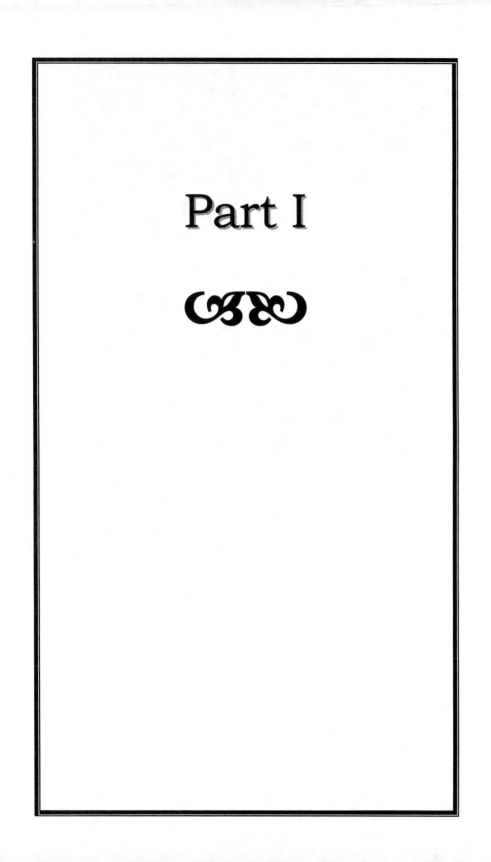

Mom and Dad on November 8, 1932.

1

Early History of the Veres Family

Béla Veres (my father, also known as Apú) was born on July 29, 1905 in Miskolc, a city located in the northeastern part of Hungary. He studied business as a trade.

Klára Lerner (my mother, also known as Anyú) was born on March 17, 1912 in Budapest, Hungary. She was a seamstress. Béla and Klára were married on November 8, 1932 in Budapest. The wedding took place in a Jewish synagogue.

Apú's father's name was Veres István (our grandfather), a bootmaker by trade who died of malaria on the Italian front as a soldier during World War I. Apú was about eleven years old when his father died. Apú never really had a father, but he loved him very much during that short time.

István and Klára Veres had had five children, but only four of them survived. The first one died at childbirth. The oldest, Béla (our father), was followed by three girls: Irén, Bözsi and Eta. Eta is the only girl who had a child, a boy named Miklós or Micú for short. Bözsi had a child, but the child died at a very early age. Irén never married.

The Nazis took our grandfather on Anyú's side, Rottler Miksa, away. (In Hungarian names, the family name comes first.) As they were marching the collected Jews toward the Nazi camps, he fell and broke his leg. Instead of giving him medical help, the Nazis shot him and left him to die. Our grandfather's name is listed in Israel as murdered by the Nazis.

Our grandmother on Anyú's side, Rottler Lerner Janka, an orthodox Jew, survived the Holocaust. After her husband was taken away she went into hiding in a small village. Both she and her husband were Jews from Poland and those Jews were rounded up early, maybe in 1939 or 40. When the Nazis finally captured our grandma, she was dressed as an old woman (she wasn't old then). She told her captors that she was looking for her husband who had left her. The Nazis used her as a cook in their kitchen. The Nazis took her for a German since she conversed with them in perfect German (she spoke the "Hoch Deutsch" dialect). She also spoke Polish, Hebrew and Hungarian.

Our uncles Ármin and Sámuel, Anyú's brothers, and her sister Baba also survived, as did Baba's husband Mihály/Misi.

The marriage of my father and mother caused Apú's side of the family to break away from him; they did not attend the wedding. The birth of the first child, Zoli, brought some peace between the newlyweds and Apú's side of the family. With the exception of Eta, Apú's youngest sister, it took them a long time to accept my mother (if ever) as a member of the Veres family.

In his younger years Apú had wanted to become a Protestant minister and had entered ministry school. Later he quit the ministry school and went on to become an apprentice in the business field. When a Jewish mother gives birth to a child, the child automatically becomes a Jew regardless of the father's religion. My father converted to Judaism. All the Veres boys were thus born as Jews. In 1943, Apú was 38 and Anyú 31 years old.

My oldest brother Zoli was born on January 26, 1935, Laci on June 19, 1937, Pista (me) on July 9, 1941, Gyuri October 26, 1943 and Jancsi on March 9, 1945, just a few months before the end of World War II. All of us boys were born in Budapest.

We were five brothers: Zoltán/Zoli, László/Laci, Stephen (István/Pista), George (György/Gyuri) and John (János/Jancsi), the children of Béla (Apú) and Klára (Anyú) Veres.

We lived on the third floor of an apartment complex in 15 Dobozi Utca (Street), VIII District of Budapest, until early February of 1945. The house we lived in had a yellow star painted on the front door. In our apartment complex, the apartment on the first floor facing the street was empty since the Nazis had deported the Jewish family that used to live there. To deter the Nazis from coming into our apartment, Apú put up a Christmas tree right at the front window of the apartment. This made the Nazis believe that the house had only

Christians living in it. This was a risky move, since the whole neighborhood had a large Jewish population. I guess the plan worked or at least helped.

During the Holocaust years our mother Anyú wore a yellow star on her overcoat every time she went out of the house to do errands. Zoli had a yellow star sewed on his overcoat also, according to Anyú. All Jews had to wear it during the Nazi occupation for easy identification purposes.

Our father, Apú, didn't have to wear one since he was Protestant by birth, although he had converted to Judaism when he married our mother (that was the condition to marry his bride). Apú went through the circumcision ceremony at the age of 26, which is an extremely dangerous procedure at that advanced age. According to Anyú, he almost died after the operation. Today, the medical profession is more advanced, compared to Hungary in the 1930s. Obviously, our father loved his bride very much, for he gave up his own religion and was willing to go through that painful operation.

Since Apú didn't have a Jewish sounding last name, didn't look Jewish, and his birth certificate listed him as Protestant, he was left alone. This gave him the opportunity to hide and protect Jews from the Nazis.

When Laci was born and when Anyú found out that he was a boy she started to cry. Laci was the second child and she wanted a little girl. My parents tried again and another boy, I, was born.

One day, as Anyú was all dressed up and ready to leave the apartment with her sister Baba, Apú walked in unexpectedly and asked where they were going. Anyú said they were going to see a doctor because she did not want another child, due to the struggling conditions our family was in. Apú's reply was that if we could feed and take care of three children, we'd be able to take care of one more. By not aborting the pregnancy the new baby, Gyuri, was born in October 1943.

During the air raids, the sirens would go off, signaling that everybody should get into the bomb shelter located under the apartment as quickly as possible because the incoming airplanes were bombing. Those air raids took place mostly in the middle of the night, although eventually a bomb destroyed our apartment in the daytime. We had to dress very quickly. It was winter and it was always cold. In the total darkness we had to find our way to safety, climbing down the steps from the third floor to the bunker. Many days the sirens went off several times. At times like those we just stayed in the bunker. Apú built a nice little cubicle for us at one corner section in the bunker. We spent many nights there squeezed in with our neighbors like a bunch of sardines, but we children didn't care since we didn't know any other way. We also spent lots of nights with rats, spiders and many other friendly creatures.

During the air raids, airplanes dropped bombs on all the bridges that connected Pest with Buda, and on railroads, water supply tanks, and buildings everywhere. One day a bomb hit our complex, completely wiping out the side of the building where our apartment was, and destroying most of our material belongings. Dust and panic were everywhere. Women put wet towels and handkerchiefs around our faces to protect us children from breathing in all that dust. All the adults acted incredibly fast to protect everyone, especially the children. Amazingly, no one got killed, to the best of my knowledge.

After the bombing we were forced to stay in the bunker. There was no water available, so Apú decided that a hole should be dug. The digging began, but just as we were reaching wet ground, someone ran in yelling that it was snowing outside. The digging stopped, for all of a sudden there was drinking water available from the snow.

One day when we were in the bunker, three Nazis appeared in the courtyard. Actually, they were the Hungarian Nyilasok, members of the Nazi Party in soldier's uniforms. They were looking for Jews to be deported. Apú went to greet them flanked by Zoli on his left and Laci on his right, holding their hands tightly. Zoli was eight and Laci was six years old. They faced the three soldiers with their captain in the middle, a pistol in his hand and the other two on either side of him with loaded rifles on their shoulders. Apú asked them if he could be of assistance to them, to which they replied that they were looking for Jews in hiding. Apú replied in a loud voice, telling them that he was a true Hungarian and that he would not hide Jews. He said to Zoli, "Zoltán, szavald el nekük a Talpra Magyar (recite for them the poem 'Stand up, Hungarians!'). Let us show them that we are dedicated true Hungarians." Zoli jumped forward, in front of the soldiers, and recited the poem. When Zoli was finished, he saluted the Nazis and grabbed

Apú's hand. The solders left and Apú, with Zoli and Laci, went back to the bunker.

After they got back Apú had to change his pants for he had shit in them from being so scared. He took a tremendous chance on his family and with the rest of the Jews' lives that he was protecting. Apú did not look scared to Zoli or Laci at all, but like the bravest of the brave! We were all as close to death as one could be, for Nazis did not hesitate to shoot people on the spot.

The poem "Stand up Magyars!" has a very patriotic theme. Petöfi Sándor, the great Hungarian poet and patriot, wrote it in 1848, during the Hungarian revolution staged against the Hapsburg Empire of Austria. Here is the poem that possibly saved our lives in English translation (I hope it is close):

Stand up Magyars! (Hungarians)!
by Sándor Petöfi

Stand up Hungarians, Your country is calling.
The time is here; it's now or never.
Are we to remain slaves, or are we to be free,
This is the question, take your choice.
To the God of the Magyars'
We take our oath
That we'll not remain slaves!

According to Anyú's recollection, at one time she was taken away by the Gestapo and was put in a camp named "Tatárza." Apú took us children, Zoli, Laci, Gyuri, and me, to the gates of the camp. Apú was holding Gyuri in his arms while the rest of us were standing next to him. This was around May of 1944; Zoli was nine, Laci was a month shy of seven, I was two months shy of three and Gyuri was seven months old. How strangely does destiny work!

An announcement came through the loudspeaker telling all mothers to step aside if they could prove that they had a child less than one year of age. As luck would have it, Anyú saw us children, with Apú holding Gyuri in his arms. She went to tell the captain that her husband was at the gate holding her seven-month old child. When they let Anyú out of the camp, Apú told her, "Nobody, not even God, will ever take you away from me again." Anyú was 32-years old at that time.

She has prayed and thanked God many times since for not aborting her pregnancy. Gyuri saved her life and in turn gave us children a loving mother.

The Russians were coming into Budapest during the early part of January 1945, pushing the Germans back to Germany. The Russian foot soldiers went from house to house sweeping the enemy out of their hiding places. One early morning the shelter door was kicked in, and a couple of Russian soldiers stood in the doorway with machine-guns pointing, screaming, "Germansky! Germansky!" They were looking for German soldiers. One of the alarm clocks went off to their right and caused them to get frightened. They emptied a fusillade of bullets in the direction of the clock, smashing everything in its way. Luckily, no human was killed. Apú told them, "No Germansky here," and offered them something to drink, including perfume, which they drank. The soldiers made Zoli hold up a candle because they were looking for women to satisfy their pleasures. In the dark the women were hastily covering themselves with dark material to make themselves look old and undesirable. Those Russian soldiers were from the region close to Mongolia, judging by their faces. Eventually they left.

To pass time more pleasantly, Apú, with others, built a theater stage in the courtyard and people got on stage to act, in order to provide some form of entertainment for all of us. According to Laci, some of them were really funny. A large piece of rug hung above the stage to act as a curtain. When the show was ready to start the rug was pulled up to let the show begin. In one of the acts, a man and a woman looked in each other's hair for lice, which were plentiful those days. Our parents constantly checked our heads.

Around the middle of February of 1945, about two months before the end of the war in Hungary, Apú used loose lumber to build a box about three feet wide, four-and-a-half feet long and three feet deep. He then proceeded to attach it to a sled we had. Anyú was put inside the box with Gyuri and I and some of our material possessions, which weren't many. A bunch of blankets kept us warm. Anyú was getting very close to delivering the new baby (this was in March). World War II did not officially end until the summer of 1945.

Apú had a house in Rákoscsaba, an outlying district of Budapest, where his mother and two sisters lived with their families. We hit the road with Apú pulling the loaded sled with a cord over his shoulder. Zoli and Laci pushed with all of their might. Laci in the back and Zoli, being older and stronger, on the side at the edge of the road to hold the loaded sled from turning over. Rákoscsaba was about 16 kilometers (10 miles) from our apartment. The winter was very cold and the snow under their feet was crunchy. In the middle of nowhere a truck approached us from the opposite direction, loaded with Russian soldiers. One of the soldiers threw a loaf of bread to us. The fresh bread landed in the snow; now we had something to eat, maybe for the first time that day. We made it to our grandmother's house. Everyone was exhausted. We stayed there until about June of 1945.

One day our parents disappeared, and a few days later Apú returned to us riding on a military truck, and as he jumped off he yelled, "Fiú gyerek! Egy fiú gyerek! (It's a boy! It's a boy!)" Jancsi was born!

Our family portrait taken in 1950:
Top row, myself, Laszlo and Zoltan
Mom, Grandma, George, Dad, and John in the lower row.

2

Just After the War

As the war raged on in Europe and many other places in 1945, we heard rumors of a possible Allied invasion in Europe. Every night my father would listen on his short-wave radio for the latest war news. The radio was set on a very low volume so nobody would know that we were listening to Radio Free Europe and turn us in to the Gestapo. We prayed for a quick end to the war and the safety of our family. Anti-Semitism in Hungary had became more evident and more open during the war years. During the war the Germans killed more than 205,000 Hungarian Jews in concentration camps. Daily reports of allied advances against the German Army on several fronts were broadcast on short-wave radio, and many felt that finally, the war was almost over.

As D-Day began and Allied forces landed in Europe, our hopes and spirits were lifted. The end to the horrors of war and killings was finally on the horizon. At last the liberation of Europe from German occupation was underway. Day after day the people of Hungary waited for the American and British forces to roll down the road, but that never happened.

During the war the Soviet Union had lost millions of their people to the German army. The Russians wanted revenge. This led to an agreement by the leaders of the Allied forces at Yalta in early 1945. It was agreed that the Armed Forces of the Soviet Union be given the go-ahead to push the German troops back to their homeland from the East. The Soviet Army was given the opportunity to liberate Hungary, Poland and the rest of Eastern Europe and march toward Germany. At the same time, the American and British forces were liberating Western Europe and were likewise marching toward Germany.

The people of Hungary hoped that Western parachute troops would descend on their capitol, but that did not happen. In the autumn of 1944 the Germans were turned back by the Soviets. The Soviet army smashed their way to victory in Eastern Europe and once again Hungary's fate was decided by her geographical location.

By January of 1945, the Soviets were deep into Hungary and were pushing toward the capitol, held mainly by tough German units. By mid-February, Budapest was under Soviet control, and their march toward Germany was unstoppable. The Yalta Conference of February 1945 sealed the fate of Hungary and the rest of Eastern Europe. As the Second World War ended, Hungary was under Soviet control.

The joy of our liberation was short-lived. It was just a change in players as we went from German occupation to Soviet occupation. Once again, Hungary came up on the short end of the stick, as had happened for so many years before. The United States helped to rebuild Western Europe, while Hungary and the other Eastern countries were left to the mercy of the Soviet occupational forces. I must give some credit to the Soviet forces — they stopped the murdering of Jews by Nazi sympathizers and anti-Semitic organizations. Hungary did have a great deal of anti-Semitic groups.

The Soviet occupation troops engaged in large scale looting and rape. Under the Communist regime the dreaded state security authority, AVO, was set up. The AVO was a well-equipped military unit under the control of the Communist regime. They carried out the dirty work of their superiors. Hungary was flooded with Soviet propaganda. The teachings of Marx, Lenin, and Stalin were forced upon the school children of Hungary. Hungarian history was belittled while Russian history was glorified.

My earliest clear memories begin from 1948 on, when I was about seven years old. Growing up under Communism was something that could never be understood by someone unless he or she had the misfortune to experience it.

Soon after the war was over, we moved back to Budapest, to our new apartment. Our new residence was located on 21 Karácsony Sándor Utca 4th floor. (In Hungary the first floor equals the second floor in the United States.) This was a luxury apartment by Hungarian standards with three bedrooms, kitchen, long hallway, bathroom and a small room off the kitchen area where the maid slept. For a short time we had a maid. The apartment was totally empty with the exception of a mattress on the floor, and that is where we slept. Slowly we got some furniture. Life was going on.

There was a bakery down the street from us that was closed, for the Nazis had taken the owners away. I think their name was Engel. Apú somehow reopened the bakery and with the help of others they fired up the ovens. Thus bread was again provided for the neighborhood. Food was scarce. The bakery was producing bread day and night to keep up with the demand. Laci remembers being in the bakery with Zoli and possibly with me, helping with the work. I'm not sure if we were much help. Laci liked the smell and the freshly baked bread tasted delicious. People brought pots full of uncooked beans to be baked in the oven. The baked beans were set on the floor waiting to be picked up by the costumers. One day one of the adult helpers stepped into one of the pots, kicking over everything. We kids were laughing. He wasn't. As Jancsi would say, "Can't he take a joke?"

The bakery business stopped when a man by the name of Hidas turned Apú in to the police for being against the Jews during the Nazi occupation. He was put in jail, but at the trial a few days later he was acquitted. Jews from the neighborhood showed up at the trial, telling the judge that because of Béla Veres, they were alive today, for he had hidden them and protected them from the Nazis.

Our parents tried lots of small business ventures, including selling calendars, salt, pesticide, and cooking oil at the local market. There was an open market near where we lived, something similar to a farmers market here in the United States.

I started to work at a very early age. When I was just five years old I would help sell cooking oil at a local market with my mother. I was told later in life that I was a very good and handsome salesman. A few years later when I was seven or eight years old, I would help my grandmother at the same market to sell butter, cheese, eggs, and salami. I also used to hang out and help after school at a little grocery store next door to our house. Working at the market and the grocery store was something I liked because I did not have to think of homework or school; also my family needed the money. The family

that owned the grocery store next door was just wonderful to me —
they were like a second family. My mom felt comfortable with me
being down there and I learned a lot about dealing with customers at a
very young age. I was happier working than doing almost anything
else, which is true even now; I just don't like to sit around and do
nothing.

During the Christmas season decorative ornaments were sold by
our parents in the warehouse building located at the bank of the
Danube *(Duna)* River. A stand was set up by Apú, always beautifully
decorated by him to attract more and more costumers. Zoli and Laci
helped, especially Zoli, for he was a great salesman too, while Laci
was very shy as a helper. It was always very cold at the warehouse and
they did lots of moving around, jumping, etc., to keep themselves
warm.

During the spring and summer months Anyú would get hold of old
bicycle tires and we would cut rubber bands out of them and sell them
to housewives at the market. They were to be used for many different
purposes — mainly for sealing jars of cooked tomatoes or different
types of cooked fruits with plastic wrap, to be preserved for the winter
months. Anyú tried many different things in her lifetime to augment
the family income, and it was always for the children.

Since Anyú was a seamstress, she worked at a clothing business out
of our home. Apú acted as tailor; with the use of patterns he cut fabric
to be sewed by Anyú. Apú decided that he should take different
clothing items to the market *(vására)* outside of the city of Budapest to
make money. Suddenly, instead of making dresses, men's shirts were
produced at our home. Apú's sister, Eta Néni, traveled in from
Rákoscsaba every day to help with the operation. They worked
extremely hard at the sewing machine, pumping the treadle hour after
hour. It seemed to us that Anyú was at the machine when we children
went to bed, and she was at it when we woke up.

Besides shirts, Apú also sold pants, coats and complete suits to the
farmers. It was a hard job getting on the train day after day, visiting
different towns, setting up tents early in the morning in rain, snow or
sunshine, to be ready for the first customer. Sleeping at train stations
or on the train's wooden benches is not an ideal situation, but that
didn't bother our dad, for he had a major responsibility to his family.
Sometimes the market was good and sometimes it was terrible. This
would keep him from home for many days or weeks at a time. He had

clothing-filled containers shipped from one market to the next open market. To save on shipping costs, my father lugged several duffel bags, like heavy suitcases, with him on the bus or train. He made enough money to send five boys through school, provide them with nice clothing and house them in a nice apartment. We were considered middle class under Hungarian standards. We did not belong to or sympathize with the Communist Party.

In 1950, the Communist regime nationalized the private businesses, factories and farms. Loyal Communist Party members were put in top positions in factories and businesses. This added to the steady decline in national production. Farmers were deprived of their farms and forced to work on the now-government-controlled collective farms. Discontent among them created a plunge in production and led to food shortages. Much of Hungary's output was shipped to the Soviet Union — items such as wheat, corn, trucks, aluminum, and wine. This was our repayment to our liberators, the Soviet Union.

As the years went by we were robbed blind by the Russians and were forced to surrender to Communist ideology. One by one we lost our rights and our liberties. We lost our freedom of speech, freedom of religion, and freedom of the press. We had no choice but to give in to an overwhelming power that had a large military force stationed in our country and the rest of Eastern Europe to enforce their ideology.

One day the Communists took away all of that little business our parents had created and Apú was crushed. On August 16, 1951, I was home with my mother and two younger brothers when we heard a knock at the door. My mother answered the door and I saw her talking to two men in the doorway. In a very short time Mom began to cry and became hysterical. The men came into the apartment and went into each room. They were looking for inventory of our business. They found some in a closet and put a seal on the door. They were government agents and were nationalizing our business. I was only ten years old at the time and I didn't understand the meaning of the events until years later. The government took our business, complete with all inventory, without compensation to us. As the agents were leaving the apartment they saw a large framed family picture on the wall with Mom, Dad and the five boys. One of them turned to my mother and said that he was very sorry and then he walked out. In just a matter of minutes we lost everything we owned. Apú had kept most of our money in his business inventory and had only taken out enough money from the business to pay the bills and feed the family. We were left with very little money and no jobs.

The same fate awaited thousands of other Hungarian business owners and farmers as the government nationalized all businesses and farms. My father was not home at the time and did not find out what had happened until a couple of days later, when he came home from a business trip. I wasn't home when he arrived so I don't know of his first reaction when Mom told him the news. The next few weeks were very difficult for us. My father was forced to go to work in a factory, learning a new trade. At that time my oldest brother Zoltan was studying at a university in Budapest. My father could no longer afford to pay for the university and was forced to remove Zoltan from school. The events devastated my father; as he was now forced to send Zoltan to get a job and help support the family. Zoltan was sixteen and a half years old and was a very good student. His teachers begged my family to keep Zoltan in school, but we just couldn't afford it.

Very few dared to oppose the Communist regime. Opposition members of the regime were banished to remote villages or eliminated by the AVO. During the 40s and 50s many governments were put into power by the Soviet Union, only to be replaced quickly when they fell out of favor. Several of our leaders were jailed and some were executed for not carrying out Soviet orders. After the death of Joseph Stalin in 1953, the reign of terror in Hungary started to slow down.

The war, the Nazis, and finally the Communists were gradually getting to my father and, according to Anyú, he almost committed suicide! He was gradually cracking up, which pretty much explains his fiery temper. Both of our parents must have gone through some incredible hardships and stresses in their lives.

Apú was a strong disciplinarian and had a mind of his own. I didn't agree with his philosophy that only men are rulers of the house and everything has to be done their way without questioning the decision — remember the movie "Fiddler on the Roof"?

We children, all grown, will never understand the hardships and the toll all of that took on Apú. Besides everything else I have already described he also served as a soldier in the Hungarian Army. He had to report many times for duty, disturbing the progress of his life when he was in his late 30s. He fought on the Russian front, and was there during the retreat over frozen fields when the Russian Red Army pushed the Germans and Hungarians back. Hungary had joined the Germans in the fight against Russia, thinking that they would beat the Russian army, but they were proven wrong. Many of his friends and soldier colleagues froze to death in the process, having no shelter or food. Surely these situations affected him and at the same time made him a stronger person and a survivor! Will we ever understand and comprehend all this?

The apartment building in Budapest where I lived until 1957.
It was run-down and a sad site to see.
Photo was taken by me on our visit back to Budapest in 1998.

3

A Communist Ruled Childhood

My father became a very angry and bitter man and he would take his frustration out on us many times. Dad worked very hard in his life to support his family but his anger was often uncontrollable. The smallest thing we did wrong would set him off and he would smack us around. He always had a bad temper, but because he had been away so much before it hadn't seemed as bad. I was at the receiving end of a share of his anger, as were my other brothers. He became very bitter and a changed man after the loss of his business, as things turned really bad and did not change for many years.

I had started first grade in 1947. The school was a few miles from where I lived in the 8th District in Budapest. I was doing fairly well in the lower grades but that changed in the fourth grade. I got bored in school and hated to do my homework. When my mom asked me if I had any homework to do, I would tell her that I had already done it in school.

My father was a dictator in our house and would listen to nobody. He would make up his mind on something and nobody could change his mind or try to reason with him. None of us or any of our relatives would dare to challenge his orders. Talking back to him was not a good idea. It would bring instant response in the form of a slap on the face or a spanking on our rear-ends. Sometimes he would hit us so hard that for many days it would be painful to sit down on a hard chair. Many times we were punished more harshly than we should have been for the mischief we caused. His belt was his favorite weapon and when he took his belt off, we knew we were in a lot of trouble. Few discussions with Dad were possible — even Mom was afraid of him, for he also yelled and screamed at her.

On one occasion when I was about 10 years old, I got into big trouble with the law and then with my father. It was about 4:00 p.m. on a mild sunny Saturday afternoon. I was at a playground with my best friend, Tommy. Tommy had a soccer ball with him and we had started to kick the ball around when two other kids asked if they could play also. We had seen these two other kids at the playground several times before. We only knew them by their first name, but we assumed that they did not live too far from the playground. We said sure. We played soccer and were just fooling around, having a good time. But about fifteen minutes later the other two boys picked up some rocks and started to throw them at a passing streetcar, hitting the side window several times. The conductor stopped the streetcar and started to run toward us.

As he approached us, the kids throwing the rocks started to run, but Tommy and I just stood there. Why should we run? We didn't do anything wrong. We stayed there and walked slowly towards the soccer ball we were playing with prior to the incident. In just a few seconds an angry conductor grabbed Tommy and me and started to scream at us. He told us that we broke his window and we were in big trouble; he started to drag us back to his streetcar. We tried to tell him that it was the two other kids and that we had done nothing wrong. We told him to let us go.

That was not to be the case. He dragged us onto the streetcar and had a couple of older men hold us while he went back to his driver's seat and started the vehicle. We were scared, not knowing what he was going to do with us. A couple of stops later the conductor saw a policeman near an intersection. He stopped the streetcar and went over to the policeman. They talked for a little while as the conductor pointed toward us and told his side of the story. They walked back to the streetcar; the policeman took us off the car and then to a police station, which was a short distance away. Now Tommy and I got really nervous and started to cry, but it did not help. They questioned us and wanted to know who cracked the window. By this time we were horrified and frightened because they did not believe us. We finally gave them the first names of the two kids who threw the rocks, but we did not know their last names or where they lived. They asked us our names, where we lived and which school we went to. The two other kids were about a year older than Tommy and me, so we didn't know what school they attended. They called us liars and put us both in a cell and locked the door. Now we were hysterical.

We were sitting in jail for the first time in our life and it wasn't even our fault. Finally around 9:00 p.m. they took us from the jail to a room near the front door. Sitting at the table were my father and Tommy's mother, talking with the interrogating policemen. Our parents were not very pleased as they started to yell at us. We also got slapped around a little. After a few minutes of being chewed out by our parents, we were allowed to leave the police station in their custody. We had been locked up for more than five hours.

The one-kilometer walk toward our house was terrible for me. My father yelled and slapped me on the head and face all the way home. I knew that this was just the beginning and that he was going to beat the heck out of me once we got home. I told Dad that we hadn't done anything wrong and that it was the other two kids who cracked the window. I told him that they had run away and we didn't, because we hadn't done anything wrong. There was no reason for me to run because I didn't throw any rocks at the streetcar. But the more I protested my innocence and Tommy's, the angrier my Dad got. Once we got home he took off his belt and spanked my bottom so hard that it bled from the lashes. My mother could not do anything about the punishment. Her pleas didn't do any good as he continued to spank me harder and harder. She left the room, as she could not bear to watch it. He was cursing me and telling me to shut up. He told me that I was stupid and an idiot for not running away. So I got punished for not running away. I felt betrayed by my own family, and for weeks I was very angry with my father. I was restricted to our home after school for many months, and I kept away from my father during that time out of fear.

That was the worst beating I ever got from my father, but it wasn't even close to the punishment my younger brother John would get. While it took many weeks for my behind to heal from the whipping I got, the scars that John got would be with him for the rest of his life. One day when John was about eight or nine years old, he stole something from a friend (I think). My father found out about it and really went crazy. He wrapped John's hand with a cloth, put some kind of flammable fluid over it and ignited it. John's hand was on fire while we all screamed, including my mom, at my father to stop it, which he finally did by dousing it in water. I will never forget that horrifying day; I would have never expected him to do such a horrible thing. I knew that he was mean when he got angry, but this was not something a normal person would do to his son. My mother, George, John and I were the only ones at home. I hated my father for a very long time because of what he had done to John.

In school, things got much worse for me in the early 1950s. We were forced to learn the Russian language. This got me very angry. The only subjects I liked in school were Mathematics, Science/Chemistry and Choral Singing. I hated all other subjects, especially History, and now the Russian language. I liked working and preferred that rather than school or homework.

I became a headache for my mother. She was called into the principal's office on many occasions because I wasn't paying attention in class and wouldn't do my homework. When the teachers would ask for my homework I would tell them that I had accidentally left it at home or that I was sick. They stopped buying that answer eventually. Our history teacher did not take my actions lightly. Besides giving me low grades, he would pick me up by my hair and force me to walk around on my tiptoes as he was pulling me up. It hurt a great deal but I refused to give in and continued to ignore History as well as the other subjects I hated.

In my mind I did not care who was the king of another country or who ruled Rome a hundred or more years before I was even born. What use would that be to me when I was working in a factory in years to come? I wanted them to teach me about tools and equipment. I wanted to learn a trade. I felt that Math and Science should have been enough, and maybe a little sports on the side. Most of the time I did my math and science homework while we were in other classes. I sat near the back of the class so my teachers did not see me doing homework on other subjects. I'm happy to say that I was good at some things in school. I was the best in my class in Math and in the top three in Science/Physics.

I could not understand that first you had to be a kid, go to school, play, do homework, get into trouble, grow up and then learn a trade. I was impatient and stubborn. I wanted to work more than anything else. I was told many times to just be a kid and that there was plenty of time in my life to work after I finished school. But I was just eager to get started and to make money at an early age. At age eight, I got interested in model airplanes. At first, I built ultra-lights, then rubber-powered planes out of balsa wood. It became my hobby.

At age eleven I began to sell homemade products at the local open market. Canning fruits and vegetables is a commonplace activity in most households in Hungary. Our house was no different. Making jam was quite easy; our family canned fruits every year. After canned fruit is cooked, it is put into a glass jar and covered with cellophane wrap, which is held in place by one or two rubber bands. The problem was that rubber bands were not easy to buy, so as I mentioned earlier, Mom decided to make and market our own. Mom would buy used bicycle tire inner tubes and I would cut them up into different widths. We would put 25 into a package and sell it at the market. We also knitted nylon shopping bags that we sold at the market, also my mom's idea. I made the special knitting tools out of wood, but I had help in the making of the nylon bags. We all tried to help the family financially as much as possible. I preferred making and selling things to going to school or doing homework. My mother never had to push me to work, as I was self-motivated and eager to do it. Most of the things we made we learned on our own. We lived a very simple life in Hungary, along with most of the ten million other citizens of our country.

Living under Communist control was a trying time for most Hungarians. We had lost our freedom: freedom of speech, religion, free enterprise, free press, our businesses and farms. We were not allowed to leave the country. We were all prisoners of a closed system and were only able to read and listen to Communist propaganda as the newspapers. The government also controlled the radio broadcasts.

At age twelve I started to fix electrical appliances such as irons and lamps. Electricity fascinated me and I would take most electrical appliances apart and figure out how they worked. There were about twenty-six apartments in the building where we lived. One day, when I was working on a broken electric iron in the kitchen, one of our neighbors came over for a visit with my mom. She saw me repairing the iron. She was very impressed with the way I fixed it and with the way I handled the tools. My mom told her that I could fix almost anything that broke, and proudly showed her some of the things I had repaired or built. It didn't take long for my neighbor to bring over broken lamps and small appliances for me to fix. Within a few days I had all the items fixed and returned in good-as-new condition. Word got out quickly in the building and I was called by other neighbors to install doorbells, light fixtures, repair wiring, irons and many other things. For a twelve-year-old I was doing pretty well.

At age thirteen, I started fooling around with radios and record players. These were the old tube type receivers. I kept expanding my knowledge in electricity and electronics, which came in very handy in my later years.

School was not getting any better for me as I was working more and studying less. I studied just enough to pass at the end of each year. I got top grades in Math, Science and Music, but barely passed in the other subjects. I had a feeling that the reason I got passing grades in the other subjects was because the teachers did not want me back in their classrooms again. They were glad to get rid of me and I was relieved to be away from them. Most of my teachers were over fifty years old and some were over sixty. My favorite subject in school was Math. Numbers and formulas fascinated me. I was the best in our class in Math and Algebra and I used to represent my class in Math Bowl. I won several times, and Janos, my math teacher, was very proud of me and the honor I brought to him and to our class.

Other than my math and science teachers, none of the other teachers showed much love towards me. My Russian teacher just plain hated me because I was the only student in class who refused to speak Russian in her class. From the very beginning I knew that this class would be my worst subject. My thinking was that I had no intention of going to Russia, so why should I learn something that would be useless to me. My teachers did not share my ideology.

Near the end of my last year of school in 1955, my family hired a college girl named Eva to tutor me twice a week in History and Russian so that I would get passing grades and be able to graduate from school. My mom and dad were afraid that I might flunk and would have to remain in school for another year. I wasn't very happy about it but I had no choice. My father had made up his mind and that was final and not negotiable. Eva lived not too far from our house and I would walk, not very happily, to her house for a two-hour lesson twice a week. Too bad that she did not tutor me in going out with girls or about sex! I would have looked forward to the tutoring sessions with much more enthusiasm. She was a very nice-looking girl about 20 or 21 years old, with a great personality and a beautiful smile. She used to tell me that with just a little effort on my part, it would be easier for her to help me graduate. I gave her just that, very little effort, but I guess it was enough, and it paid off.

The last year in school required us to take a final test that would account for about forty percent of our grade. This was very important because if you did poorly all year and did extremely well on the test you could end up with a better-than-just-passing grade. The day finally arrived and I nervously went to school for the big test. We were told to bring only a couple of pencils with us, some blank paper, and nothing else. No books or written papers.

As I went to my class I was pleasantly surprised when I saw my math and history teachers sitting at the front desk. On the desk in front of them were some thirty to forty gray manila-sized envelopes containing the test papers. One by one each student was called to the front desk and was told to select an envelope. We were to go back to our seats and not open the envelopes until the teacher directed us to do so. Some of the students would just pick up the nearest envelope while others would sort through a bunch of them. Some even put them toward the light to see if they could look inside.

When it was my turn, I went to the desk where Janos, my math teacher, was sitting. I didn't go near Imre, my history teacher. I had started to touch some of the envelopes when Janos shoved a gray envelope into my hand and pushed me from the desk. He looked at me and told me loudly that it didn't matter which envelope I took because I had no chance of graduating this year. His tone was harsh and took me by surprise, as I thought that Janos was my friend. Now even he had turned against me. I would have accepted it from most other teachers but not from him. Imre had a smirk on his face as if to agree with Janos completely. I felt betrayed and as I walked back to my seat I was ready to cry.

After all of the students had received their envelopes we were told the rules of the test. We were given three hours to complete the entire test, which contained all subjects other than music. We were allowed to go to the bathroom and get a drink of water, but only one person at a time, and we could not take anything with us such as our tests or working papers. In other words they didn't want us to cheat. Imre looked at the clock and directed us to open the envelopes and start on the test. Angrily I opened my envelope and took a quick glance at all the test sheets, which amounted to two or three pages per subject. My eyes had a hard time focusing because I was a little teary-eyed from the comments made a few minutes earlier by Janos. As I flipped through the pages, my eyes started to clear up and my body started to fill with confidence. This was quite unusual for me while I was in school. I had all the confidence in the world when I was working or when I had a tool in my hand, but never when I was in school other than in my math and science classes.

In just a few minutes my anger disappeared and I was ready and eager to get on with the test. I also wanted to finish in less than three hours. The more I looked at the papers the more confident I got and the smarter I felt. My mind started to wander and I started to get a little excited because the test looked easy at first glance. I looked at the test papers quickly once again just to make sure that my eyes did not deceive me. In a few minutes I had totally calmed down and was ready to prove them all wrong, but my mind continued to question why this test looked so easy. It had to be the tutoring with Eva, or perhaps I was smarter than my teachers had given me credit for. The answer to the puzzle was staring me right in the face.

I looked around in the class and everybody was either staring at or starting on the test. Feeling much better, I looked toward my history and math teachers. Imre was busy reading a book, but Janos was staring at me. I was no longer angry with him nor was I on the verge of crying, as was the case less than ten minutes before. Upon making eye contact, his face lightened up and he gave me a little wink. His face turned serious again as he turned away from me and looked toward the other students. What a show, putting me down in front of the class, and then shoving an easy test into my hand in order to help me in my time of need! Now this was the Janos I knew and loved. He was so proud of our team and me when we were victorious in the Math Bowl, and of the credit he received as our teacher. He had never had to yell at me in the three years I had him as my math teacher. Now it all made sense to me. I loved Janos and I will be forever grateful for his help at a time when I needed it badly.

I finished the test in about two hours, and then decided to look it over one more time and change some of my answers. I glanced at Janos several times and I know he looked at me many times. We must have made eye contact four or five times. I know he saw the confidence on my face. When I got home my mom was very nervous and wanted to know how I did. When I told her I thought I did really well she didn't believe me, until I received my report card a few days later. I got an A+ for Math, an A for Science and Music and a B for Gymnastics. In other subjects I got a C, with a C- in Russian. I made it! We were all very happy, especially my mom who had been very nervous about the test. I went to Eva's house and showed her my report card. She was thrilled and gave me a big hug. She was so proud of me! My father didn't say very much when my mom showed him the report card. I still tried to stay away from him as much as possible.

My oldest brother Zoltan had gone to work at the post office after my mother took him out of school. There he met a co-worker, an older gentleman who was a musician. He played the clarinet. Zoltan found out that this man was also teaching clarinet lessons on the side. A little later, Zoltan decided to ask him if he would teach him. My father agreed on the condition that the teacher would provide Zoltan with a loan instrument because we could not afford to buy one at that time.

Zoltan started with clarinet lessons and shortly afterward my next oldest brother, Laszlo, also asked if he could take lessons. My father agreed but then decided that my two younger brothers and I should also take lessons. I wasn't very excited about this but I could not talk my father out of it. I was forced to practice daily. Of the five of us, John and I did the worst. John wanted to play the drums, which he later did. I wanted to work rather than practice the clarinet. Going to school and then practicing the clarinet daily was no fun for me.

Zoltan liked jazz and swing music. His idol was Benny Goodman. Laszlo loved classical music and operas. He was later accepted to the Bartok Conservatory of Music in Budapest, which is a very famous school in Europe. Of the sixty eighty applicants, only he was chosen. My family was thrilled and very proud. Zoltan formed a band and they played a lot of American songs, but with Hungarian lyrics and titles. That was the only way they could get away with it. Zoltan loved to entertain and perform in front of an audience. He was doing very well. They had gigs almost every weekend.

My brother Laszlo was also doing well in music and in sports. He played in the minor league of one of our top major league soccer teams in Budapest. He was an all-star defenseman in the minor league and he had a great future in soccer. I used to go to many of his games and I even served as a ball boy at one or two. I tried out for the same teams' younger division, playing right wing for half a game, but I was too skinny and was afraid of contact. I was also too slow for a right-winger. I was not good enough to make the team but I was thrilled just to have the uniform on. I had a lot of fun that day and I'm glad they gave me the chance, even though I knew that the only reason they let me try out was because Laszlo was my brother. Laszlo's nickname was "Rabbit" because he was so fast. Because he was built well he was asked to pose for a statue of a sports figure. That statute was later displayed at one of our sports stadiums in Budapest. Laszlo also practiced the clarinet more than any one of us. He took it very seriously and would make it his life.

In 1955, at the age of fourteen, I graduated from school. I wasted no time and went to work as a machinist trainee. Living under Communist control we had very little choices as to where we would work and what schools we could go to. I was glad to get a job in a factory where they were making truck-mounted water-drilling equipment. The factory was about fifty minutes by public transportation. We never had a car while we lived in Hungary and we never owned a television either. I had to get up each morning by 5:30 a.m. in order to get in for my shift, which was from 7:00 a.m. to 3:30 p.m. As a trainee I spent two weeks on the job and two weeks in trade school learning subjects related to work. Math and Metallurgy were two of the more important subjects. We did class work on the many different metal-fabricating machines we would be using, such as lathes, milling machines and bridgeports. Thank goodness I no longer had to learn Russian and History. I was a changed young man.

I did well in trade school and in the shop. There was heavy emphasis on Math and Trigonometry, which was great for me. The first machine I learned to work on was a 12" belt-driven lathe; it was about thirty years old. That was typical for the equipment used in Hungarian factories. Most of the equipment in our factory was very old and worn out. The government owned the factory and did not believe in investing a great deal of money into new or modern equipment. Hungary was a very poor country and we also had to pay for the upkeep of the occupation forces of the Soviet Union. Technology in Eastern Europe did not keep pace with our western neighbors. The western countries got financial help from the United States while our resources were drained and exported to the Soviet Union. Collective farming did not produce crops as in the West. There were no incentives to work hard, as the Communist government now owned everything. The plant where I worked was inefficient and poorly managed. Most of the management were political appointees. People got ahead if they were a member of the Communist Party. I was not a member nor interested in politics.

I was gung-ho when I started to work at the factory and was eager to learn as much as they would show me. The machine shop teacher was an old machinist named Tibor. He had been teaching this trade for more than twenty years. He demanded respect and pushed the class more than some of the students cared for. If you did not pay attention or could not keep up with his class he would transfer you out. This was good for some of us because the size of the class went from thirty down to about eighteen in just a few months. I did not mind because we were able to learn more using several different machines, including the milling machine and the bridgeport. On a lathe machine, we would make round metal, brass, or aluminum parts. A milling machine cuts metal in a different way from a lathe. A stationary cutter shaves metal off a block of steel or brass in a one-way movement. A bridgeport machine uses a rotating cutter to shave metal off the piece being worked on.

At the factory I had met my best friend Micklos (Micki). We had many things in common and would do things together after work. He lived far from my house; therefore we never got together on a weekend, only at work or after work. I was content and was doing very well. Things were calm at home. I was in the top three in my trade school class, which was quite unusual for me. What a change! Nobody had to nag me to do my homework or go to school. I could finally do what I had wanted to do for several years: work and make money. The money I made was given to my family and I would get an allowance for transportation and maybe a movie once a month or so.

Food was in short supply after the war. We could not afford to buy beef so Mom would buy horsemeat and cold cuts, which looked and tasted like beef. Dad never knew that he ate horsemeat, which he did for a very long time. We could not buy chocolate, oranges or bananas as they were considered luxury items. Mom would sometimes buy two oranges on the black market, which she would than peel and each of us would get two sections. Sometimes she would also get some chocolate, which was a real treat, but we could not tell anybody that we were buying things on the black market.

At this time my father was working as an expresso machine repairman. Mom was doing some part-time alteration work; Zoltan was still working at the post office. Laszlo was working as a truck repairman and now I was working as a machinist trainee. My two younger brothers were still in school. In late 1955 my oldest brother Zoltan was drafted into the Army. After basic training he somehow talked his commanding officer into forming a band. This helped him while he was in the Army because band members got better duty assignments.

The early months of 1956 were uneventful for my family and I, as for most Hungarians. We worked very hard under difficult conditions. Now that four of us were working, Mom was able to do things that were not possible a few years before. She stopped buying horsemeat and bought oranges more often on the black-market. The salary that I was making as a trainee was however very little the first year. We got raises only once a year, depending on our grades.

We were not very religious as the Communist government closed the churches and temples after World War II. Grandma kept a kosher house but we did not. I was never at a Jewish temple in Hungary.

My second year started at trade school and I got a fairly good raise by Hungarian standards of the time. I had barely started the year when events changed my family's life forever, as well as the lives of tens of thousands of other Hungarians.

4

Revolt in Hungary

I do not have first-hand information of all of the events that took place from October 23rd through November 14th, 1956. The events described here include information I found in books, on the Internet, and reports by the United Nations and documentaries I have seen over the last forty two years.

In neighboring Poland, political unrest had culminated in a mass walkout by factory workers on June 28 of that year. More than fifty thousand Poles marched in the procession with signs and banners demanding free elections and the removal of Soviet forces from Poland. A clash with the police resulted in the death of more than fifty people and the wounding of hundreds, but the crisis continued. The political unrest in Poland seemed to touch off a chain of events in Hungary.

Several days prior to October 23, students and professors took advantage of the Polish uprising to publicize their demands. In Budapest, the capitol, students and writers took the lead in formulating a march. This was to be held on October 23rd. A series of demands was circulated in factories. They were also posted on trees and billboards.

Monday, October 22, was like most other days for my family and me. I went to work at around 5:45 a.m. and after returning home I started a small two-day side job in our building. There was no sign of any revolution or disturbance on the horizon. The people of Hungary were going about their duties.

Tuesday, October 23, also started out to be just an ordinary day. I left home as usual and was at work at my usual time before the buzzer rang at 7:00 a.m. As soon as I arrived at work I knew that something was going on. I saw our factory workers in small groups looking at a sheet of paper, which was passed around. People were whispering all around me. I didn't know what was going on at the time and proceeded to walk toward the locker room where we changed into our work clothes. I was just over fifteen years old. At that time I knew very little as to what was happening in the world other than what I read in Communist controlled newspapers. I did not understand, nor was I involved in politics or political organizations.

When I entered the locker room I found most of my co-workers at a bench reading some leaflets. Micki saw me coming in and invited me to join the group. He showed me a leaflet being distributed by some factory workers, who had gotten it from their friends at a university.

I was a young, unsophisticated factory worker who did what I was told and minded my own business. I was growing up living in a totally closed society, controlled by a puppet regime of the Soviet Union that had brainwashed us with Communist propaganda all my life. We were told in school that the Western Imperialists were our enemies and the Soviet Union had liberated us from these monsters. We owed them our gratitude and our lives. Now, for the first time in my young life, I started to put together little bits of information that I had heard from my friends or had overheard when my father was listening to Radio Free Europe.

My father had never discussed politics with me because most of us feared the Secret Police and their brutal manner of handling dissidents. We were not allowed to listen to or use the short-wave radio at home. Dad used to put it on late at night with the volume turned very low in order for our neighbors not to hear it. You could trust no one and had to protect yourself and your family—that was just the way of life for us. I had heard rumors about the June Polish uprising and arrests of opposition leaders at work and on the radio, but I never read about it in the newspapers.

Now I read the flyer and was listening to the guys as they were discussing some of its demands when the one-minute warning bell sounded. The discussions stopped and we headed to our work area.

The first few hours were very quiet but I felt tension and excitement all around the factory. I saw that more than the usual number of workers were going into the bathroom and staying for longer times. Around 9:15 a.m. I went to the bathroom and saw twelve to fourteen workers, young and old, discussing the flyer and the planned meeting at Petöfi Square. They planned to march to the statute of General Bem, the hero of the 1848-1849 War of Independence, who was of Polish origin. The gathering of the students at Petöfi Square was most fitting. Sandor Petöfi was a famous Hungarian poet who was very outspoken against foreign occupation. It is Petöfi's poem, "Arise Hungarians," that states: "Now is the time, now or never. Should we be slaves or free? This is the question you must choose." This had sparked the 1848 revolution against our Austrian rulers.

I just listened and didn't say a word while I was in the bathroom. The more I heard, the more confused and nervous I got. I decided to go back to work. Just before 10:00 a.m. Micki came over to me and told me that he was leaving the building after lunch with other factory workers. He asked me if I wanted to go with them. I told him that I couldn't because my father would get mad at me. I told Micki to have a great time. He knew that I was scared of my father because he was very strict with us. He accepted my answer without hesitation or question. I don't really know why I said no to Micki, as he was my best friend, but I was so scared I didn't know what to do.

My family had always sheltered us from politics. This was done mostly out of fear and because we were Jews. Anti-Semitism was evident in Budapest, which forced our parents to keep my brothers and me mostly at home when not at school or work. We were not allowed to practice our religion; I didn't study Judaism at home or anywhere else.

Just as we started to eat lunch, two other flyers were circulated and read by most of us. It was evident from the two scheduled marches and the three different versions of flyers I had seen at work that day that the march on Budapest was not centrally organized. One of the plans was to march to Parliament, assemble in the square, make some speeches and present a list of demands to our government. One list had sixteen demands; one had ten, while the third had fourteen. The lists had similar demands but each had the following:

The immediate withdrawal of all Soviet troops.

A new government headed by Imre Nagy.

New general elections based on secret ballot and participation by a number of parties.

Freedom of opinion and of the press.

Reorganization of the Hungarian economy and return to the free enterprise system.

Freedom for youth organizations.

Removal of Stalin statues.

The replacement of the national emblem.

Micki and I listened to some of the comments of co-workers and elderly factory workers. It was clear to me that many of the elderly workers were more cautious than were the younger kids in the 15 to 20 year age group. Later, as Micki was leaving, he told me they were going to Petöfi Square. We said our good-byes and I told him that I would see him tomorrow. I could tell that he was a little nervous, but he was more sure of himself and street-smart than I was. This would be the last time we would see each other.

By one o'clock on that day, a large crowd had already assembled around the Petöfi Statue. Most were university students and factory workers. The crowd was electrified by the reciting of Petöfi's poem "Arise Hungarians." There was another march to the statue of General Bem by the Hungarian Writers' Union around two o'clock. After the ceremonies and some speeches, the crowd proceeded to Parliament Square. The ranks of the marchers grew by the thousands as workers, leaving factories to go home, joined their numbers. The marchers filled Parliament Square. They carried flags, banners, and homemade signs. By six o'clock their numbers reached almost 200,000. The crowd sang patriotic songs and the national anthem time and time again as dusk settled over the city of Budapest.

The rest of my day at work went as usual. The locker room was quieter than normal as we showered and dressed and went our separate ways. The trip home seemed longer than usual. Everything looked normal, but most Hungarians were not aware of the events that would put Hungary in the middle of the spotlight for weeks to come. I got home around four o'clock and continued the project I was working on in the building from the day before. My mind was on work and the completion of the project before dinnertime.

On the same evening another demonstration by a large number of students was underway at the Budapest radio station. The station had been commenting on the demonstrations from the government's point of view. A delegation from the crowd was allowed into the building and attempted to negotiate with the station director to have him broadcast their demands. The radio station was guarded by the hated AVO. During the early evening hours an additional 210 AVO troops were ordered to the radio station by the Communist government. As the crowd got larger, it began to press against the gate.

Back at Parliament Square, shouts of the crowd, "Bring Imre Nagy to us," were heard inside the walls of Parliament. Since early afternoon the Politburo had been debating what to do about the demonstrators. The crowd knew it. The lights at Parliament Square were turned off by order of the government, but the darkness did not alter the mood of the crowd. Paper torches were lit and the singing and chanting continued louder than before. Fear of the consequences of what might happen when all the paper was exhausted brought the lights on again, to the delight of the assembled. At the urging of his supporters, Imre Nagy was brought to Parliament Square to speak to the demonstrators. The shouts of "We want Imre Nagy" continued until he appeared on a first-floor balcony.

Nagy (pronounced "nody") was a symbol of the revolt against the Soviet Union. As an agricultural expert he had held several government posts in postwar Hungary before serving (1953-55) as premier. His "new course" de-emphasized heavy industry, stopped forcible collectivization, and loosened police controls. He had been increasingly critical of the Soviet influence in Hungary. Denounced for Titoism, he was removed from office (Tito was the Communist leader of Yugoslavia who had already broken with Stalin). However, Nagy's expulsion from the Hungarian Communist party in early 1956 was rescinded at the request of rioting students shortly before the October revolution began.

From the balcony, Nagy waved several times in order to quiet the crowd spoke briefly. He promised reforms and called for negotiations with the Communist party. He also called for discipline, calm, and for everyone to go home; then he left the balcony. The demonstrators decided to call it a night and began to leave the square, heading for home. Some of them were already at major boulevards when the news was heard that AVO troops had opened fire on the crowd at Radio

Budapest. Disbelief and outrage was felt everywhere as this news spread across Budapest and the country.

Shortly after 9:00 p.m. at the Radio Building, tear gas bombs had been thrown by the AVO from the upper windows into the crowd. The crowd became more excited and within a minute or two the AVO opened fire on the crowd, killing a number of people, and wounding many others. On orders by the Central Committee, army units were sent to the Radio Building to reinforce the AVO. Demonstrators not too far from the Radio Building stopped the troops. The soldiers then allowed the crowd to take over their weapons. Soon the Radio Building was under attack by the crowd and a siege was underway.

Several hundred special police, who were ordered in to repel the revolutionaries, refused to fire on them. The students and factory workers raided arms plants, police stations, and army barracks throughout the night. Scattered firing had broken out all around the city. More army and police units were joining the ranks of the demonstrators. The AVO was ordered to defend the Radio Building at all cost, but the demonstrators finally seized the building in the early hours of the following morning.

Meanwhile, at Stalin Square, another large crowd had gathered to overthrow the fifty-foot-high bronze statue of Joseph Stalin. Ropes, chains and a heavy truck could not topple the statue. Then welders' equipment was brought in. Workers quickly burned holes into the legs of the statue. This time, like a giant tree, they managed to topple the metal effigy and hammered it into bits.

The insurgents ordered a general strike for Wednesday the 24th. With all factories closed, thousands of workers and others became freedom fighters. Ordered by the Communist party, Russian armored columns poured into Budapest with lightning speed, with the objective to spread fear, paralyze the city and crush the uprising. Bands of freedom fighters formed locally. Resistance to the Russians was spontaneous, but confused. They lacked unified leadership. All over Budapest there was fierce street fighting. Using improvised hand-grenades and Molotov cocktails, the freedom fighters destroyed most of the Russian armor engaging them. Soldiers and cadets from several barracks joined the freedom fighters. Anti-Russian feeling was expressed by the burning of Soviet books and propaganda.

Also on Wednesday morning, October 24, the Minister of Defense ordered Colonel Pal Maleter to lead a formation of tanks against the insurgents in the eighth and ninth districts. Colonel Maleter refused to put down the resistance. He changed sides and took charge of the revolution. The revolution spread from Budapest to other major cities in Hungary. After the massacre at the Radio Station, AVO men were hunted down with a vengeance and hanged from trees.

On Sunday, October 28th, the Communist Party accepted the revolution and its achievements. A new cabinet was formed headed by Imre Nagy. Colonel Pal Maleter was designated as Deputy Minister of Defense. A cease-fire was ordered and the people of Hungary were told that the Russian troops were to be replaced by a democratic police force. The AVO would be abolished. For the next few days there was confusion. Some Soviet units withdrew, some advanced, and some didn't do anything. There were reports that fresh troops were crossing the border into Hungary while negotiations were underway. For several days there were scattered shootings and on Wednesday, October 31st, Budapest Radio reported that Soviet troops had left the capitol during the night. These troops however, remained on the outskirts of the city.

The pressure on Nagy was heavy from endless meetings with large numbers of new and varied political parties. He was also aware of the violence on the streets and the Soviet troop movements in Hungary. On November 1st, reports reached Nagy that the Russians were not retreating but were reinforcing their units. More than 75,000 men and 2,400 tanks were crossing into Hungary from Czechoslovakia, Russia, and Romania. The entry of further Soviet troops into Hungary forced the Nagy's hand.

He summoned Soviet Ambassador Andropov, and expressed his strongest protest against the entry of new Soviet troops into Hungary. He insisted on the immediate withdrawal of these units. He also informed the Soviet ambassador that the government of Hungary was withdrawing from the Warsaw Pact. In the early evening hours Nagy, in a broadcast to the nation and the world, declared the country's neutrality and the break with the Warsaw Pact. In one diplomatic note he requested that the Secretary General of the United Nations put the Hungarian question on the agenda of the General Assembly, which was about to meet to debate the Suez crisis. He also asked the United

Nations Secretary General to ask the great powers to recognize Hungarian neutrality. At the same time in Budapest, Cardinal Mindszenty joined Prime Minister Nagy in making an appeal to the West for help.

In the U.N. Security Council, meeting in a special session on November 2nd, the Soviet delegate took the floor to deny the reports that additional Soviet troops had crossed into Hungary. While he was actually speaking, Soviet troops were encircling the city of Budapest. Nagy, however, still believed that the ongoing negotiations with the Soviet Union would conclude with an agreement that Soviet forces would be removed.

Negotiations continued between the representatives of the government of Nagy and the Soviet military delegation. At around 8:00 p.m. on November 3rd, the Hungarian negotiators, headed by Colonel Pal Maleter, entered a fortified camp of the Soviet headquarters in Hungary at Tokol, near Budapest. By this time, agreement appeared to be certain, with only a few minor details to be settled. The Soviet generals received them warmly and everything seemed to go perfectly in the office where the talks were taking place. Near midnight, about twenty armed guards stormed the room and arrested the Hungarian delegation. The Soviets had used the negotiations as a ploy to cover their military preparations and to capture Maleter. Soviet troops were on the move now with the support of armored columns of Soviet tanks and supporting vehicles in battle formation.

The city of Budapest was abruptly awakened shortly before 3:00 a.m. on Sunday, November 4th, by explosions, intense artillery barrage, and the roar of fighter-bombers. Strategic points were bombed from the air. While the city and key towns were under attack, this time by an overwhelmingly ruthless force, Premier Imre Nagy took to the airwaves. He told the citizens of Hungary that Soviet troops had launched an attack in the morning against the capital with the intention of overthrowing the legal, democratic government of Hungary. He called on his armed forces and the people of Hungary to defend the city and to resist the Soviet attack at all costs. He appealed to the free world to save this tiny nation that was fighting for its freedom.

Active radio stations transmitted their desperate appeal to the United Nations and the outside world in several languages. The small Hungarian Army, which was joined by freedom fighters, lacked leadership and heavy weapons and was no match for the invading Soviet forces. The attack was so overpowering and widespread that in only a few hours Russian troops occupied strategic centers, airfields, railways, highways and crucial bridges. In less than three days the Soviet forces crushed most major resistance, but fighting continued in urban pockets. All resistance ceased on November 14th.

In the United Nations, American ambassador Henry Cabot Lodge deplored the intervention of the Soviet military forces to repress the Hungarian people. While the United Nations and the free world looked on in disbelief and condemned the Soviet armed invasion, the people of Hungary were left to fight the Soviets alone. Reprisals against the freedom fighters and sympathizers were swift and deadly. Secret sentences were hurriedly carried out and detention camps were once more filled with over 20,000 prisoners. Deportations began; scores of young men were loaded onto trains and were sent to Russia. Nagy had taken refuge in the Yugoslav embassy when the Soviets counterattacked on November 4th. He was later kidnapped, convicted without a public trial, and executed at a secret location. Hungary was once again under Communist control with a puppet regime controlled by the Soviet Union. It is estimated that more than 23,500 were killed.

The Hungarian revolution of 1956 was unique in that a small country rose against one of the great superpowers. The Hungarian uprising aroused the interest of the free world, but worldwide condemnation of the Soviet Union was no help to the freedom fighters of Hungary. The Hungarian spirit and the will to be free was however, not broken. And the people of the free world saw for the first time, on their television screens and in their newspapers, the evils of Communism.

Laszlo and Zoltan in 1955.

5

A Desperate Journey

During the revolution my family and I spent much of our time in the bomb shelter in the basement of our building. Most of our neighbors were also there. My mom was a nervous wreck because we had not heard from my oldest brother Zoltan, who was in the army at that time. News reports of heavy fighting by army units alongside the freedom fighters and heavy casualties on both sides were reported. There were a couple of other families in the shelter who had sons in the army and they were in the same predicament as my family.

When there was a lull in the fighting we would go outside, but only within a few blocks of our house. In the early days of the revolution we saw streetcars and buses that were turned over. They were used as barricades by the freedom fighters. We saw several burned out military trucks and a burned out tank. I saw many civilians carrying rifles over their shoulders and noticed damage to buildings. We finally heard from Zoltan by phone that he was OK and would be home within a few days. But that was not to happen.

When the Soviet troops attacked Budapest on Sunday, November 4th, we were asleep. We were awakened just before 3:00 a.m. by loud explosions and artillery fire. Grabbing our blankets, we rushed to the shelter in the basement of our building wearing only our pajamas. At times the noise was unbearable as continuous machine gun, mortar and artillery fire ripped through the air. Most of us cried as we listened on our radio to the speech by Premier Imre Nagy asking for help from the free world. The scene in the shelter was one of horror and disbelief as adults wept openly, hugging each other, trying to comfort one another. The news on the radio got worse by the hour. We all felt that the Hungarian army had no chance against the invading troops. We held out hope that the United Nations would come to our rescue. But the pleas for help from the West were in vain.

For two days and nights we stayed in the shelter, not knowing what was happening in the city other than what we heard on our radio. In the late afternoon on November 5, someone ran into our shelter yelling that there was smoke coming from our fourth floor apartment. My father ran upstairs with a neighbor and found Zoltan's mattress burning from a large caliber bullet. They put the fire out and came back downstairs to the shelter. My father was visibly shaken; had my brother been in bed at that time he might have been killed. Most of the gunfire stopped on the third day. On November 6, we left the shelter for good. When we went outside we could not believe the extent of the destruction all around us. Burned out tanks and trucks, heavily damaged or destroyed buildings, and Soviet tanks holding key positions at every major intersection.

Words cannot describe the way we felt and the emptiness in our hearts. For the few days prior to the Soviet invasion there had been joy in the streets of Budapest. We had been free and we had high hopes for the future. That hope had been smashed once again by a ruthless evil empire. Hungary once again lost its opportunity to shape its own destiny.

I was not a freedom fighter but I sympathized with their goal. I was more confused than ever. I could not understand why the United Nations would not help Hungary in its hour of need. At the age of fifteen I was naive and scared. I was not aware of the politics within the United Nations or of the veto power of the Soviet Union.

Zoltan's army unit had sided with the revolution. After the revolt was crushed by the Soviet troops, Zoltan and most of his buddies, fearing reprisals, escaped into Austria on November 5th. A few days later, my other brother Laszlo also escaped into Austria. News that young men were being rounded up were circulating in the city and had forced his decision. The only things he took with him were the clothes on his back and his Selmer clarinet. Mom was devastated at her sons' leaving of family and country. Chaos ruled in all of Hungary. No one knew what was going to happen or how brutal the reprisals would be and against who. The borders with Austria were mostly open from October 24 to the end of November while troops were brought into the city to crush the revolution. After the failed revolt, more than 200,000 people left Hungary, hoping to start a new life in a new country, anywhere they could be taken in.

In December, the borders were once again sealed tight and escape from Hungary was more difficult. This turned to almost impossible by early January 1957. My father was torn between staying or leaving. He was afraid to uproot the rest of the family. In the early evening hours in mid-December, Zoltan came home, to the surprise of everybody. He begged my father and mother to come to Austria while it was still possible. My father blew his cool when he saw Zoltan. He screamed and yelled at him, calling Zoltan crazy and reckless to take such a chance by coming back. He could have easily been caught and turned over to the AVO. Dad refused to listen to Zoltan and ordered him to go back. He told him that he had better not come back home again. The joy on my mom's face was short-lived as she saw her firstborn son for only a very short time. Before Zoltan returned to Austria he talked our Aunt Baba and her family into escaping with him to Austria. It was a very dangerous thing that Zoltan did and could have cost him his life, and he was only 21 years old at the time.

After the revolt was crushed there were reprisals against many leaders and loyalists. The AVO was once again back in full control, eliminating anti-government troublemakers. I did not work in November or early December. The Communists shut down factories, on orders from the government, in order to bring law and order to the city and the surrounding towns. Finally, in mid-December we were allowed to go back to work. Tension was still very high in the city as a large number of Soviet troops were kept at strategic locations, especially in Budapest. I was very nervous on my way to work on the first day back on the job after the revolt. While en route I could not believe the devastation in some parts of the city. Entire blocks had been completely destroyed by the Soviet troops. At the factory, only about half of the workers showed up on the first day. Micki was not one of them.

At lunchtime I talked to some of my other friends and asked them if they knew where Micki was. Nobody knew where he was or if he was all right. For more than a week I did not hear from Micki or from his family, even after I went to his house and left a note on the front door. The following week I learned that Micki was wounded in the chest and was recovering at his grandmother's house. He would be back at work by the end of January. At home, things were very quiet. We did not discuss the whereabouts of my two older brothers. Only our very closest friends knew that they had escaped into Austria.

Slowly, the country got back to normal. People were afraid, and uncertainty was visible everywhere. We had not heard from my brothers in Austria since Zoltan had come home in mid-December. There was no jubilation at our house or in the capital when the New Year arrived. But people were going on with their daily lives and our family tried to go on without our two older brothers.

In the late hours of January 7, 1957, our father awakened us. We were told to get dressed and to keep very quiet. Within ten to fifteen minutes we were all dressed and walking quietly down the stairs in order not to awaken anyone in the building. My father didn't want to use the elevator. That would have made noise and could have awakened one of our neighbors. My father gave me a bag to carry and he carried a backpack and a large handbag. Once we exited our building, a tall young man in his late 20s met us. He briskly rushed us to a waiting truck down the street. The only other person I saw was another young man who was behind the wheel of the truck. My father told us to get on the truck quickly and quietly. Once in the canvas-covered truck, we were pushed to the front behind some wooden crates and potato sacks. There I saw one of our neighbors, Szofi, and her family. After everybody got in we were told to keep very quiet and not to move around. The two young men pushed boxes behind us so no one could see us from the road. At this point I felt something very special was going to happen, but our father didn't tell us anything. It was quite cold, as it was in the middle of winter. We huddled close together for warmth.

After about five minutes of traveling, the truck stopped and we picked up another person. It was my grandmother, who lived not too far from us. Once she was on board and seated next to us, the truck started up again. This time the truck did not stop for hours. The trip was rough and long, compounded by our sitting on boxes and on the floor of the truck. We traveled on narrow bumpy roads to avoid checkpoints. After about a five-hour trip the truck pulled in behind a farmhouse, where we were unloaded and whisked quickly inside. I had no idea where we were, but I had a feeling that we were about to leave Hungary. Later on I found out that the name of the city was Sopron and we were on the outskirts of it.

We stayed at that house for several days and were allowed outside only when we went to the outhouse behind the building. An old couple lived in the house and it seemed the truck driver was their son. A couple of days later another family joined our group at the house. A second family followed them the next night. The farmhouse was not big enough for all of us, but we only had to be there another few days. I overheard the taller man telling my father and some of the other families that it would not be much longer. The weather was cold and windy, but the ground was bare. This was causing our delay.

On the twelfth of January we awakened to light snow that turned to heavy, with gusty winds of about 25 mph. It came down harder as the day progressed, and by nightfall we had more than eight inches of snow. Around eight o'clock in the evening we were told to get ready because we would be leaving in fifteen minutes. We left by way of the back door and headed toward the snow-covered farmland behind the house. Twenty-three of us left the house; this included four families and the two guides who would lead us to freedom. Later on I found out that my father and the other families had hired these men to smuggle us out of Hungary and into Austria. The deal was that we would leave them all our furniture and other belongings and pay 10,000 forint, which was equal to four or five months' wages. For this they would provide transportation to a farmhouse near the border; then when the visibility was low, they would guide us into Austria.

The two guides told us to keep very quiet and to stay close to them. There would be no flashlights or smoking allowed. The ground was covered by more than ten inches of snow by ten o'clock and it was still coming down as we made our way toward the border. At times we turned left, then an hour or so later we would take a right turn. The snow turned to freezing rain and the wind was gusting, making our travel much harder as the night wore on. At times the tall guard would drop back a little to where we were and tell us to pick up the pace. We were falling behind the lead group. Our family and Szofi's family walked slower because of my grandmother and my youngest brother, 11-year old John, who had a hard time walking in the deep snow. At times we were not able to see the lead group and followed their footsteps only. It was very dark; the ice and snow were coming down much harder than earlier that evening. The handbag I carried was getting heavier by the hour. Icicles hung from our clothes and bodies. By eleven o'clock both groups were walking much slower than when we had started out. At times we fell 60 to 100 yards behind the lead group. At around 11:30 we heard a loud "HALT" (in Russian), ordered in a strong strange voice.

We hit the ground at once and did not move for more than fifteen minutes. At that point we knew that Soviet border guards had captured the lead group. They were ahead of us by less than eighty yards. As they were led away, we stayed motionless on the ground and extremely quiet for another five minutes. Our faces were getting numb from the ice-covered snow, which covered more than half of our bodies. After the group was led away, my father told us to get up and get going, but we had a major problem. We had lost our guides and had no idea as to which way to go or how much farther. At the start of our march to the border there had been a total of twenty-three of us. This group was now reduced to ten. It was only my family and Szofi's family, and we were left in unfamiliar territory. We were tired and shaken by the events of just a few minutes earlier, but we had to move on or we would also be captured, or would freeze to death.

As we walked by the area where the rest of the group had been captured we were able to see a lake at a distance of about twenty yards. The visibility was less than sixty yards as we reached the edge of the water. It was clear to us that we had to cross the lake; otherwise the guides would have taken us toward a different location. Just to the right of us was a large bush with a very small rowboat tied to one of the branches. After a short discussion between the two families, it was decided that we would cross the lake in groups of three or four. One person would bring back the boat to pick up the next group. My father, my grandmother and George were the first to cross the lake. My father came back and took my mother and John and me. I brought the boat back for the next group and took Szofi's husband and son across. He went back to bring the rest of his family across. At the point of crossing, the lake was about 250 yards wide. Rowing was difficult because of the heavy jackets we had on and because we were totally exhausted. When everybody was accounted for, we started forward on an unknown heading, only guessing as to which way we should go.

The snow and wind tapered off around 1:00 a.m. as we continued to walk. In these hours we had seen no sign of life anywhere.

By this time we were near total exhaustion. We were lost and we had no idea which way to go. Around 3:30 in the morning we were ready to give up. My grandmother and John could hardly walk any more. We were desperate and we started to yell for help as we continued to move forward, but our screams went unheard. Ever so slowly we kept moving forward, yelling for anybody to help. At this point we didn't care if Soviet border guards captured us. At around 4:30 a.m. we spotted a small light in the distance to our right, halfway up a small hill. We turned and started toward the light, which at times was hardly visible. We yelled louder and louder as the light got closer. It was clear that the light was moving toward us and we gathered all our strength as we marched forward toward the light.

A little while later the light stopped coming toward us, but we were still moving toward it. We kept yelling as loud as we could. By this time we could hardly move. We were totally exhausted and our voices were getting weaker by the minute. We could hardly talk, never mind yell. A faint voice came from the direction of the light. Lacking strength, we yelled back as loud as we could and asked for help. The voice came back in German, telling us that we were still in Hungary and we needed to come to them. My grandmother translated for us, and after realizing what was happening, we jubilantly forced our bodies to move forward again. We headed toward that small beacon of light while yelling to them that we were coming. We didn't know if the light belonged to Russian or Austrian border guards, but at this point we didn't care. We just wanted it to be over, regardless of the consequences. It took us another seven minutes before we reached the border guards, who welcomed us to Austria. We were all crying from the joy of making it safely into Austria. We hugged and kissed both border guards over and over again and kept thanking them for saving our lives.

After being found by the guards we had to walk for another forty-five minutes to a guard station. There we were put on a truck and taken to the barracks some thirty minutes away. Once inside the barracks, the border guards made us remove our frozen clothing and gave us some army blankets, hot tea and food to eat. They took us into a large room with many portable beds where we could lie down. I was so tired that I didn't even wait for the food. After some hot tea, I took off my clothing and wrapped myself in a couple of army blankets. I slumped onto the bed and in less than a minute I was sound asleep. I slept for more than fourteen hours, but not as long as some others.

My father and grandmother were up when I awoke. Grandma was talking with some people in a corner of this large room. I still could not believe that we had made it and were finally free. What a difference a day makes! A day earlier we had nearly frozen to death in the snow-covered fields at the border. The realization started to sink in that fate was on our side that memorable night. Because we could not keep up with the younger and faster-moving families, we had been successful in reaching our destination. January 13, 1957, will always have a very special place in my heart. It is the day when freedom was ours and we started a new life in a new world. Forever I'll be grateful that my grandmother slowed us down, thereby saving our lives and enabling us to live free for the rest of our lives. Thanks, Grandma!

The following day we were taken by bus to a refugee-processing center in Vienna where they gave us a quick medical examination and interviewed each of us. They also put us up for a couple of days. At the center we met many other Hungarians and everyone listened to each other's accounts of the escape from Hungary. From the processing center we were taken by bus to a refugee camp in Korneuburg, which was only 15 or 20 miles from Vienna. The trip was exciting. For the first time in months, everyone was happy. Our days under Communist control were finally over. We had left behind almost everything we owned. We were now on our way to a new way of life. We were ready and determined to start over.

Part II

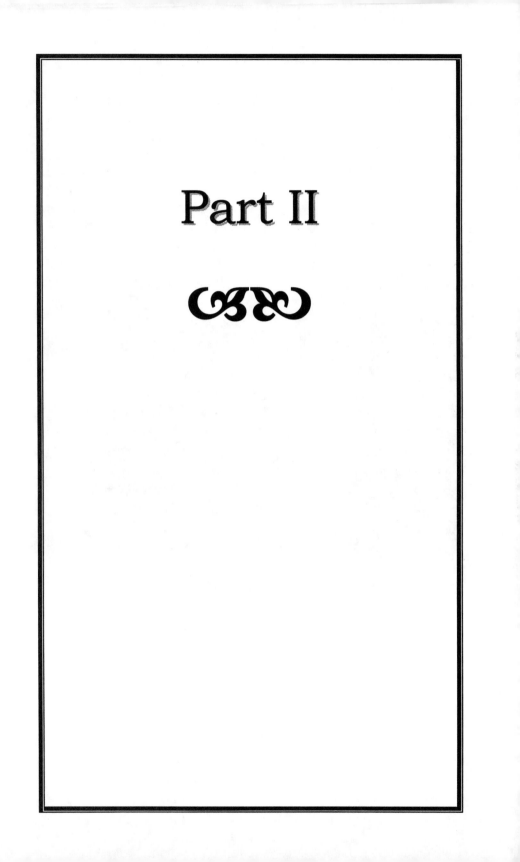

Myself, John and George in Korneuburg, March 1957.

6

Refugees – Austria to the United States

We arrived at our new temporary home at the Hungarian refugee camp in Korneuburg around 11:00 a.m. on January 16. It was a slow trip. Most of us were a little nervous. We didn't know what was going to happen when we got to the camp, or how long we would stay there. The camp, like most of the areas we passed, was covered with snow. It was a small army base, which had been turned into a refugee camp and processing center.

Upon arrival we were given a tour, and shown the sleeping quarters and the mess hall. We were advised of camp procedures. We were taken to a large room on the first floor of one of the buildings. Our living quarters looked like converted dormitories with several large rooms on each floor. Each room had about forty to fifty army-style bunk beds. We could take whichever empty cot we wanted. We were told to keep all our belongings under the bed because there was no other storage space available. That didn't bother us because we only had the clothes we were wearing, a backpack, and two small handbags. Father put our few belongings under his bed. It didn't take long before our floor was filled with new arrivals. Some were younger families with young kids, which made our room quite lively.

The following day we were taken to a building that had several rooms filled with used clothing. We were allowed to select a limited amount of clothing: a sweater, a jacket, and a pair of shoes. We also received a pocket-sized Hungarian-German dictionary, which I kept in my back pocket at all times. It came in handy when I tried to communicate with Austrians who didn't speak Hungarian. In early

April we also received a Hungarian-English dictionary because we were planning to go to the United States. When I left Hungary I had never spoken German or English, therefore it was very hard to communicate with anyone other than fellow Hungarians. Our family was very lucky that my grandmother spoke fluent German and my mother also spoke some German.

In just a few days we adapted fairly well to our new home, thanks mostly to the people who operated the camp. They were extremely helpful to all of us, as they understood the difficult times we were facing. The camp was set up mainly as a processing center for Hungarian refugees going to countries all over the world. With the help of the International Red Cross we were able to find my two older brothers. They were both living in Vienna. Zoltan and Laszlo were already speaking some German because they had been in Austria for three months. Laszlo had gotten a job as a diesel mechanic in Vienna.

Laszlo would come to visit us on most weekends and to give Dad some of the money he saved. Both of my older brothers had applied for admittance to the United States. Shortly after arriving at the camp, we filled out all the required forms and also applied. Going to the U.S. was very difficult. The quota allocated for Hungarians to immigrate was only a few hundred each year. At that rate it would take us sixty or more years before we would be allowed into the country! Uncertainty as to whether my family would be allowed to immigrate to the United States would cast a dark shadow over us for months. There was not very much we were able to do, other than to wait and try to make the best of a difficult situation.

To pass the time we practiced our clarinets, which we had brought with us. We also tried to learn German. My most memorable recollection during our stay in Korneuburg was the total lack of privacy. For the first month, we lived and slept in a large room along with 40 to 50 noisy strangers. In late February, we moved into a small room vacated by another family. This gave us more privacy as well as peace and quiet. On a daily basis we went to the main office to look at the bulletin board and check on our application for entry into the U.S. In early March a talent show by Hungarian refugees was to be held at the camp. My two younger brothers and I decided to perform as well. George and I would play the clarinet while my youngest brother John would play the drums on a borrowed set.

We were the opening act and we felt it would be most appropriate if one of the two songs we were to play would be an American song that we had often heard my oldest brother Zoltan play. Zoltan was a big fan of Benny Goodman; he used to play his music, but with Hungarian lyrics. The first song we played was Benny Goodman's big hit, "Sing Sing Sing." The curtain was down when we started to play and after about 4 or 5 seconds we had the curtain raised slowly. The crowd loved it; we had started the program off on the right foot. We did fairly well and we had a lot of fun performing. This was the first time that John, George, and I played together on stage and in front of a live audience. After the show, they had a little party backstage for the performers, and it was at that party that we had our first taste of Coca-Cola. We had never had it before and we were a little excited because we knew it was American. I didn't think it was anything special, but my brother John liked it very much and still drinks it daily.

The days went by very slowly. There was little to do other than just mark time. Almost daily, buses filled with Hungarians would depart the camp on their way to a new homeland. Many countries offered financial incentives for doctors, engineers, and skilled tradesmen. Australia was one of the many countries offering great incentives, as was Brazil and several other Latin American countries that were welcoming skilled professionals with open arms. One of my father's best friends and his family, who were going to Australia, had their papers processed in just a few weeks. We had applied only to the United States and so we hoped for a miracle. Zoltan liked American music, especially jazz, and he wanted to go to the U.S. I guess that was the reason we only applied to the United States, but I'm not sure on that. I never discussed it with my family.

Our prayers and the prayers of thousands of others were finally answered when word came that the Congress of the United States, at the urging of President Dwight Eisenhower, had passed a new law. It authorized the US Government to allow tens of thousands of Hungarian refugees to emigrate to the U.S. and relieve Austria of some of the 200,000 refugees.

This was the miracle we were praying for, but there was a catch, which created a great deal of anxious moments for us and thousands of others. Under the law passed by Congress, the refugees would have to be sponsored by friends, relatives, or religious organizations. These sponsors would have to take full financial responsibility for the sponsored families. It would also be on a first-come, first-served basis, which meant that refugees who had arrived in Austria earliest would be taken first. Some of the early arrivals in Austria, like my two older brothers, were quickly sponsored into the U.S., but we were near the bottom of the list.

Zoltan was the first to arrive in the United States. He first lived in Washington D.C., and then he moved to New York City. Laszlo arrived on March 11, 1957, and also lived in Washington before he moved to Cleveland. They were both sponsored into the U.S. by Jewish organizations. Because we had arrived in Austria near the end of the exodus, our chances for entry into the U.S. did not look very bright. Many Hungarian refugees were sponsored by relatives who lived in America, as was my Aunt Baba and her family. They were quickly processed. My grandmother joined my aunt and they all went to New York City where Baba's brother-in-law and sponsor, Laszlo Grunwald, lived. My father asked Baba if Laszlo would also sponsor us. For whatever reason, she never asked Laszlo if he would. That is what we understand, but we don't know the reasons behind it all. Because of this matter, my father did not speak to Baba for many years. After arriving in the U.S., my aunt and grandmother moved to New Jersey, living not too far from each other.

Not having relatives who could sponsor us, we turned for help to the Red Cross and to Jewish organizations. This was a very difficult time for us, not knowing if we could join Zoltan and Lazlo, who were already in the U.S. We pleaded with the agencies, telling them that once we reached the U.S., we would not be a burden to the country or to anyone else. The family should be united and be allowed to start a new life as a whole family. Things did not go easily and we had many sleepless nights. Finally, in mid-April, we received word that we had a sponsor. Within the next ten days we would leave the camp and head for the United States.

Our dream had finally come true. Once again a helping hand had come to our rescue. Our savior this time was none other than HIAS - Hebrew Immigrant Aid Society, a Jewish organization, which guaranteed all costs for our family. For more than a century, HIAS has had an extraordinary impact on millions of Jews. For generation after generation, HIAS has provided essential lifesaving services to world

Jewry, through its mission of rescue, reunion, and resettlement. As an expression of Jewish tradition and values, HIAS also responds to the emigration needs of other people who are threatened and oppressed.

On that guarantee, we received our visas from the U.S. Embassy. On April 21, we left Korneuburg by bus, heading to the airport in Vienna. We boarded a chartered plane, destination: the United States. The flight made stops in Iceland and Canada and took slightly over thirty-six hours. It was a very rough flight and many of us got airsick. We could hardly wait for the plane to land. Finally, it was over and our plane landed in New York City. We were finally in the land of our dreams. It was a very emotional moment as we departed the plane and stood on American soil for the very first time.

After landing in New York City, we were taken by bus to Camp Kilmer, which was located in New Jersey. Camp Kilmer was an old army base that was re-opened temporarily and was to be used as a processing center for Hungarian refugees arriving in the U.S. The date April 22, 1957, is a memorable day for my family and me; it was the start of a new life in a new country, with high hopes and anticipation.

At the camp we were given complete physical examinations. We stayed at Camp Kilmer for only two weeks, filling out many forms and applications and waiting for word as to where we would be sent next. While at the camp we had a great deal of help from the American Red Cross and CARE. Both organizations distributed clothing and also provided us with shaving razors and much more. With the help of the Red Cross we were able to track down Zoltan and Laszlo. This was a great help for my family. We finally knew where everybody was and that they were all right. There was nothing to do at the camp other than just wait, which bored me to death. We were eager to do something and get on with our lives, but things moved slowly. Finally, news came that we were being transferred again.

Several Jewish families, including us, were taken from the camp to a small hotel on Lafayette Street in Manhattan, New York, for further processing. We arrived at the hotel around 7:30 p.m. and were met in the lobby by representatives of HIAS. They welcomed us to the United States and assured us that within a few days we would be on our way to our final destinations. In just a few minutes they took us up to our rooms in order to put our things away. Then they took us down to the first floor HIAS meeting room for a short orientation. They informed us as to what would happen next and what was expected of us while we were at the hotel. Some of the HIAS workers spoke Hungarian and all spoke Hebrew or Yiddish. After a very short and informal orientation they took all of us to the dining room for a nice dinner. Then we were advised to go to our rooms and sleep. Breakfast would be served the next day from eight to ten, after which we were to go to the HIAS room for processing.

It was just after nine in the evening and as advised, we went up to our room. It had been a long day; the trip from Camp Kilmer to the city had taken a lot out of us. We were dead tired.

Shortly after getting to our room, my father gave me a dollar and told George and me to go downstairs to get some stamps because he wanted to mail a letter to his sisters in Hungary. Why he couldn't wait until the next morning I'll never know. We complied with his wishes, as we had no other choice. This very simple task would turn out to be a most frustrating experience for George and me. Looking back now, I can only laugh at the sequence of events that happened that night, but at that time it was no laughing matter.

We went downstairs to the HIAS room, but it was closed. So, I figured we would go to a store on the street and get some stamps. In my back pocket I always carried my Hungarian-English pocket dictionary that we had been given in Austria. I looked up how to say, "Where could I obtain stamps, please," and I also wrote it onto a piece of paper. At that time I did not realize that the dictionary which was given to us was Hungarian to British English, not Hungarian to "American" English, and that there was a great deal of difference between the two. At 9:15 p.m., with the written paper in one hand and a dollar in my pocket, George and I went down to the street. We were so innocent!

Once on the street, we tried to stop some people to ask where we could buy stamps, but nobody would stop for us. It looked like people were afraid of us. I was fifteen and George was thirteen years old. We were not used to this, but looking back I couldn't blame them. I would have been scared to stop for two teenagers late at night in a so-so area of New York City, especially the way we were dressed. We just kept walking down Lafayette Street, taking in the scenery and looking for a store where we could buy stamps. We tried to stop and ask for help from more than 25 people of all ages, men and women alike, but it was no use. No one would stop and help us. We were puzzled, but refused to give up. We were determined to buy our stamps even if it took all night, because going home without them would have been much worse.

For more than forty minutes we walked, and there were still no stamps in sight when we made our daring move. We saw two big black policemen with nightsticks in their hands walking a few yards ahead of us. I decided to ask them for help. This was unusual for us, as we normally tried to stay away from the police, but this time was different. I tried to explain to them what we wanted, but they just could not understand my English pronunciation. On the verge of tears and totally frustrated, I showed them the piece of paper I had written out, and kept pointing to the word "stamps."

My insistence paid off, as I think they finally understood what we were trying to say. They told us to follow them for a couple of blocks. The taller policeman then pointed toward a corner drugstore across the street and told us to go in there. In our own way, with our very limited vocabulary, we thanked them for their help, relieved that our confrontation with the New York Police Department was successful. When the light turned green, we crossed the street and proudly walked into the drugstore. Once inside, we happily stood in line at the counter.

After waiting in line for about five minutes we finally reached the clerk. Once again we told our story, but he could not understand us. After showing him the paper and pointing at the word "stamps," he too finally understood.

He pointed to a corner of the store, where we saw a machine with what looked like stamps in a display case. By this time the people behind us were getting quite upset, as we were holding up the line. We were only a few feet from success as we rushed toward the machine. But we were stopped cold again as we tried to figure out how to get stamps out of the machine with a dollar bill. We needed change. Out came the dictionary once again as I looked up the word, "change." Determined to succeed, I was finally able to convince a male customer to help us by pointing to the stamp machine and the dollar bill in my hand, and repeating the word "change" over and over again.

At last it worked. He helped us to get change, and by my pointing to the airmail stamp he got us the stamps we needed. With teary eyes we thanked him and left the drugstore, holding on dearly to our stamps. It was finally over and we felt like we had run five miles. By this time it was after 10:15 p.m. when we started our journey back to the hotel. By 10:45 we got to our hotel and proceeded to go back to our room with our prize possession. Satisfied with our monumental achievement, we proudly opened the door to our room.

Upon entering, we immediately sensed great tension. My father was irate and started to scream at me for being out so late when he had only sent me out to get stamps. I tried to explain to him what had happened, but he just refused to accept my explanation. He kept calling George and me stupid and irresponsible. He just didn't get it. I was going to tell him that next time he should get his own stamps, but I thought better of it. I kept my mouth shut and once again let him take his anger out on me. Mom didn't say a word, which we were used to by now. Mom came to us a little later and tried to explain that they were very worried because we were out so long. They thought that surely something had happened to us. Mom's justification did not make me feel any better. Angrily I went to bed.

It took me some time to fall asleep that night, as I was hurt and mad at my father for giving us hell, and at my mother for not standing up for us. George and I had had a tough enough time that evening. While lying in bed I was also trying to figure out why all those people refused to stop. It took me years before I understood. This was just the beginning, and it would take a long while before I would master the language well enough to be understood. It would be only one of many frustrating experiences, but one that I will never forget.

The next morning we had a buffet breakfast, which was new to me and I'm sure to my younger brothers as well. After breakfast, the HIAS room was already a scene of bustling activity. We saw one of the other families that came with us from Camp Kilmer as we sat down to wait for our turn. We were given an information sheet which we read carefully. After waiting ten minutes, Mom and Dad were told to sit next to a table while we were to stay in our chairs, which were only a few feet from the desk. We were able to hear almost everything that was said.

The HIAS worker, a very nice lady in her 40s, was extremely helpful. She spoke some Hungarian and also Yiddish, which made it easier for Mom to communicate. She was going to be our contact with HIAS while we stayed at the hotel. We were to stay in touch with her, once in the morning and once in the afternoon each day until we left the hotel for good. She took some information from Mom and Dad, such as the type of work we did in Hungary and what we were capable of doing, what our educational background was, the size of our family, and so on. Mom told her that she had two other sons who we hoped would be joining us prior to our leaving the hotel. After getting all the information from Mom, the HIAS worker told us that within the next few days we would be advised as to which city we would be sent to. We were given numerous information sheets, and we were also given some money to use while we were under their care.

The hotel had many Hungarian refugees already and new families were coming daily, while other families were leaving each day. Things were happening, it was starting to get exciting, and we felt good. We were not just marking time.We knew it would be only a short time before it was our turn to leave. The morale in the hotel was very positive and upbeat, thanks in most part to the dedicated HIAS organizers who worked so hard on our behalf. Most of them were volunteers and they put in long hours to help the Hungarian refugees.

We were free to come and go as we liked, so long as we stayed in touch with HIAS. There was always something that needed to be discussed. They also told us which areas to avoid, and interestingly, one of the areas was the one where George and I went in search of stamps. We should have gone the other way on Lafayette Street but we had made it back safely, and that is what mattered.

The weather was mild in the city, around seventy degrees. For early May it was really nice. That gave us a chance to walk around our neighborhood, avoiding the bad areas just as we were told. Mostly we just took in the sights. The merchandise in each store overwhelmed us. I was especially amazed by the abundance of oranges and other fruits that we had been only able to buy on the black market in Hungary. When we were out window-shopping, we bought very little because of the limited amount of money we had. I knew that someday we would walk into these types of stores and would buy almost anything we wanted.

I studied my dictionary and I would try to translate the headlines in newspapers. It was a very slow and frustrating process because our language was so different from English. In Hungarian you pronounce a word the way it is written; that is not the case in English and this caused my next embarrassing moment.

On our fourth day at the hotel I was walking down one of the streets in our neighborhood when I saw a person buying an ice cream cone through a double serving window at the sidewalk. On such a beautiful day it would have been great to have such a treat, so I looked in my dictionary for the words for buying ice cream. Confidently I approached the empty window. I told the young man behind the window that I wanted some vanilla ice cream, but I guess it didn't sound anything like that. He didn't understand what I wanted nor did the second man who came over to the window a short while later. For more than two minutes I repeated my request for "ice cream," but to no avail. Then I took out my dictionary and started to look up the word "vanilla."

As I was thumbing through the dictionary, another customer stepped up to the window next to me. He ordered and then received an ice cream cone. I quickly closed the dictionary and kept pointing and saying "that," "that," and "that." Then he said something to me that I didn't understand. He probably wanted to know what size and what flavor ice cream I wanted. I didn't understand him and just kept pointing at the ice cream for which the other customer was now paying. Within a few seconds he handed me a strawberry ice cream cone with two scoops just like the other customer ordered. I gave him all the money I had, which was all of fifty cents. Being very honest, he gave me back 35 cents, the correct change. It wasn't the flavor I wanted, but I didn't mind, as I would have taken any flavor at that point.

This episode became one of the most cherished memories of my young life, yet it was just another one of the many new and sometimes frustrating experiences that I will never forget. Episodes similar to these happened quite often and were now just a part of our lives. Going into Jewish stores made things much easier for us when we were with Mom. But for us boys, each day was a challenge once we left our hotel. We knew that every day we would learn something new, but eventually things would get easier. However it didn't get easier for a very long time! I was too embarrassed to tell people of my ice cream and stamp experiences until a long time after they had happened.

One of our big concerns passed when my brother Laszlo joined us a couple of days later at the hotel. We saw progress made each day as more and more of the refugees were sent on their way by HIAS to their new homes. Some of them had been at the hotel only two or three days before we arrived. We were getting excited, waiting impatiently for our turn. About a week after our arrival at the hotel, we were told to see our HIAS contact immediately. We all looked at each other with a great deal of anticipation as we had the feeling that this could be the moment we were waiting for. We quickly went to see our counselor.

As usual, she welcomed us warmly and had Mom and Dad sit at her table. She told us that our time had finally come and that we had some options as to where we might want to live. We were all a little surprised at this. We knew so little about the United States that it didn't matter; we were just glad to be here and we were eager to get on with our lives. She told us that we had several cities we could choose from, and she gave Mom a few sheets of paper that had the names of the cities and some information about each one. One of the cities on the list was Boston. She also gave us a map on which she had circled all the cities with a marker. She told us that we would have to make our decision by that afternoon.

It was up to us, but it would only be a guess on our part as to which city would be better for us. We took all the papers with us and with the adrenaline now flowing; we went upstairs to make our big decision. Neither my two younger brothers nor I were involved in the decision-making. Most of the cities were in the northern part of the country, but we knew nothing about them other than what we had heard from others and the information on the few sheets just provided by HIAS. Laszlo had heard that Boston had good schools, and with that information Dad decided to take Boston. Laszlo had lived in the country longer than we had and had more experience here than us. So the decision was made.

Dad didn't want to waste any more time or wait until the afternoon. He went downstairs to the HIAS office with Mom and Laszlo and gave them our decision. We were told that it would be only a day or two before we were sent on our way to Boston and we were told to stay close to the hotel. Now things really started to move. Later that same afternoon we were told that we would be leaving New York by train for Boston early the next morning. We were overjoyed and most of us cried with anticipation. We could hardly believe what was happening. I had a very hard time falling asleep that night. We said good-bye to our friends that night and wished all of them good luck. We all had a great deal in common.

The next morning we had an early breakfast and a warm sendoff by our HIAS counselor. She gave us our bus and train tickets and told us which bus we should take to the train station and where we had to go once we got into Boston. Everything was written down in an item-by-item order, very easy to follow. The HIAS staff was very professional in everything they did, and we were impressed by their skills under difficult circumstances. Our counselor also gave us some cash to have on us. She wished us good luck and gave a kiss and a warm hug to each one of us. She was a beautiful person who truly cared about us and all the others she helped. It was also great to have Laszlo with us, because he spoke English better than all of us put together.

It was a beautiful, sunny May day as we left our hotel and walked to the bus stop, which was only a block away. We had several bags to carry, including the heavy winter clothing we did not now need to wear. We only had to wait a few minutes for our bus and in no time we were at the train station. We had fun looking around, and ten minutes prior to departure we boarded: destination Boston. It was a very exciting time for my family and me, but we were a little nervous as the train left. We didn't mind the more than seven-hour trip to Boston; it was long but beautiful. Many thoughts and questions came to mind during the trip. Did we make the right decision in choosing Boston and would the people in Boston accept us? We had waited a long time for this moment. We were scared, but ready to start our new life in a new country. We held our heads high and beamed with excitement as the train slowed down and pulled into North Station. Our dreams and prayers were finally answered. The months of waiting in camps and in processing centers were now behind us. It was the first time since leaving Hungary that we had traveled without an escort, and it felt great! We were truly free and we were almost "home."

7

Boston here we are

The 16th of May, 1957, was a beautiful warm day in Boston. We arrived on schedule in a strange city that was to be our new home. After receiving some directions from a porter, we walked to the bus stop and continued to our next and final destination. While on the bus we kept looking all around as we tried to see everything that was out there. Before we arrived at our apartment we had to transfer to another bus heading to Dorchester.

Finally, we arrived. It was a third floor apartment on Nightingale Street in Dorchester, next to Franklin Field. Some of the neighbors knew that a Hungarian refugee family was moving into the apartment that day. They were on their porches, waiting for us to arrive. Some said hello and waved to us as we entered the building. We smiled, waved back and went upstairs. The apartment was mostly empty. There were a couple of kitchen chairs, an old GE one-door refrigerator and some mattresses on the floor in each of the bedrooms. In the refrigerator we had milk, eggs, bread, jam, and fruit. The apartment also had a gas stove and a few cabinets that contained some dishes and silverware. The apartment floors were bare wood and in need of sanding and refinishing. We didn't expect much so we were not disappointed. We were ready to get on with our lives. We had lived under worse conditions in the past and survived. We would do it again. We had faith in ourselves and in our abilities.

We checked out the apartment and the large front porch. While we were unpacking our few belongings there was a knock on the front door. To our surprise it was a neighbor from a couple of houses away.

She had a tray full of cookies in her hands and had her two daughters with her. She introduced herself and her daughters, and we each introduced ourselves as well. As I recall, her name was Maria. She welcomed us to the neighborhood and told us to call on them if we needed anything. Maria, younger than Mom, told us that they were Italian and had lived in the area for some time. There was more hand communication than verbal, because we understood very little of what they were saying, but we nodded a lot. Maria took us to the front porch and showed us where she lived. She pointed and waved to some of the neighbors, and I think she was telling us their names. It was obvious to Maria that our apartment was nearly empty and that we could use some furniture. As she left, we thanked her for the cookies and her warm welcome. She smiled and gave Mom and us a big hug before leaving. That visit was very special to us in more ways than we imagined at the time.

Prior to departing the HIAS office in New York, we were given the phone number of the local HIAS office that we were to call after arriving in Boston. The following morning, we called that office and were told that they had jobs lined up for us. We would start on Monday. That was only a few days away. It was the best news we could have hoped for. We were all very thankful and excited. They also advised us that the rent was paid through the end of May and for the full month of June. After that time, it was our responsibility to make the rent payment, which was very reasonable. The job offers were minimum wage jobs at a dollar per hour for each of us. With our limited English, we didn't expect much more at the time. The next couple of days were some of the most emotional and unbelievable days since escaping from Hungary.

Maria must have told her friends in the neighborhood that we were very poor and in need of help. She took it upon herself to solicit furniture, clothing, and other household items for us. We were surprised at the generosity of our neighbors. They invited us into their homes and offered furniture and clothing to us. We graciously accepted just about everything that was offered. In the first week, we received furniture almost daily. The very first thing we received was a kitchen table and chairs from an elderly Jewish couple who lived next door. It was followed by a couple of area rugs from Maria. Within a few days, we also had a large sofa, which turned out to be a pain in the neck to take up to the third floor since it was very heavy. Slowly our apartment became more livable and we had more clothes. We named our neighbors by the items they gave us, such as the carpet lady (Maria) and so on.

I wasn't much for standing around and doing nothing. On Friday, two days before starting my job, I left the house and looked into the availability of night schools. By the time I came home that afternoon, I had signed up for English and Machine Shop at a trade school. I wanted to learn English as fast as possible and my only choice was to go to adult education at night because I would be working in the daytime. I signed up for English on Tuesdays and Thursdays and Machine Shop on Mondays, Wednesdays and Fridays. I was able to join the English class at once, but had to wait a few weeks for the machine shop class to start.

The very first weekend my brothers and I went down to Franklin Field, which was just down the street from us. We watched the kids play baseball there. Baseball was new to us and we had a very hard time learning the rules of the game. In Hungary and all of Europe, the big sport is soccer, plus some basketball. Within a few weeks we got friendly with some of the neighborhood kids, but communicating with them was hard and at times very frustrating. As months went by, we started to play baseball. I liked to pitch while George liked the outfield.

One of the kids I met was Joel Satin, who lived on Talbot Avenue, across from Franklin Field. He played the saxophone. I told Joe that I played the clarinet and he got all excited. Later on, he introduced me to Bobby Gruenin, who lived on Browning Avenue. Bobby was a drummer. I also met many of their other friends, including Rose Lipsky, who would play a very important role later in my life. When I had time, Joe would invite me to Bobby's house to join him and Bobby in a small band. I was not familiar with any of the songs they played, which made it much more difficult for me. I was playing the clarinet and later on the alto saxophone, but I wasn't very good at either one. I didn't have time to practice enough, and music wasn't one of my top priorities. Some time later at Bobby's house, I met another friend of theirs named Al, who was a singer and played the guitar. He was very good.

My parents got friendly with the Jewish couple next door, who were very kind and generous to us. Knowing that we didn't have a TV, they invited us over to watch theirs. It would be many months before we had our own TV. Mom was able to talk to them in Yiddish, and she would translate for us. One program we all watched was the Ed Sullivan show, which was the favorite show of our hosts. Most weekends we would be next door, watching that show. They would translate and give a little background on the acts.

I started my job on that Monday in downtown Boston on Washington Street. It was a sandwich shop and I was the busboy and dishwasher. This job didn't last very long. I worked 56 hours the first week and when I received my pay envelope, the amount of money I received did not look right. I went to the owner who was working at the cash register, and in my limited vocabulary, I asked what were all the deductions on the stub. He showed me the deductions for taxes and a dollar per day deduction for food. He had taken six dollars more from my check than he was allowed to. I tried to tell him that I brought my own lunch from home every day and I took from my pocket a used bag that held my sandwich every day. He didn't want to listen and told me to move away from the cash register and let the customers pay their bills. I got very mad and started banging on the register counter, demanding my money. Whether he understood me or not I will never know. I told him that I would kill him if he didn't give me the six dollars. I was a very shy boy, not yet sixteen years old, but in just a few minutes I had matured a lot. I refused to be ripped off. I had worked very hard for that money and my family needed every penny I earned. My persistence and refusal to back down paid off. He took six dollars from the cash register and threw it at me. I took the money, gave him the finger and quit. I had learned the finger gesture from a friend only a few days before. Needless to say, I did not use him as a reference on future job applications.

Now that I was an expert busboy, I was ready to go on to bigger and better things. This turned out to be a job at the Beth Israel Hospital in Brookline. The bigger but not better things were larger pots and pans to clean in the hospital kitchen. My father was also working at the hospital as a laborer. My brother Laszlo was working at Embo Shoe in Roxbury. I had already started my English classes, and each day I would learn new words, but my accent was horrible. Learning English was very difficult for me and for my father. I had a hard time pronouncing words correctly that had "th" ("think," "that," "thirty," and so on). My lips and tongue were not made to learn English. They got in my way. I would also mispronounce words that started with V and W. I didn't have the proper sounds for those letters, which made it more difficult when I had to give someone my name, Veres. My younger brothers enrolled in the local school system. They were able to learn English much faster than those of us who had to work. George learned the fastest and had the best accent, but Laszlo also did well. Zoltan stayed with us in Boston for only a short time, then he moved back to New York. At this time, John was 12 years old, George was almost 14, Laszlo was almost 20, Zoltan was 22 and I was almost 16 years old.

I worked at the hospital daily, from eight to five, then stopped for a quick sandwich and went to night school. Night school was very helpful. I didn't mind the long days, five days a week. I knew that in order to get a better-paying job, I had to learn English. Slowly but surely, I was learning the English language and doing well in the machine shop class. In just a few weeks, I gained more confidence and was able to communicate better. I switched jobs from the Beth Israel Hospital to a boiler control rebuilding company in Boston. I had always loved electrical work, and when I saw the ad in the paper for this job I jumped at the opportunity. It paid $1.25 per hour — that was a 25% raise over my previous jobs. I was doing well and I learned a lot about oil burner controls. This came in very handy later in my life when I had my own mechanical construction business.

The company was a small business with about 14 employees. There was a major drawback that I was not aware of when I was hired. In late July, a few of the employees were let go, but I wasn't very concerned. The owner was very pleased with my work, knowledge, and work habits. I got to work early and I worked hard, but it didn't do me much good. In early August, at quitting time on payday, I was given my paycheck and the bad news. My boss told me that I had done a great job and I would be called again when they needed me in the future. At first I didn't understand what he meant until one of my fellow workers explained it to me. When I was hired, they hadn't told me that this was a temporary, three-month job. I was very surprised and upset when I found out. As I found out from my co-worker, the company had only four full-time employees. Prior to the heating season, they would hire additional workers for a few months only. Several months later they would let them go. I nearly cried as I left the building and headed for home, unemployed and very mad. But, by the time I got home I felt a lot better and I was no longer angry with my boss. It was just a part of life and there was nothing I could do about it.

I knew that for my next job, I wasn't going to be washing pots or pans. I also knew that I was not proficient enough in English to work in a machine shop yet. On Saturday and Sunday I checked the employment opportunity section of the *Boston Globe* paper closely and circled a few ads. I also talked with Laszlo, who told me that he probably could get me a job at Embo Shoe, where he worked.

The interview Monday at Embo Shoe went very well and I was hired immediately. The following day, I started in the same department as Laszlo. For a sixteen-year-old, this was a good temporary job until I learned enough English to go to work as a machinist. Working at Embo Shoe was different and it was fun, plus I was making more money. I was used in many departments, and most of the jobs I did were piecework. The faster I did the work, the more money I made. In order to make more money I worked overtime on Saturdays as much as possible.

Things were going along fairly well at home; all of us settled into our daily routines. Laszlo was accepted into the New England Conservatory of Music in Boston. In 1958, Laszlo got his driver's license and later bought a used 1951 Chevy for $400 on credit, so now instead of taking the bus, we drove to work in his car. Things were looking good. We owned a car.

I wanted to also get my driver's license. I asked Laszlo to teach me how to drive, which he did. I got my driver's license on my first try and I was very excited. On some occasions when Laszlo didn't use the car he would let me borrow it. The '51 Chevy was a very good car. Later on, I bought the car from Laszlo with money I had saved from my weekend side jobs. It was the policy at our house that each one of us who worked would give the money we earned on our regular day jobs to our parents, until we were twenty-one years old. We got an allowance only, and that wasn't very much. Laszlo, Dad, and I supported the family. My side jobs, from which I could keep the earnings, were in the form of repairing radios and later TVs in the neighborhood. I used the money to buy tools, test instruments, and for the purchase and upkeep of the '51 Chevy. Laszlo no longer wanted to own a car at that time in order to save money. My first car and what a thrill it was! I was only eighteen years old. It was a great first car and served me well.

As soon as my father learned the language a little better, he left Beth Israel Hospital and went to work at a restaurant equipment supplier for better pay. He would continue to repair and rebuild used restaurant equipment until he started his painting and paperhanging business with the help of John.

In mid 1959, we moved to a much nicer and larger third floor apartment on Blue Hill Avenue in Dorchester. It was only a few blocks away. Luck was on our side again, for we met who would become our very best friends the day we moved into the new apartment. After the movers left and we were unpacking, Mom wanted me to put the heat on. I went to the thermostat and turned it on, but after ten or fifteen minutes we felt no heat. I looked around the house to see if there was another switch somewhere but could not find one. When it came to repairs in the house, it was always me, "Steve," and still is today. I decided to go to the basement and see what the problem was. I had a hard time figuring out which fuse box belonged to which apartment, so I decided to knock on the first floor apartment door and ask for help from our neighbor.

To my good fortune, they were home. Sylvia Goodman opened the door and I introduced myself and told her that we had no heat. I asked her if she knew which one of the fuse boxes and furnaces belonged to the third floor. She told me that she didn't but maybe her husband, who had just come home from work, might. Her husband Saul came to the back door and said that he would be more than happy to help me. With flashlight in hand we went to the basement. He took me to the wall where some furnace switches and controls were mounted. He saw that the third floor heater switch was off and told me to put the switch on. I flipped it on and we heard a click at the furnace control. In a few seconds the furnace started. He also showed me where all the fuse boxes were and also the storage areas for each tenant. We stayed in the basement for another minute or two to make sure that the heater would stay on. He then came upstairs with me to make sure that the thermostat settings were also correct. I introduced my family to him, and when he heard that we were Jewish he was thrilled. He invited us for coffee after we had a chance to unpack because he wanted the rest of my family to also meet his wife Sylvia.

It was another helping hand, which turned into a friendship that is still alive today. My parents were 20 to 25 years older than the Goodmans, but it was a wonderful relationship. Our families became very close. Later on, when Sylvia had kids, my parents or I would baby-sit for their new daughter Sheila, and later on Kenny, their son. My father adored Sheila. Dad always wanted a daughter; this was as close as he came until he had granddaughters. Every time we go back to Boston, we visit our good friends the Goodmans.

While we lived on Blue Hill Avenue my parents also met a very nice older lady, who lived next door on the first floor. One day while they were talking, she told my parents that she was thinking about painting and wallpapering one of the rooms, which was only painted at the time. Knowing that we could use the money, she asked Dad if he knew painting and paperhanging, to which he said yes. The fact was that although painting was not a problem, we had never done paperhanging before. My father was not afraid to try something new and was willing to undertake this project. That decision would change his life. She asked Dad how much he would charge her if she bought the materials and Dad supplied the labor. Dad gave her a very low price because he wanted to do it for her and he thought it would be an interesting thing to do. That was the understatement of the year. Boy, did we learn a lesson!

She gave Dad the job and special-ordered the wallpaper at the local paint store. A few weeks later she received the wallpaper. She called us and told us that we could start any time. Dad told her that he would do the job during the next two weekends. This turned out to be a family affair. Dad told me and my younger brothers not to make plans for the next two weekends because we would all be working next door. A few days before we started the job, we picked up some brushes and other supplies we would need. We also asked the store clerk a lot of questions. We took a crash course on painting and preparing a painted wall for paperhanging in just a few minutes. I became a critical part of this undertaking. I had to do most of the translating for Dad and I knew a little about painting but nothing of paperhanging. The store clerk was very patient with us and was very helpful. He had a hard time understanding us and we had a hard time understanding everything he said. Once again we nodded a lot; we didn't understand most of what he said.

On Saturday, we sanded, patched, and primed the woodwork, walls, and ceiling. On Sunday, we painted the wood trim and the ceiling with the first coat. A few days later, after work, my father painted the second coat with one or more of my brothers while I was at school. At that time all paints were oil-based and cleanup was much harder than with the latex paint that is available today. The following weekend we started to wallpaper, but had a problem as soon as we opened the roll. To our surprise, it was very heavy wallpaper, and to add insult to injury, it had a design on it. It was beautiful and expensive. An experienced wallpaper hanger should have installed it, not amateurs like us. It required much more work than we had anticipated. We had to match each piece, which is much harder especially when you work at a corner. The smartest thing would have been to stop as soon as we opened the first roll and saw what we were up against. That would have required us to admit that we were wrong to undertake the job, which is something no Veres ever admitted to before, to the best of my knowledge!

Dad would never let inexperience stop him in anything he undertook. I inherited that stubbornness from him. Many times I tackled and then mastered new undertakings, and this turned out to be quite useful, especially after I started my own business later. But there was no time to panic now. After a few choice words and curses from my father, in Hungarian of course, we proceeded with the hanging of the wallpaper. We cut to length and pasted the first piece and put it on the wall. As soon as we hung that first piece, we knew that we had a problem and we were in for a very long day.

The hung strip of wallpaper kept peeling off the wall because it was too heavy. We had to hold the hung paper in place and let it set for a while before we could set the next piece. Having only one stepladder didn't help us either. We fetched a couple of chairs from our apartment — we didn't want to mess up her nice chairs. We were not the right contractor for this job. We did not have the right tools for the job and were unable to read the instructions that came with the wallpaper and the paste. We had nothing going in our favor, but we didn't let that influence our decision, and continued with the job.

It turned out to be a very long and frustrating day as we forged on, determined to complete our agreement, regardless how long it took. At times we could have used ten or more extra hands to help hold the wallpaper on the wall. After we hung the first few pieces, my father made the paste heavier, which helped a lot. This is what is called "on the job training," but the best was yet to come. We rolled the seams while we held the wallpaper against the wall to remove the excess paste. We didn't finish the wallpapering until late that night. Dad decided to do the touch-up painting and cleanup the following day, Sunday. We were hungry and exhausted as we went home that night, but glad the day was finally over. We had completed our very first wallpapering job. We were proud of our accomplishment and ourselves. However, our joy was short-lived. We could not believe our eyes when we went back the following morning to finish the job.

Just after 9:00 a.m. we went back for what should have been a little touchup and cleanup. Upon entering the room we were amazed and shocked at what we saw. At every seam there was shiny dried glue facing us, and fingerprints on the wallpaper all around the room. Something had gone very wrong. We had screwed up bigtime. We hadn't washed down the wallpaper very well, especially at the seams and where we had been holding the wallpaper with our glue-covered hands.

Every time I think of this job now I burst out laughing, but it wasn't funny at the time. We tried to wash off the glue, but it was already dry and our efforts did very little. Rubbing much harder would damage the paper, doing more harm than good. My father was very upset, and started in cursing as he had the day before, again in Hungarian. Thank God he didn't know how to curse in English! Demoralized and embarrassed, we proceeded to touch up the trim and cleaned up the room. Now, it was time to break the bad news to a wonderful old lady who was so impressed by our hard work.

Telling her the news was my job, as Dad had very limited use of the language. I tried to explain to her what the problem was and why it had happened. We told her that we were very sorry. I also told her that we would buy new wallpaper and that we would re-do the job at our expense. She felt very bad for us, because she saw how embarrassed we were and how hard we had worked. My father kept saying to her over and over again the words, "Very sorry." She told us that she had hated the previously painted wall and that she could live with the wall, as is. She didn't want us to re-do the job and she refused our offer to not take her money. I told her that this was unfair for a poorly installed job, but she insisted and made us take the money. We were sincere in our offers, but she refused because she knew we could put that money to good use. The money we charged her amounted to probably less than ten cents an hour. We remained very good friends while we lived next door to her.

We earned our money the hard way that time and learned from our mistakes. The bad job didn't deter us from undertaking other jobs in the months to come, but we would not use that first job as a reference either! These jobs led my father to quit his other job and start his own painting and wallpapering business after John had finished school.

In 1960, Laszlo left Embo Shoe and joined the Army for a two-year hitch. This left only Dad and I to support the family, as both of my younger brothers were in school. Laszlo was stationed in Arizona where he met his wife-to-be Linda. He was in the Army Band and his unit was sent to Germany for about a year. After he was discharged from the Army, he decided to live in Tucson, and went into teaching music at a Tucson high school. I got Laszlo's job at Embo Shoe, which was embossing the leather sole with a heated die on a small hydraulic press. This was a piecemeal job and I was making much more money than before. I also started night classes at the South Shore School of Refrigeration & Air Conditioning in Quincy. My brother George also took the same class. Bill, our teacher, had his basement in the house converted into a classroom and a workshop. The three-hour class met twice a week and was broken into two phases. Half the time in class was spent learning the fundamentals of refrigeration and air conditioning; the other half was shop work. It was hands-on training and I enjoyed it a great deal. I wanted to have a second trade just in case I didn't like machine shop work.

Now was the time politics entered my busy life. This would create problems at home. I became a big John F. Kennedy fan and read most news accounts about his campaign for the Senate and later on for the White House. I was fascinated by his charisma and the way he would inject humor into some of his answers in response to reporters' questions. I knew very little about American politics, but that soon changed after I started to follow JFK's campaign. I just couldn't get enough of him on TV or in the papers. My father didn't like Kennedy because he came from a rich family and because he was young. Dad liked Nixon. The many JFK posters and banners I brought home would get my father very upset, but I didn't care. He was my candidate and I was an enthusiastic supporter. Dad and I would argue about politics and he would tell me time and time again that I was too young to understand things. That may have been true in part, but I told Dad that we were not in Hungary now and things were different here. I idolized JFK and convinced several of my older friends to vote for him at election time.

I had started taking music lessons on Saturdays to improve my reading and technique. I was no Benny Goodman, and our band wasn't great, but we had a lot of fun when we practiced. On some occasions we even played as a band with Al, the singer and guitar player, at some gigs. Because of my busy work and school schedule, I had very little time to meet new friends or to have an active social life. Other than knowing a few of the girls through Joel and Bobby, I never dated a girl until late in 1960, when I was nineteen years old. It was a very nice date with a girl named Rosalyn, who lived in the neighborhood. We went to Nantasket Beach and then we went on some rides at Paragon Park across the street. Because of my limited finances we kept the rides to only a few. While driving her home, she moved close to me and leaned her head against my shoulder. For reasons I don't remember I never asked her for another date, but I did see her at the homes of some of my friends. I was very shy when I was out with my friends, especially when we were in the company of people I didn't know, or girls. My limited knowledge of the English language was mostly responsible for this. As years went on, that changed, especially on a very memorable night in early 1961.

Most of my friends belonged to the B'nai Brith Young Adults (BBYA) organization, and because of that, I also joined the local chapter. That was the best decision I have ever made. At the BBYA there were social events and club dances in addition to the regular meetings. I was afraid to go to the club dances because I didn't know how to dance, so I decided to learn how. From our local library I took out books on how to dance and I practiced at home. It was much different when I had to dance in front of people. I felt that everybody was watching me, which really wasn't the case. My very first dance was at the Boston YMCA on a Saturday night. I danced only twice all night due to lack of courage. It cost a dollar per night, and I would go to four more YMCA dances before attempting my first dance in front of my friends. At the YMCA dances I watched others and saw that I was not the only one who didn't know how to dance. Each time I went, I danced more, and finally, I decided that I would go to our next BBYA chapter dance. It was a very good decision.

On January 14, 1961, the Brookline/Brighton/Newton Community Center hosted a dance and some of us decided to go. This was my first social event with this organization and I will be forever grateful to Rose Lipsky, a friend of mine who also went to the dance. We decided to meet in front of the G & G Restaurant on Blue Hill Avenue in Dorchester. Those of us who had cars would drive our friends to the dance. Rose needed a ride and asked me if I would drive her and her three girlfriends to the dance. Being a nice guy, I told her that I would, and after introducing me to her friends, we got into my car. One of the girls was Elaine M. Dores. I met her for the first time that night. Rose sat in the front seat and the other three girls sat in the back. Elaine sat in the middle of the back seat.

The trip to Newton took us about a half-hour and en route, on several occasions, I looked into my rear view mirror and saw Elaine. I liked what I saw and I know she saw me looking at her a few times. I knew only a few people at the dance and was very nervous until I finally asked Elaine for a dance. It took me more than thirty minutes after the music started before I asked her. I was no Fred Astaire and it showed, but at last I was on the dance floor, showing off my skills (or lack of them). This was only my sixth dance and I could only dance to slow music. After our first dance we sat down because they were playing music I didn't know how to dance to.

From the first minute I met Elaine I knew there was something special about her. A little later I asked her for another dance and she said yes. This time I was more relaxed and wasn't worried about other people watching me. Normally I wasn't much for talking because I still had limited knowledge of the English language, but that night was very different. At one point when the girls went to the ladies' room, Rose told Elaine to be patient with me because I was very shy and didn't talk very much. Elaine just laughed. She told Rose and the girls that I had hardly shut up while we were dancing.

The fact was that she was quite right; I felt so comfortable with her that I just kept talking as though I had known her for years. I didn't shut up all night. She was a very good-looking girl, wore a lovely red dress, and had a pageboy hairstyle. We danced several times, which was a record for me at a dance. At around 10:20 p.m. I told her that I had to leave because I had to be home before 11:00. I said I would be more than happy to take her and the other girls home. She and her girlfriend Estelle accepted my offer, but the other girls went home with some of our other friends. I took Estelle home first, then Elaine. She lived on Kerwin Street in Dorchester. When I got to her house, I stopped in the middle of the street in front of her house and let her out without walking her to her door. What class! What manners! But the fact was that I didn't know any better. She didn't seem to mind and thanked me for the ride. She told me that she had a good time at the dance. I told her that I had a great night also and we said our goodbyes. It was quite a night for me. She was wonderful! She made me feel very comfortable.

The following Saturday I decided to call her and ask for a date for that evening. She told me that she wished I had called earlier in the week, but she had to refuse as she had another date. I stayed home that evening, feeling a little hurt, but I got over it real fast. Acting on her hint that I should call earlier in the week, I called her the next Tuesday for a Saturday night date. She accepted and I was thrilled. A second date with the same girl was a new record for me. I was coming out of my self-imposed closet and becoming more social. When I picked up Elaine that Saturday night I met her family and found that their TV was not working. I went to the trunk of my car, got my TV repair toolbox, and fixed their TV. I became an instant hit at her house.

We went to the Boston YMCA, where we danced. We also went bowling. Elaine and I started to date on a regular basis and after that day, I never dated another girl. On February 14, I sent Elaine a valentine card which read, "To Someone too Nice to Forget." I also brought her mom a beautiful vase and flowers. It put a dent into my limited finances. What a guy!

At the BBYA dance I told Elaine that I worked at Embo Shoe in Roxbury, only to find out that she worked just a couple of blocks from me. I could hardly believe it! Things were going along really well between us. We dated most Saturdays until the day my father decided that we were moving to Union City, New Jersey. I had known Elaine for only a little more than three months, but I liked her a lot. I was very upset over the move, but I had no voice in the matter.

On April 1, 1961 we moved to New Jersey. From the very first moment we got there, I let my parents know that I didn't want to stay. I wanted to go back to Boston. My family had never met Elaine and they didn't even know that I was dating anyone, nor would it have changed things. In fact, it might have made things worse.

I didn't want to look for a job in Union City. Within the first three weeks I got a rash on my neck and body. The doctor told me it was because I was getting myself worked up over the move. He gave me some cream to use, and told me to relax and to stop worrying. I refused and my rash got much worse. I had to wear a scarf around my neck to hide it in public. I had become a rebel with a cause, and this was just the beginning. Finally my father realized that it was a mistake to move to New Jersey, and on May 30th we moved back to Boston. I newer knew why we moved to New Jersey or what made him change his mind, but the decision to move back to Boston made me very happy.

Me, Joel, Al and Bobby on drums not shown in 1961.

The day I fell in love, January 14, 1961.
Elaine and I are at a BBYA dance. This is our first dance together.
41years later I'm still smiling and we are still in love.

8

Getting a Job at Keystone Camera

Upon returning to Boston, we moved to 12 Theodore Street in Dorchester, which is just south of Boston. It was a nice first floor apartment, which was a relief after having previously had two third floor apartments. Shortly after moving in, we bought a used RCA/Whirlpool washing machine for Mom. This was our very first washing machine. It was time to give Mom a break. The machine was six or seven years old and came with only a thirty-day warranty. Several weeks after the machine was out of warranty it broke. When I came home that night after school, which was around 9:30 in the evening, Mom told me that the washing machine had died. I told her that I would take care of it on the weekend, which was a few days away. She got upset with me and asked me what she would do until then with the dirty laundry. I told her that for 47 years prior to having a washing machine she had managed quite well, and that I was too busy with school and the side jobs I was doing. She had no other choice but to wait because it was Steve the family repairman who would have to fix the machine. The next Saturday, I fixed the machine by replacing the automatic timer. It was the first time that I repaired a washer.

After we moved back to Boston I decided to get a job in a machine shop instead of going back to Embo Shoe. I made appointments and hit the road for what I hoped would be a much better paying job. I went on several interviews, but the shops rejected me because at nineteen I was too young. Some potential employers felt that I had exaggerated about my experience on my application. I was not exaggerating, but they still didn't believe me. Finally, after four or five rejections I got a job in Roxbury at the Automatic Screw Machine Company. The pay was no better than at Embo Shoe, but I felt I had a better future there. I was finally a machinist. It was the trade I had learned in Hungary and went to school for at night after working all day here in the USA.

The machine shop was a small job shop operation employing ten to twelve people and it was running two shifts. Lou, a very nice, elderly Italian man owned it. On many occasions I had to work longer hours and Saturdays in order to complete some projects on schedule. Because of my busy work and school schedules, I was only able to see Elaine on weekends. I would meet most of her friends at gatherings at her house. Her closest friend was Rita Steir. Most of Elaine's friends are still friends of ours more than 40 years later. The first few times at Rita's house I was very shy, but slowly I became more talkative and outgoing. Elaine and I would double date with Rita and her boyfriend, Stan Speigelman, on a regular basis. We became the closest of friends and still are today.

In just a few months I became Lou's top machinist and got a raise. I was now making around $65 per week and had just turned twenty years old. Most of the work we did was piecework and it was hard for him to get qualified machinists who would work under those conditions. Later on I also became Lou's set-up man for the screw-machines and for most of the other machines as well. Most of our work was short or long-run production of parts made from steel, brass and aluminum on our lathes, bridgeports, grinders and screw-machines. When we made only a few pieces of a complicated part the job was exciting; other times it was boring when we had to make 10,000 pieces of the same thing. That is the nature of a machine shop and that is why automatic screw-machines are used in most shops. They run unattended most of the time, once the machine is properly set up. Only reloading of the stock is required. An occasional spot-checking of the product is performed to make sure that it's within the required tolerances.

At times business was slow and Lou had to lay off a few of our machine operators. On many occasions we were told not to cash the paychecks for several days or weeks because there wasn't enough money to cover the checks. It was a tough, cutthroat business. Too many machine shops, not enough business to go around.

One of our new friends and neighbors on Theodore Street was Earl Bornstein. He and his wife came over one night to introduce themselves. They were thrilled when they found out we were also Jewish. Earl was my dad's age and worked at Keystone Camera in Dorchester as a machinist. He became a friend of my father and would come to our house about once a week. They had one thing in common; they were both chain smokers and smoked the same brand of cigarettes. Only my father and my brother John smoked. The rest of us did not pick up the bad habit. After Mom told Earl that I was also a machinist, he would ask me what I was doing at work.

If I was at home, Earl and I would talk shop. I showed him some of the parts I was making at work. On one occasion I showed him a drawing of a very complicated part that I was producing. Earl didn't believe that I had the experience to do it because I was only twenty. To prove to him how good I was, I brought home the part when it was done. He was impressed. We talked about how much money I was making and he told me that I should be making much more. He knew that besides not making enough, I was also not getting medical benefits, nor did I get paid holidays or vacations. Earl told me that he got paid holidays and a paid vacation each year on top of full medical insurance for his family. I was impressed and told him so.

A few months later Earl came over and wanted to talk to me about a vacancy that was coming up at Keystone Camera. He told me that a co-worker was leaving in a week or so and that he had talked with his boss, Mike Shapiro, about the possible job opening. He had told Mike about me and had asked him to give me a chance at the job. Mike told Earl to have me come in for an interview. I accepted the invitation, but did not tell my parents about the possible job offer. I told Earl to tell Mike that I would come by at 3:00 p.m. the following day.

A few minutes before three I met with Mike Shapiro and his assistant in Mike's office at Keystone Camera. I had with me some drawings of the parts I had been making the last few months. Mike was impressed. He asked me many questions as to my experience on different machines and if I had made any jigs or dies. He also asked me how much money I was making at my present job. I told him what my strengths and weaknesses were and that I had made a few jigs. I had not made a die up to that point, but I saw no problem in making one. I told him that I was making $65 to 70 per week and sometimes more when I worked overtime.

He showed me some drawings of jigs and dies and asked me which one of those I could make. I looked at the drawings for just a short time and told him that they all looked very easy and that I could make all of them. I told Mike that I could make much more complicated ones than those. His assistant looked at me as if to say who did I think I was kidding. Mike just shook his head as if he was just not sure.

He finally told me that he had a hard time believing that a twenty-year-old kid had as much experience as I claimed to have. I got angry and lost my temper with him. I told him that I was not a liar and all I wanted was a chance to prove it to him and any others who doubted my ability. I added that a person should be hired on his or her experience and not because they are young or old. I also told him that working in a machine shop for ten years or more does not necessarily make you an experienced machinist, even if you are 35 or 40 years old. I told Mike I was good and I could prove it in just a few weeks, or I'd quit and save him the trouble of firing me.

Mike was taken by surprise and was speechless for a few seconds. He finally said that I was right. He was tapping on the table with a pencil in his hand and just gazed at the drawings he showed me earlier. After thinking for a minute or two and shaking his head, he finally made his decision. He told me that Earl spoke very highly of me, and based on what Earl told him and what I told him, he was willing to give me a job, but not at the salary I was making presently.

He explained to me that they were a union shop and they had grade levels 1 to 14. Once you are hired at a certain grade level they can't put you back to a lower classification. He told me that they had several twenty-year-olds working there at grade levels 13 and 14 but he would start me off at grade level 12. That would be $1.45 per hour. Once I showed him what I could do he would raise my classification to the level of my experience. That starting level was much less than I was making, but he sounded sincere and after only a short hesitation I accepted the job. I told Mike that I wanted to give a two-week notice to my present employer because I was his only set-up man. Mike said that was fine and he shook my hand. He told me that I would be working at a bench next to Earl and that he was looking forward to seeing me in two weeks. I thanked him for the job and shook his hand once again and that of his assistant, who still had his doubts about me.

I left Mike's office and stopped at Earl's bench, which was only several feet away. I told Earl that I had gotten the job and that I would be starting in two weeks. I told him that I would be working at the bench next to his and asked him if that was the empty bench to his right. He said yes and he congratulated me and smiled. I was very excited and could hardly wait to go home and tell my parents the good news.

At last I had finally gotten a job with lots of opportunity and plenty of room for advancement. I was overwhelmed with excitement as I arrived at home and went to tell the good news to my mother. After I told her that I took a new job the very first thing she asked was how much money they were paying me. I told her that I would start at $1.45 per hour, but once they saw what I could do they would pay me more. I tried to explain to her how a union shop works and the different grade levels they had, and so on. She asked me if I had talked this over with Dad before accepting the job and I told her that it had all happened just this afternoon. My mom looked puzzled and nervous as to what my father's reaction would be. We didn't have to wait long.

Dad came home a short while later, and I told him excitedly about the new job at Keystone Camera, the same place where his friend Earl Bornstein worked. His very first question was how much money I would be making. I told him the whole story and that this was a great opportunity for me, and that after six months of employment I would also be eligible for fringe benefits. My father turned angry and started to yell and scream at me for letting them take advantage of me. I told him that he was wrong. Mike Shapiro seemed to be a very honest man, and in a short time I would be making much more than I was making currently.

I tried to explain to Dad that I knew what I was doing and that it was *my* life, but he just got angrier. He told me to call Mike in the morning and tell him that I had changed my mind, and that was final. Looking him in the face, I said no. I told him that in a few months I would be twenty-one. This was my decision to make. It was my future and I was taking the job. He blew his top. He raised his right hand and was ready to smash me in my face, but I grabbed his arm just short of my face and forced his hands to his sides. I couldn't believe what I was doing. For the very first time in my life I stood up to my father! I refused to let him beat me up. My body was filled with anger and my hands kept up the pressure on his arms. This time I had to stand up to him, even if I was only twenty years old. After a minute or more of this I told him that it was over! I pushed him away from me and went to my room.

Instead of being happy, my family had turned against me. I felt abandoned and betrayed. My father kept cursing and yelling for about thirty minutes after I went into my room. Mom came into my room after a short while and in a soft voice told me to apologize to my father; I had no right to talk to him the way I did. I got mad again and told her in a loud voice to forget it. It was Dad that needed to apologize, not me. That evening changed our relationship for years. We didn't say a word to each other for many months and hardly spoke to each other for the next two or three years.

The following morning I gave my two-week notice to Lou, who was devastated. He told me he needed me and he would give me a raise, but I said I was sorry, that I had made up my mind. I told him that if he wanted it, I would work every night for two or three hours, plus Saturdays, to do set-up for him until he found someone to replace me. He accepted my offer and wished me good luck.

The ride home that night after school was nerve-wracking for me. I didn't look forward to it. On my way home, I decided that I would give my parents all the money I made evenings and Saturdays at Lou's, which would more than make up for the pay cut I had taken. Dad was home watching TV when I got home that night and I went directly to my room without saying a word to anyone. A few minutes later Mom came into my room and again begged me to apologize to Dad, this time for her sake, but I stood my ground. I told her that I was not a kid anymore and that I knew what I was doing. I would do it with or without their blessing. I told her that I had given my notice to Lou that morning. Mom called me a stubborn boy, and then unhappily left my room.

For the next two weeks tension was very high at home. You could cut it with a knife. The money I would make at Keystone Camera and the second job at Lou's was going to be much more than I'd made before, but still my father wasn't happy. Dad and I didn't say a word to each other nor did we look at each other. Once I got home I would stay in my room doing my side jobs until it was time to go to work the next morning. My social life was zero.

Finally, it was time to start my new job at Keystone Camera. I was a little nervous the first day. Earl was not yet in when I arrived at work about fifteen minutes early. I put my toolbox on my workbench and went into Mike's office. He got out of his chair, shook my hand and asked me to sit down for a few minutes. He gave me a little overview as to how they operated and how jobs were assigned. Then he gave me a blueprint for my first project. It was a very simple jig. He told me that the raw materials for the job were in a box on my table and that he asked Earl to show me around and introduce me to my co-workers. We shook hands and I thanked him for the job, and then headed to my workstation. I started to put what few tools I had away and was looking at the blueprint of my first project.

Earl came to work a few minutes before starting time, which was at 8:00 a.m. He came over to my bench and welcomed me to the machine shop. He looked at the jig I was to build and asked me if I had any questions. I told him "no problem" and that I would finish it in less than three days. He smiled and then took me around and introduced me to my co-workers. I had already introduced myself to some of them near my workbench. I was eager to get started on my jig but I had a problem that needed to be discussed with Earl. One of the requirements of the job was that I needed to have a certain number of hand tools and measuring instruments. At grade level 12 ,where I was hired, I did not have to have many tools but once I got into higher grades I would need to buy a lot of expensive tools. That was a problem for me and I asked Earl if I could talk to him at break-time. He said sure.

I told Earl that at my previous job they had provided almost all the tools that were required; therefore, I had no need to buy a lot of tools for myself. I told him that I would buy some tools every week but I had a very limited amount of funds because I gave my parents all the money I made and I only got an allowance. I told him that I was doing side jobs in repairing radios and TVs and I would use that money to buy tools. I asked him if I could use some of his calipers and micrometers because I had not bought any of those yet. I would not damage them and it would be a big help. Earl told me that as long as I put them back in the same condition that I took them, he would have no problem with it. I was relieved and I thanked him for his generosity. I showed him my toolbox and the limited quantity of tools I had. He took from my toolbox my 0-1" outside micrometer and examined the friction/ratchet on it. He liked it and told me that it was better than his was. He might just borrow it a few times when he needed a good micrometer. I was thrilled and told him OK, as long as he put it back in the same condition. We both laughed.

The following morning I showed Earl a list of tools I was planning to purchase the first month. I asked for his advice as to which of those tools I should get first. He looked over my list carefully and put a number next to each item in the order I should purchase them. He also put a few other tools on the list, ones I hadn't even thought of.

Working at Keystone Camera was the best thing that could have happened to me. It gave me a great opportunity and I took full advantage of everything that was available to me. I finished my jig in slightly less than three days, to the delight of Mike, and he gave me my next project. I looked over the drawings and started on it, but something did not seem right with the design. I stopped working on the jig and looked at the design time and time again, just to make sure that I was correct in my thinking.

I went over to Earl at the lathe he was working on and told him that I needed to talk to him about a problem I had with my new project. At first he thought that it was above my capabilities, until I showed him the drawing and what concerned me. I told him that I felt the design was flawed and would not last more than a week in production. Earl was not an expert in jigs or dies. He was an expert lathe operator, but did have some experience in building a few jigs. He did agree with me though, and told me to see Mike. Mike would tell me if I was right or not. Nervous and unsure of myself, I started for Mike's office, but turned back just before entering and went back to my workstation. Mike must have seen me and came out of his office. He saw a puzzled look on my face, came over to me, and asked what was wrong.

On the verge of tears, I told him that I had a problem and I didn't know what to do about it. I told Mike that in my opinion the design of the jig was flawed, but I didn't want to make enemies after being on the job for less than a week. It was no way to start a new job. I could tell some of my co-workers were looking on, wondering what was happening. Earl was at a lathe machine but kept looking at me, and just smiled and nodded. Mike told me to relax and not to worry. This was not the first time that one of his tool and die makers improved on a design, and it probably would not be the last. He smiled and told me to come into his office with the blueprints. I was more relaxed now as we walked into his office to discuss my problem. I told him that when I got a project I liked to look over the design and visualize how the tool will perform under working conditions. I liked to know why an engineer did something a certain way. I also told Mike that on bigger jobs I would take home the blueprints to study them because I wanted to learn more about engineering and that someday I wanted to be an engineer myself. I also asked him if it was OK for me to take home the blueprints I was working on in order to study them and learn from them. He said it was no problem. We then turned our attention to my jig.

Mike was good at listening and making people feel at ease around him, and it definitely worked on me. I was no longer nervous and occasionally even managed a few smiles. Now it was time to get down to serious business. I unfolded the blueprint on his desk. I wasn't looking for trouble and didn't want to get anybody else into trouble. I showed him the hold-down clamp design and the area I felt was weak and unsafe. I told him that I was not an engineer but I wanted someone else to look at it before I started the job. I said that I had no problem with making the jig; I just needed someone else to tell me if I was right or wrong. I felt that it was my obligation to the company to bring it to their attention. A breakdown in production could be very costly for the company and someone could get hurt.

After looking at the blueprints for a few minutes Mike told me that I was 100% right, and asked what I would do differently on the jig. Those were the words I wanted to hear, and they removed a great burden from my shoulders. Mike thanked me and told me that I should never be afraid to speak my mind or voice my concerns.

Now, with much more confidence, I told him that I had used several different types of hold-down clamps that would be strong enough to withstand the production run. I asked him for a catalog of a particular clamp manufacturer so I could show him the ones I liked and used on the jigs I had made before. I flipped through the pages until I found the clamps I was looking for and pointed them out to him. Mike looked at one and told me that he would agree on that clamp. He asked if I would like to modify the jig the way it should be done or whether he should have the engineering department do it. I told him that I would be more than happy to sketch a revised design for him. He told me to get moving; what was I waiting for? I borrowed the catalog and some tracing paper, and then thanked Mike for his help and we shook hands. I was excited and hurried back to my worktable.

On my way back I stopped at the lathe where Earl was working and told him what had happened. He just grinned and gave me a slap on my back. Quickly I went to my table and proceeded to make room on it. I moved things to the side and started to redesign the jig. Once I started, I also decided to change a couple more things, which would make the jig faster to load. Instead of a sketch I decided to make it a neat drawing. I took my time because I wanted it to be just right and I wanted to impress Mike. It worked! That redesign and that day changed the life of this poor Hungarian refugee for years to come.

I took the finished drawing into Mike's office and showed him the revised design and all the changes I had made. His face lit up as he viewed it. After a few minutes of looking at the drawing and glancing several times at me, Mike stood up and shook my hand. He told me that the design was great and to get started on it at once. He was very impressed. I was on cloud nine as I headed from Mike's office toward my workstation. It was a very emotional morning. What a triumph! It was not yet noon, but it seemed like I had been working for more than a full day. I gave the thumbs-up sign to Earl, who had an ear-to-ear smile on his face.

Earl and I sat together at lunch and I showed him my drawings. I pointed out to him the changes I had made and I could tell by his expressions that he was impressed. I told him that Mike liked the design and had given me the go-ahead to start fabrication. Earl was very happy for me and told me to keep up the good work. Just after lunch I started the fabrication of the jig and I had the parts department order the new hold-down clamps for me. The afternoon went by fast, but by quitting time I was very nervous again. The events of the morning had taken a lot out of me and I almost didn't go to my second job that evening, but I did. Once I got home from my second job I said hi to my parents, but as usual my mother was the only one who replied to me. As usual, I went to my room and worked on some radios and televisions I had to repair.

Things at Keystone Camera were going along better than I anticipated. In my second paycheck I had already received a two-grade raise and more money. I thanked Mike for the raise and told him that I really appreciated it. I was glad I took the job. He told me that he had wanted to raise me three grades, but personnel told him that only two grades were allowed. He told me that Earl had told him that my father was very upset with me for taking the job at a much lower scale. He also said that the way I was going, it wouldn't take very long before I made more than before.

In just a few days, my redesigned jig was completed and sent to the inspection department for approval. Every jig and die was inspected to ensure that it was within the tolerances allowed. I was well into my third project, a small die, when I was advised that my jig had passed inspections with flying colors. That, of course, made Mike and me very happy. In my fourth check I received another two-grade raise, which made me classification 8. When I gave the check to Mom I told her that I had gotten another two-grade raise and was making more money than at my previous job. She told me to give the check to Dad and tell him that I got another raise. I refused and as usual just went to my room.

After working nights and Saturdays at Lou's for more than four weeks, I decided to tell Lou that I couldn't do it anymore. I would work for only one more week. He had already hired someone to replace me but the other guy was not as fast as I was. After some discussions with Lou, I agreed to help him part-time, but not on Saturdays. I had too many side jobs and I also needed some sleep. I was averaging 65 to 70 hours a week of work, including my side jobs.

As the weeks and months went by, I was given more complex and larger jigs and dies to build. I also received new classifications and more money. My father still refused to acknowledge that he had been wrong, which made me very mad every time I got a raise. At times when Earl was over at our house, he would tell Dad how well I was doing and how pleased my boss was with me, but my father just changed the subject. Earl tried to help me, but it was no use. My father was too stubborn.

Later on, after I turned twenty-one, I gave my parents only part of my paycheck and used the rest of the money to buy more and better tools. It felt good to have high-grade tools that belonged to me. Earl was impressed with the new tools and used them regularly. I was pleased; I had used his tools for months and it was payback time.

A few weeks after I started my job at Keystone Cameras I found out that if I wanted to go to school at night to study subjects related to my work, they would pay a percentage of the cost. Depending on the grades I got, they would pay up to 100% of the cost. I jumped at the opportunity. After looking into several schools, I decided to enroll at the Wenthworth Institute in Brookline, which was starting a class in early September. I took a one-year course in Design Engineering and I loved it, but my poor hand printing skills prevented me from getting an A in the class. I had to be satisfied with a B and was reimbursed 85% of my cost, which made me very happy.

I was still taking night classes at the South Shore School of Refrigeration & Air Conditioning in Quincy. Now I went to school every night of the week and loved every minute of it. I had sacrificed my social life for night school, but I wanted to have options as to what I would do for the rest of my life. I also felt that the engineering classes I took would be helpful to me in the future. This happened much sooner than expected, and it happened in a very big way.

9

A Big Opportunity

My job at Keystone Camera was going extremely well. I was very happy with my progress, but little did I know that something big would be happening in the next couple of months. I was given more and larger jobs to design/build and I did them all without a problem. My schooling came in handy when I was designing a new tool. My drafting skills also improved immensely. Earl and I became very close friends and he enjoyed looking over the designs I was making. Only three or four employees were allowed to design and build tools in our machine shop, and I was one of the select few. Some of the more complicated dies or jigs we would subcontract out to an outside company.

Dies and jigs perform different functions. A die is placed in a press and stamps out a piece of metal from a sheet or a coil of metal. Dies are made for large quantity production. It is not feasible to build a die if you only make a few pieces. There are single-stage dies or multi-stage (progressive) dies. For example: if you make 10,000 metal wall brackets, you would build either two single-stage or one two-stage die. A single-stage die would punch the holes and pierce the flat piece out of a sheet metal coil. The second die would bend the piece 90 degrees. If you make a two-stage die, the first stage would punch the holes and cut part of the metal, and the second stage would bend it and make the final cut. A more complicated part like computer housings would use a multi-stage die.

Jigs are used for holding a piece of material in place while work is performed on that part. There are simple jigs that can be made in just hours, while more complicated ones take many days.

Each month I bought new hand tools and measuring instruments with money I made on my side jobs. As time went by, I had to borrow fewer tools from Earl and eventually I had more tools than he did. Many times he would borrow my tools because they were better than his. Good tools make better mechanics. It was now time for a surprise in my life and a break I didn't expect.

I was working at my bench on a die I was close to finishing and testing when Mike came over and told me that he wanted to see me after the break. I asked Earl if he knew what Mike might want, but he was clueless as well.

I went to Mike's office right after the break, but he was busy. He was discussing something with his assistant and with the chief engineer from our tool-engineering department. He told me to wait outside for a minute, which I did. Once he finished with the others he sent them on their way and asked me to come in and sit down.

He closed the door behind me, which meant that he was not to be disturbed. There were large windows in the front of his office and anybody could see who was in his office at any time. He told me to relax because he saw a puzzled look on my face. He told me that everything was fine, but he needed to talk to me about a very special project. Mike told me about a progressive die they wanted to make, which would be a first for our company. All progressive dies used in our production facilities were made by subcontractors and none of them were as complex as the one he was thinking about making in-house. He pulled out a blueprint of a part and a preliminary drawing of a progressive die design that was only 10 or 15 percent completed. He told me that the engineering department wanted another six to eight weeks to design the die. He wasn't sure if they could design it correctly and the company didn't have eight weeks to spare.

He said that he needed the proposed die designed and built within four months. If not completed on time, it would delay a new projector our company was introducing. I was his choice for this project. I told Mike that there were others who had more experience than I and they probably could do the job better than I. He leaned toward me, put his hand on my shoulder and told me not to underestimate my ability. In his opinion I was the only one who could do it. He wouldn't be talking to me otherwise. Mike also told me it took days for him to convince Mr. Schwartz, the owner of Keystone, and others that we could make this die. He told me that this was a great opportunity for me but it was my decision to make. I was not yet twenty-one, and this would be the biggest decision yet I would have to make in my young life. What a moment, what a great opportunity!

I was speechless for a few seconds. I told Mike that it would most likely take thousands of hours to make and weeks of design work before any of the parts could be fabricated. He told me that he knew it was going to be a tough job but we could do it. Time was a big factor. He had to make a decision that day, and I had to give him my answer before lunch. He told me that he would give me all the manpower I needed. I could pick my own assistant and most of the other people who would work for me on this project. He gave me a hard pat on my shoulder and told me to take the drawings, look them over carefully, and let him know before noon.

I went back to my workbench and tried to make my decision before noon, just as Mike asked. The more I looked at the drawings the more difficult it looked, but at the same time I was getting excited. The thought of doing the largest project in-house at Keystone got my adrenaline going. I started to scribble in a notebook my thoughts about the design and how many men it would take to make it. It didn't take me long to realize why Mike wanted to make this tool. This progressive die would do the work of eight separate dies. It would save up to 75% of production labor cost and could therefore save a lot of money for the company. In less than an hour I was convinced that I could do it, and I went to see Mike in his office. He was in there talking on the phone and told me to sit down. He told the person on the other end of the phone that I was walking into his office and then he hung up the phone. I figured he was talking with one of the people that would make the final decision.

With the blueprints in my hand and a smile on my face, I told Mike that I was willing to undertake this project and that I would do the best I could do. I told him that I wanted his assurances that he would give me the manpower I needed when I asked for it. It was a deal. He then told me not to discuss this matter with anybody until a decision was made whether they would or would not make this die. I don't know who was more nervous, Mike or I. With a broad smile on his face he got up, shook my hand, then quickly left the room and went downstairs. I went back to my work area and proceeded with the completion of the die I was working on.

At lunchtime Earl tried to question me, as did others, about what was going on in Mike's office. Everybody knew that Mike's door was hardly ever closed, and when it was, that normally meant that someone was in big trouble. I had no choice but to lie to Earl. I told him that Mike wanted to know how I was getting along with my father and if things were improving at home. I didn't know what else to say and I was not really sure that he believed me. Earl didn't pursue the matter any further, which was a relief to me. He saw me looking at some blueprints but he didn't ask me about them. Perhaps he felt that I wasn't going to talk about it.

After lunch I finished and tested the die I was working on, and around 2:00 p.m. I took it to the inspection department. From there I went to Mike's office for the next job. Mike was not in and I did not see him on the floor either. I went to my work area, put all my tools away, and cleaned up my work area. Still no sign of Mike, so I decided to take out the drawings and spend some time on them, at least until Mike came back. I looked around the room and started to put the names of co-workers on a piece of paper that I wanted on my team, if the company proceeded with the project. I crossed some of the names off the list and put new ones on, until the list was finally complete. I wanted people who got along with me, would work hard with me, and would not resent me as their boss. I also started to do preliminary sketches of sub-assemblies for the die. I had nothing else to do and I figured it was better than doing nothing.

Finally around 2:45 p.m. I saw Mike heading towards his office. He signaled to me that he wanted to see me. We both went into his office, but this time he didn't close the door. He told me that the project was a go and asked me how much longer I would be with the die I was working on. I told him that it was finished and already sent to the inspection department. I told him that I had started preliminary work on the progressive die and had a list of workers I wanted for the job. I gave Mike the list and requested that Larry, a tool and die-maker, be assigned as my assistant for the duration of the job. I also told Mike that within two or three days I would be ready to start fabricating some of the parts. He shook his head in disbelief and told me with a smile that I wasn't wasting much time in getting going. He told me that he would review the list and would let me know if it was acceptable to him. Some of the men were working on other projects that were also important.

The following morning he called me into his office and told me that all but one of the names were OK with him. He suggested that I use one of the other milling machine operators as a replacement. We agreed and he directed his assistant to call the listed people into his office at once. Within two minutes his office was filled with my team. Mike stood up from his desk and made me stand to his right. He told the men gathered that I had been put in charge to design and build the largest and most complex die ever built at Keystone Camera. He told them that it was going to be a progressive die and would take thousands of hours to build. Each one of them was going to be a part of this undertaking under my direction, and Larry would be my assistant. He said that he expected each and every one of them to do their very best and to cooperate with me 100%.

There was total silence in the room for a few seconds, after which Mike asked me to say a few words. I was a little embarrassed by the sudden fame and responsibility. I told them that this would be a team effort. I also told them that I chose them because they were very good in their specialized fields and that I wanted the best team possible. We all shook hands and they each congratulated me on my promotion. Larry seemed even more excited than I was and looked very happy to be working with me. Shortly after the team left Mike's office, the word spread, and within ten minutes everybody knew that I had been put in charge of a major project. There was no more secrecy. I would design and build our first progressive die.

Earl and other co-workers knew that something big was happening in Mike's office, and they knew they were not part of it. Earl was at his workbench just marking time, dying to hear what was going on, as were Jim and Tom who worked directly behind us. Jim or Tom could have been put in charge of this project — they had much more die-making experience than I did. I called them over to my bench because they were good friends of mine and told them what was happening. They were very excited for me and each one congratulated me. Jim and Tom almost beat me to death in fun. Earl looked at me and just smiled.

The next morning Earl told me that he had known what was going on. Mike had talked to him regarding what he thought of me doing this job. He knew that the project was a secret at the time that I lied to him. Earl was not part of my team because I felt that Mike needed him on several other important smaller projects. Besides, I would have been uncomfortable as we were such goods friends and he was about 40 years older than I. It was the right decision.

I wasted no time in starting my design, and within two days I was ready to start fabricating some of the parts. However, I was about to discover that there was a lot of resentment by others. They were jealous that a twenty-year-old kid had been put in charge of a project of this magnitude. The die could cost more than $30,000 to build.

Many felt that the main reason I got this project was that I was Jewish just like Mike, Mr. Greenberg, and Mr. Schwartz, the owner. I felt a surge of anger, but managed to suppress it. We had several anti-Semites in our department who hated every one of us Jews. They would whisper behind my back. Mike told me that this might happen. He told me to just ignore them and let him know if anybody was giving me a hard time. I was more disappointed than hurt; I refused to be intimidated by them.

Their behavior just made me more determined than ever to let my work speak for itself. I had already had a run-in with one of them who had accused me of trying to show off by working fast. The fact of the matter was that I always believed in working hard for the wages I earned. Earl and many others made much more money than I did, yet they couldn't have made many of the dies or jigs I made, but I was never jealous of them. Only insecure people are jealous of the achievements of others.

Early into the project I sat down with Larry and discussed how we were going to share responsibilities. I told him that I needed as much time to myself as possible the first few weeks in order to get the design off to a flying start. I wanted him to handle most of the communications with our team, and I wanted to hear from him only, in order to keep disruptions to a minimum. I would also give him the drawings. Larry would make the parts himself or assign them to others. I thanked him for his support and told him that I wanted to beat the time frame that had been given to us. He thanked me for choosing him as my assistant and assured me that he would do whatever it took to ensure success. I knew Larry as a hard worker; we had a lot in common and shared the same desire to succeed.

In order to get the design in ahead of schedule, I requested permission from Mike to also work at home. It wasn't for the overtime pay, but I felt the first few weeks were very critical and this would help me a great deal in getting the hardest part over as soon as possible. Mike gladly agreed, and I stopped taking side jobs until this project was nearly done. I used the kitchen table as my drafting table at home. Mom would look at the many drawings, but it was all Greek to her. Dad never came over to see what I was doing.

There were times when I got very nervous because it seemed things were not going as fast or as smooth as I hoped. At times it was like hitting a brick wall. I did not quite have the die-making experience that was required for this job, but I refused to give up. Some nights I was still working at 1 or 2 a.m., yet I was never late for work.

Because I felt that my lack of experience forced me to work so many hours more than anticipated, I would only turn in half the hours I worked at home. The first few weeks I drank a lot of coffee and I lost some weight. After the third week, we were back on my schedule and by the sixth week we were ahead of schedule.

The design was mostly completed and we now concentrated on fabricating the hundreds of parts that went into the die. I kept my team members very busy. Larry, besides making many of the parts, also made sure that materials for everybody were ordered in a timely manner. He ordered the raw materials from the supply room and special tools and kept a log. Our project had top priority.

Larry was very good and was my confidant when things were not going well. We would brainstorm on solutions. Not every idea that went into the design was mine. Larry and my friend Tom both gave me new ideas and helped when I was stuck, or just not sure about something. At the start of the job, Larry, Jim, Tom, and Earl told me that they were there to help me in any way they could. That made me very happy and grateful. They had over 100 total-years of experience between them. Time and time again, they would look at the drawings and pat me on my back, or tell me about the design features they liked.

There was a time when Tom questioned one section of the design. At first I thought I was still right and proceeded with the design, but that night I took the plans home for a closer look and sure enough, I saw the problem. I thought I was clever, but the fact is that I was stupid for not looking ahead towards the next section of the die. By the next morning I had the section redesigned and was very grateful to Tom for finding my screw-up. As soon as Tom came to work, I went to him and told him that he was right, and how grateful I was to him for pointing it out to me. Because it was found so early in the design and not a week or two later, it saved me a lot of time and aggravation. I gave him a huge hug and a kiss on his cheek. What a good friend!

Each day I was more and more confident, even when things were not running as smoothly as I wanted. Mike would come to me only on rare occasions to ask how things were going and my answer was always the same: "We are on schedule and things are going great." Sometimes it was a lie and an over-exaggeration on my part, but I didn't want to worry him because there was very little he could do. Larry and I did all the worrying for everybody; we both agreed that this was the best way to handle it.

My 21st birthday came and went without much fanfare. I was too busy with the project; it consumed all my time and energy. I had very little time for any social life. Elaine was very understanding and supportive and didn't make a big deal of it. She knew that this was important for me and she was excited for me. My friends knew about the big project I was working on and would ask Elaine how it was coming, and she would just say that it was coming along. While busy at work I got my U.S. citizenship as soon as the law allowed. I passed the test with flying colors. It was a memorable day.

Almost until the time I turned twenty-one years old, I gave all the money I made on my normal job to my parents, who gave me a $10 allowance per week. That didn't help with my social life, because I didn't have the money to go places my friends went. At times I lied and told them that I had to work. The truth was that I didn't have much money. Without my side jobs I don't know what I would have done. I would have had to give up school or the car, both of which were unthinkable to me. I scraped and hustled and barely got by. At times I wasn't totally happy about giving up my full paycheck at home, but I felt that I could live with it until I was twenty-one. That was Dad's rule!

Once I turned twenty-one, things got better on the financial end of things. The overtime money plus my regular paycheck gave me freedom like I never had before. I contributed $50 a week to my parents and kept the rest. For the very first time in my life I was able to save a little money each week and set up a savings account at a bank.

Thing didn't get any better on the home front; I just kept to myself and concentrated on my work. I hardly watched any TV and kept my distance from Dad. I didn't want arguments or fights. In our house he had been the one who made all the decisions: right or wrong. He didn't care what anybody else wanted, not even my mother. That made me very angry. It had been his show and nobody dared to question it until I did. Mom was always nervous when Dad came home, not knowing what mood he was in. He would have a fit if she didn't make soup every night or if dinner was not to his liking. He would yell and scream for long periods at Mom or us, so loud that he could be heard next door and even further.

Things didn't get any better when I decided to run my own life. He felt that I was too young, lacked his years of experience, and didn't know what I was doing. But I was the oldest son living at home at the time and I wanted more from life than just living under his rule, and I refused to be dictated to.

It was a good thing that Elaine didn't put any more pressure on me. That allowed me to focus on my job and get the project done in a rush. As weeks went by, more and more parts were finished. Good progress was being made by the team. By the end of the third month, more than 85% of the parts were already made. I felt that we would be finished ahead of schedule. Our team produced quality parts in record time and their hard work was much appreciated by me. At this point the team's confidence was radiating all over the shop. We were all much more relaxed than earlier in the project.

By week fourteen, we had already started to assemble the progressive die. It started to take shape as hundreds of precision parts were put into their proper locations. Finally, there was something to show for the thousands of hours of labor. Near the end of the job we ran into a few problems. Two of the parts, already made, were misplaced or stolen. I felt it was the latter but had no way to prove it.

We were forced to scramble and remake the parts as fast as possible. I made one of them while I had Larry concentrate on assembly work only. At this point we were already releasing some of our team members. We had run out of work for them.

On Wednesday morning, more than a week ahead of schedule, we put the progressive die into the largest punch press in our shop. We started final alignment and began to attach the final components to the die as well as the automatic stock-feeding device. I went to Mike's office and told him that we were going to test the die by 2 p.m. that day. He almost jumped out of his chair in excitement. He told me to let him know fifteen minutes before we started the press. I told him, "No problem," and went back to help Larry with the final preparations.

The day before, I had requested the rollstock from the stockroom. It was the material cold-roll-steel that was to be used for fabrication, and it had been brought upstairs for us that morning. I had hardly slept the night before, and it showed. There had been many sleepless nights since I started this project, especially in the first month of the job. At times I had my doubts and wondered if I did the right thing by accepting this project. However, as the project developed, all doubts had vanished.

We were ready to go by 1:30 but Mike told us to hold off until 2:00 p.m. Both Larry and I started to get a little nervous and decided to do another manual test of the die. We did it without stock one more time, just to make sure. With power off, we would release the clutch on the big punch press and manually turn the big flywheel. We wanted to check again to make sure that the upper part of the die went into the bottom parts without resistance. It looked great, and we also checked the vertical travel adjustments. We checked everything twice, then reloaded the stock feeding mechanism and waited for 2:00 p.m. The minutes went by ever so slowly.

Finally, a few minutes before the hour, upper management came upstairs to witness this historic moment. Never before was so much riding on any tool! Mike's reputation was on the line. With forty to fifty machine shop employees around our punch press, we were given the signal by Mike to start the machine.

With a shaking hand, I pressed the green button on the punch press, which started the motor and flywheel. For safety I decided to do the first 15 to 20 strokes slowly and manually, which meant that I pressed the foot control switch once and then released it.

This was a six-station progressive-die, which meant that I had to press the switch a total of six times before the first piece would eject. After that, each time I pressed the switch a new piece would eject. With slight hesitation I pressed the foot switch the first time. Everything looked and sounded normal. After waiting two to three seconds I pressed the switch again with the same results. Five more times I pressed the switch and the first two pieces ejected into the parts bin.

I took a quick look at both parts and rapidly passed my hand around the part to check for burrs. There were none. I flipped one to Larry to check and gave the other to Mike, who quickly looked at it and passed it on to Mr. Schwartz, the owner of Keystone. I looked towards Earl, who was across the way from me, and gave him the thumbs up signal. I pressed the foot switch and this time I kept my foot on it. The press ejected about 45 pieces in one minute. Loud applause burst from my friends, including all the engineers who witnessed this great moment.

There is no greater reward than the satisfaction that you've done something extraordinary under very difficult circumstances. My critics were silenced. They walked away from the punch press, dejected. They had wanted failure and Mike's head, but that had not happened. I asked Larry to take over the honor of running the punch press, while I flipped some of the formed pieces to my team members, to my friends, and finally to Mr. Greenberg. I also gave pieces to the engineers who witnessed the event.

There were smiles and jubilation as co-workers congratulated the team members on a job well done. The project came in ahead of schedule and way under budget. Mike sent a few of the pieces to the inspection department for measurements, but we were confident that all was well. It was finally over.

I went to each of my team members and thanked them for their help and for a job well done. I gave each a sample of the part we made for them to keep. The last, but most important team member was Larry, who was glowing with excitement. I thanked him for his help and dedication to this project. We hugged each other warmly and patted each other on the back time and time again.

After the jubilation had subsided, Mike came over to the punch press and told me that he needed to talk to me. He asked me to come into his office. There he introduced me to Yale Greenberg, who had been standing next to the big boss at the punch press just a few minutes earlier. Mike told me to sit down because he had something very important to tell me. He then dropped another unexpected bombshell into my lap.

Mike told me that Yale was the chief engineer in our camera and projector design department. They had an opening for me in that department if I wanted the job. At the insistence of Mike, the position had been held open for me for almost two months. Mike wanted me to have it. Of course, there would be more money, and no more coveralls to wear. No arm-twisting was needed and I quickly accepted the position. I was given the rest of the week off with pay. I was told to report to engineering the following Monday, 8:00 a.m. sharp. I was to wear a white shirt, a tie, and a jacket.

I couldn't believe it. I asked them if they were sure about this. Mike just nodded. They both shook my hand and congratulated me and wished me good luck. I headed back to my bench to gather my tools, but first I wanted to tell Earl and some of my other friends the news. I called Jim, Tom, Earl, Larry and a few others to my desk and I told them the good news.

At first they thought I was just kidding, but soon they realized that it was no joke. I had indeed received a surprising but well-deserved promotion. They were all happy for me and told me that they would miss me a lot. I thanked all of them for their support and guidance, especially in the early weeks when there was a lot of resentment in the shop against me. These guys had stood up for me. For that, I would be forever grateful.

Earl was speechless for a few moments and got a little teary-eyed, as was I, but he was extremely happy for me. I told Earl to keep my work area open just in case I didn't like my new job. He just smiled and went back to work, as did the others. I gathered my tools, said my final good-byes, and left for home. I was emotionally drained. It was a day I would never forget as long as I live. I was the happiest twenty-one-year-old on earth! WOW! I loved working there!

Part III

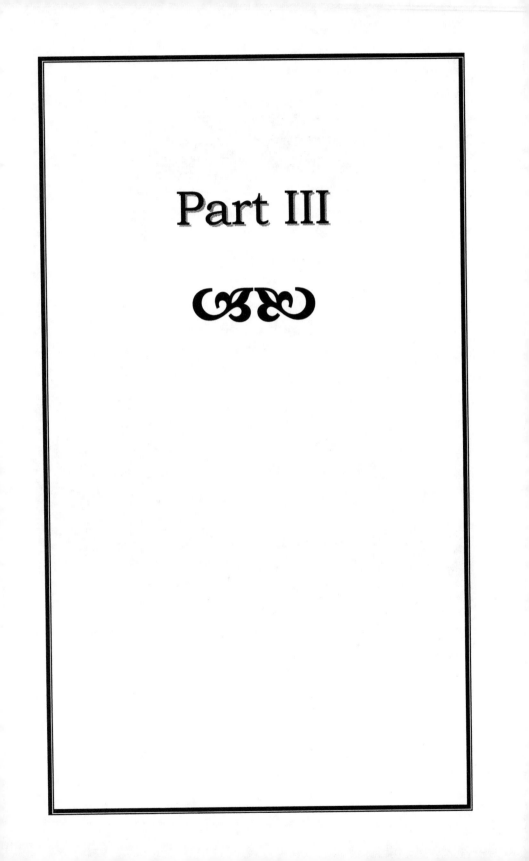

My citizenship photo, May, 1962 in Boston.

10

On to Engineering

The trip going home from work that afternoon was filled with excitement and some uncertainty. I had grown up during the progressive die project. I had learned a lot about working with others and the responsibility that comes with being in charge. If I never had to face resentment again, it would be just fine, yet there is no way to avoid it. If we are to get ahead and prosper, then we must take chances, even if some risks are involved. You need to make things happen and you must take advantage of every opportunity, otherwise, you will be bypassed and left behind. I have always believed in the motto, "work hard, play hard," whether working for myself or for others. Working hard was my life and still is today.

I always tried to set goals. Many resent those who are successful, yet the same people refuse to put the time and effort, the sweat and blood into their work. Millions of us went to school at night, after work, giving up our social life in order to get ahead. Nothing was given to me on a silver plate; I worked hard for my success and earned it.

Mike was like a father to me. He had more faith in me than my own family. Mike knew about my problems at home and made himself available, should I need to talk. I always appreciated it, and that is one of the big reasons I respected him so much. He was honest and fair but would not hesitate to give you a piece of his mind if you screwed up. He pushed me hard but I did not mind. I will always be grateful for his trust and support. He made me grow up in a hurry. Thanks, Mike!

I arrived home around 4:00 p.m., which was very early for me. I normally got home after school around 10:30 p.m. My mother appeared nervous and asked why was I home so early. She thought that something was wrong. I told her that nothing was wrong; the project I was working on was finished. It had worked great! I also told her that, as a total surprise, I had gotten a new position in the Engineering Department starting next Monday, with more money. I wanted to call Elaine, but I knew she wasn't home from work yet, so I waited. I then called and told her that I wanted to see her and had great news.

I jumped into the car and in just a few minutes I was at her house. I told her the good news. She was more excited than I was. It had been a busy day, but it wasn't over yet, as I still had school that night.

Mom told Dad about the successful completion of the project and my promotion. He never congratulated me nor did he show any emotion. Mom begged me to talk to Dad and tell him about the new position, but I refused. I was still mad at him for making my life miserable.

Next Monday morning, not knowing what to expect, I reported to Engineering wearing a white shirt, a tie and a sport jacket. I reported to Mr. Lou Greenberg's office and we talked for about fifteen minutes. He told me that I would be working for a while under Izzy Nesson, a long-time Keystone engineer. Izzy and Mr. Greenberg would be the ones evaluating my progress. He introduced me to all the engineers, but some looked at me a little funny, as if they were wondering what a kid was doing in engineering. I was just over twenty-one, felt out of place, and was quite nervous. All the engineers were over forty years old and the only thing we had in common were the white shirt, tie, and jacket we were wearing.

Finally, it was time to meet my new boss, so Lou introduced me to Izzy Nesson. Izzy was an older gentleman, who smoked a pipe and looked very serious. He was only about 5'2" tall, but was one of the most experienced engineers at Keystone Cameras. We talked about the new slow motion projector he was designing and the many parts needed. He asked me about my engineering background and I told him that it was mostly in tool and die making. I told him that I was going to Wenthworth Institute and I would do my best for him. He showed me my new workstation, which was right in front of his. Shortly after that, he gave me my first design job.

In just a few days I adapted to my new job without much trouble. I had no problem working with Izzy, and as time went by, we became the best of friends. He liked my enthusiasm and devotion to my work. I was always on time and was not afraid to ask questions if I had a problem or needed help. What a break once again! It was just like working with Mike and Earl upstairs. I helped design many of the parts that went into the new machine. This helped Izzy get ahead of schedule. But I was uncomfortable at my drafting table with my jacket on.

In less than a week, I took off my jacket and kept it behind me on the table. Nobody said anything, not even Lou, who saw me without my jacket several times. A few days later, I also took off my tie. It just wasn't "me" to wear a tie and jacket while working. I sweat easily. In just over a week, I was going to work without a tie or a jacket. This started a trend. A few days later some of the others took off their jackets, and a few also took off their ties.

I was very happy in engineering, so I asked Izzy if I should take any other classes at night. He recommended that I also take a course in Advanced Trigonometry and Calculus. Of course I took his advice, and registered for a year at the Lincoln Institute in Cambridge, Mass. After we finished the new slow motion projector, I got my own projects, but stayed close to Izzy. We talked a lot and used to bounce ideas off one another.

At home, things didn't get any better. I hadn't had money to take Elaine to nice places. Most of the time we would go on a date Dutch treat. Normally we took in a movie or dinner. We went candlepin bowling a lot. Elaine never complained, which made me love her that much more. We had clicked together from the first time we met. After I turned twenty-one I could take Elaine to places we could not afford before. I saw her on most Saturday nights, and we got along great. She couldn't come over to my house or call me at home, yet she never complained. My father would not allow us to bring our girlfriends home. She understood my situation. While I wasn't happy at home, I refused to have my problems there take over everything else.

I worked hard and learned new things each week. A lot of that had to do with my teacher, Izzy. He would stay after work and teach me about the do's and don'ts in engineering. Although he was about forty years my senior, we got along well. We both loved our job and the challenges that came with it. Our company also did some contract work for others in order to keep our fabrication facilities busy. One of my best-remembered designs was a new seat belt device for airplanes. I designed the two-piece buckle and latch assembly, and our fabrication shop produced hundreds of thousands of them. The trade name was American on the buckle. This buckle and latch device was used on most airplanes in the USA for over twenty years. We saw the buckle on all types of airplanes when we traveled by air. For many years it was the first thing Elaine and I looked for when we got on a plane. We just looked at each other and agreed that we were in good hands because we had my buckle and latch to keep us safe. I finally had created something that many people would use every day. It was a good feeling.

In spite of my busy work and school schedule, I found a little time to play music with Joe, Bobby and Al. I played at a few dance functions for the fun of it and did not get paid. My younger brother George was working for Embo Shoe at my old position.

As I was approaching my twenty-second birthday, I started to plan my future and what I wanted out of life. I decided that as soon as I turned twenty-two, I would enlist in the Air Force and become a jet pilot. In early May 1963, I went to the Air Force recruitment center to enlist, but my application was rejected. I didn't have enough college credits. I was devastated and very angry!

Ever since I was eight years old, I had built model airplanes. First I built ultra-lights, then rubber-powered planes. I loved planes and flying and I thought I would make a great pilot. Years later, I also built radio-controlled power planes. I built radio-controlled cars before kits were available for them, and also boats. I loved the hobby, and would work on my models into the early hours of the morning. I still have model cars, boats and planes today.

A few weeks after I was rejected by the Air Force, I decided to join the Army Reserves, which included six months active duty, then five and one half years of duty in the reserves. I felt it was my obligation, and I wanted to do my part to serve my country. I was also thinking about starting a business and I wanted to get my military obligation behind me. I requested starting my active duty on July 10th, which was one day past my 22nd birthday. I advised Izzy and Lou that I was going into the Army Reserves, and that I would be going on active duty in a month. They were not happy about it, but they knew that I had made up my mind. I did not consult with Mom or Dad. I told them after I signed up. My father said nothing to me, which was just fine with me.

Elaine threw a big surprise birthday and going-into-the-Army party for me. All our friends were there. Elaine put up a huge American flag, which was very appropriate. I was gung-ho USA. We had a great time at the party. Because of Rita, I had met a lot of wonderful people. Many became our friends and most are still our friends after all these years. I have been blessed with so many friends! Some knew me when I had a hard time communicating in English, but they took the time to make me feel at home. What a great bunch! The farewell got a little emotional near the end as I hugged each of them and said my good-byes.

Serving in the US Army in 1963.
Basic training at Fort Dix, New Jersey
than stationed in Fort Gordon, Georgia.

11

We're In the Army Now

I had to report to Fort Dix, New Jersey, for basic training on July 10th, 1963. My most memorable recollections are the verbal abuse we got from company sergeants, especially in the first few weeks. They constantly tried to intimidate and harass us. They bombarded us with filthy language every hour of the day. They called us everything in the book and then some. Every other word was a four-letter word. I didn't understand the point of it.

When I arrived at Fort Dix, we went to a processing center where we got a very short hair cut, for which we had to pay about $1.50. Shortly after our fine haircut, we were issued our uniforms and other required Army gear. We were then directed to put everything into our newly issued duffel bag. While waiting to be transferred to our assigned company area, I got friendly with a couple of local Bostonians, Herb and Barry. During basic training we became good friends and we hung out together most of the time. Herb came from a poor family like I did, and we had more in common. Barry came from a well-to-do family and lived in West Roxbury, a more affluent area in Boston. For a while after we were discharged from the Army, Herb and I stayed in touch. Elaine and I even went to Herb's wedding.

After lunch we were bussed to our designated company area. It was sunny and hot, in the high 90s with very high humidity. We were all very nervous as we took our short bus ride. We were ordered off the bus and ordered to double-time approximately 100 yards while carrying our fully loaded duffel bag to the designated assembly area. More than twenty screaming, yelling and constantly swearing sergeants spaced about ten yards apart forced us to run faster and faster. This was the time we got our worst verbal abuse. We were humiliated as never before. They wanted us to know that they were in charge and our asses belonged to them from now on. I tried to ignore this and did what I was told.

After running to the assembly area we had to stand in formation with an arm's length between each other. A few minutes later, while the C.O. (a Second Lieutenant) gave us a lecture as to what was expected of us, Herb fainted and fell on his face. The heat and tension had caused him to pass out. They gave him smelling salts to revive him. He was white as a sheet. It was around 1:30 p.m. It was brutal out there as we listened to our C.O. He gave us his pep talk and the staff sergeant followed him. Finally, after 45 minutes of bull, it was time to move to our next phase. We got our building and bunk assignments, and were dismissed and ordered to put our things away.

Basic training in Fort Dix, New Jersey in July and August was no fun, to say the least. It was hot and muggy every day and I was drenched by late morning. Clothing stuck to my body and was quite uncomfortable. We couldn't wait to get back to the barracks to take a cool shower. We were told to take salt tablets, which were issued to us in order to replenish the salt lost by heavy sweating. We worked long hours, with a lot of marching and training. Two weeks after basic training started, our C.O. wanted to put together a company band and asked if any of us played a musical instrument. I raised my hand along with Herb and eight others. They asked what instruments we played, and seven of us were allowed to go home on a weekend pass to get our instruments. I played the clarinet and the saxophone. I wasn't great but I knew how to read music and how to play up to a certain level.

I called Elaine to say I was coming home for two days. She was thrilled until she saw my new haircut. I was almost bald, with just a little hair up front. When I took off my hat she just laughed. I didn't look very good with no hair, but she told me that I looked cute in my uniform.

It took only an hour to fly to Boston, so I was able to stay for almost the full two days. We did form a band, but most of us were just mediocre. We did it for the fun of it, and to get out of K.P. and guard duty. That was our reward for joining the band. The only part of basic training I liked was firing our M-14s at the rifle range. I also liked the night firing, when we used tracers. Our company sergeant was an OK guy. He had many lady visitors to his private room. He had fun! Needless to say, we did not.

We had a large mess hall where they fed ten or more companies three times a day. The food was nothing to brag about. I lost over 25 pounds in basic training due to the heat, lousy food, and hard work. We got $68 per month pay, which didn't go far. We were restricted to the company area most of the time for the first six weeks, but were allowed to go to the PX a few times. After the sixth week we got our weekends to ourselves, but were still restricted to base. I was not able to save a lot from my pay. I spent it on food and other things I needed. I would write home to Elaine telling her how things were, but nothing to make her upset. There was nothing dramatic to tell, other than the vigorous training and the heat. She would send me letters, and she sealed the back of each one with a kiss. The lipstick was very noticeable. Some of the guys would kid me about it and I would just tell them to eat their hearts out. Mail call was the most popular event while on active duty. Elaine wrote to me on a regular basis, which was very much appreciated.

By the end of basic training I was in great physical condition, but weighed only 140 pounds. My eight-week basic training was finally over. When I enlisted I had to put three choices as my preferences after basic training. My first choice was refrigeration, my second choice was electrical, and my third choice was electronics. I loved all of them and to me it didn't make any difference which one I got so long as it wasn't advanced infantry training. I'd had all the training I wanted in that. Because I signed up voluntarily and was not drafted, I was to be given one of my choices unless something dramatic happened, which it didn't. Finally, with basic training finished, I received my orders. I was to report to Fort Gordon, Georgia, while Herb and my other friends went to other places for their assignments.

Signal Corps wasn't my first choice, but later on I found out why they put me into electronics. The Army was just changing from the old style vacuum tube type receivers and transceivers to transistorized equipment, and needed additional soldiers to help implement the change. Fort Gordon was much more to my liking. We had to be in school by 8:00 a.m. and after school we were free to do as we wanted to. Most of the weekends were our own. No more cursing and harassment — we left that behind in basic training and I was therefore more comfortable. Knowing how to repair radios and TVs, and knowing how to read schematics came in very handy now. I knew more about electronics than some of my teachers. Two of our teachers were good, but most of the others just followed the lessons from the book. Because solid-state radios were new, the Army didn't have enough qualified teachers. Later on, when it was obvious that a few of us were really good, we were asked if we would sign up for a longer term than the six months active duty. I said no, but agreed to help some of the officers in class who could not keep up with the rest of us. I had plans for the future, and staying in the Army longer than six months was not one of them. Had they accepted me into the Air Force, things would have been different. I would have stayed for years, maybe for a full career.

Elaine and I had already decided to get married shortly after I got out of the service. I left it up to her to find the place, and we decided on March 22, 1964.

In school we spent part of our time in the classroom learning the basics and how to read schematics, then we went into the lab to work on the latest receivers and transmitters at the Army's disposal. I liked it and was good at it. While working on our equipment we would listen on a certain frequency and would hear communications between Army units. The new equipment was much smaller, much lighter, and needed much less power to operate, yet they were more powerful than the receivers and transmitters the Army had used before.

Most of my free time in the evenings and weekends was spent at the USO club playing table tennis. There was a group of us who played several times a week. Some of us were pretty good and I was in the top five out of about thirty. I also joined the company bowling team, but in that I was just average, but it was fun and made our time pass by faster. We counted down the days and weeks and did our jobs, knowing that in a few months we would be home and back to our normal life.

November 22, 1963 was just another day at school; we were in the lab working when the unthinkable happened. A news flash was heard on our receivers: President John F. Kennedy was shot while riding in a motorcade in Dallas, Texas. I jumped up and yelled "Oh no!" Several of us who heard the news looked at each other in disbelief; most of us were in shock. Within just a few minutes an officer came into the lab and gave us the official news — the president was shot but he didn't know how serious it was. We switched our equipment onto a different frequency and were then getting direct news of the assassination attempt on the life of the President. When the news came that the President was dead, I didn't want to believe it. I started to cry. I was devastated like so many others, yet there were a few southerners in our unit who were very happy. They didn't like Kennedy, which almost got me into a fistfight with one of them.

Rumors of Cuban involvement were heard, and because our base was near Cuba, we were put on full tactical alert. We were issued our weapons and for three days we had them on us at all times. Finally, after three days of being on alert, our base was ordered to stand down. We turned in our rifles and returned to normal duty.

There had been some political discussions in our barracks in the past, which turned into heated debates at times. There was a great deal of resentment by a few of the Southerners in our unit over the actions taken by the President in desegregating the schools in the South. I was the President's strongest supporter in our unit and was not afraid to defend his actions. As a Jew, I knew firsthand some of the resentment that African-Americans were facing. I felt that all children should have the right to go to the school of their choice in order to get the best education possible and to make a better life for themselves. We are a free country and that is why the world looks up to the USA. Just as when I talked politics with my dad, the discussions became heated with strong feelings on both sides. As usual, I never backed down. I didn't agree with everything the President did or didn't do, but you have look at the overall job he was doing and what he wanted for the country. There is no way you can agree with someone 100% of the time, but that should not stop you from liking or supporting the man.

The first thing I had noticed about Kennedy that impressed me was his style and charisma that I saw on TV. I heard about him first when he ran for the U.S. Senate and I had often seen his image on TV. There was something about him that made me take notice. He talked about new ideas and his vision for a better America. I listened and liked what I heard or understood. Then I saw him in person when he dropped in for a campaign stop at the G&G Restaurant on Blue Hill Avenue in Dorchester.

I was young, new to politics, didn't speak English well, and didn't understand many of the things he talked about. But I liked what I saw and heard and so did the crowd. I got more excited as the campaign went into the final months, and after the debate with Nixon I just knew he would win. I watched the returns at home, and while it was nerve-wracking and very close, it was also extremely exciting. How thrilled I was when he won, and how upset my father was! I felt that Kennedy had some great ideas, which this country needed, and the timing for new and fresh ideas was just right.

His inaugural speech had been very electrifying and something that I would never forget. While I was new to politics, it didn't take long for me to get into political debates in a hurry. His presidency got off to a shaky start with the Bay of Pigs disaster. I felt that the President should have provided air support to the landing forces or should not have allowed the exiles to invade Cuba.

I was very anti-Communist and I wanted Castro out of power. I wanted freedom for the people of Cuba. I felt that the Eisenhower Administration, who approved the original plan, and Kennedy's own advisers screwed up big-time. It was stupid to undertake such a mission without air support and I never understood the logic of such a plan. They had a great chance and they blew it. Kennedy impressed me and the American people when he took full blame for the fiasco. He didn't blame others as he could have; he took full responsibility for it in an address to the American people on nationwide TV.

I loved his humor at the many news conferences he held, and how he made fun of some very serious issues. Problems arose, one after another, in a very short time. I was impressed with how he dealt with US Steel in the steel crisis and the many other challenges. How he faced nuclear war when he stood up and forced the Soviet Union to remove the offensive missiles from Cuba during the Cuban missile crisis. How he listened to the people and how he cared about the poor. How the Peace Corps, that he started, helped millions in Third World countries. His support for the space program and his vision for the new frontier. His trip and his speech in West Berlin, and the support to our Western Allies. The way he got this country moving and how proud we were to be Americans. How lucky I was that he came at a time when I needed someone to look up to. How lucky we all were to have him as our President, even if it was only for a very short time.

How sad I was with millions of others as we watched his funeral on TV. How we cried as John saluted the passing casket! I'm forever grateful for the leadership he provided and for the everlasting memories he etched into my mind. His assassination by a mindless coward deprived the Free World of a great leader. As weeks went by and the country went on with business under President Johnson, things were not the same. I know that I speak for a great many people when I say that John Kennedy was more than just our President. The mood of the country reflected that.

As Christmas approached, excitement and anticipation spread as we made travel plans to go home for Christmas and New Year and then come back for the last week of school. My discharge date was January 9th, but a decision was made to discharge everybody whose discharge date was no later than January 10th, and so on December 24th my active duty came to completion, to the delight of Elaine and I.

I found out that one of the company sergeants lived in the Boston area and had a car. I could come home with him if I drove. He had been up for over 24 hours processing discharge papers and was too tired. Needless to say, I agreed at once, as it would save me money. The twenty-hour drive was long and tiring, but I didn't care. My thoughts were only to be home as soon as possible. We stopped to eat, use the restrooms and get gas; otherwise it was nonstop. I paid for the fuel and the food. He slept on the back seat and left all the driving to me.

Several weeks before I was discharged from active duty, I decided that I would not be going home to live with my parents again. I wanted to start a new life and I had had enough of living at home. I didn't need to hear any more arguments or fights. I wanted to be free from yelling and screaming. Now that John was working with Dad, painting houses, my family didn't need my financial support. I called my boss at Keystone and had my job back in less than a minute. I could start any day I wanted to. That was a relief, because I needed the money and didn't want to waste my time looking for a job now that I was out.

I discussed my plans with Elaine, but my limited finances complicated matters. I had very little money saved because I had helped support my family. While in the Army, the $68 per month pay we got didn't even pay for the airline fares when I went home on leave. I needed a place to stay for a few weeks and look for an apartment to rent.

Elaine asked her parents if I could stay with them for a few weeks and they agreed, but of course, separate bedrooms. Elaine lived on the first floor of a three-story house with her parents and her sister Elanor. Elaine slept on the couch while I slept in her room. Josie, a long time family friend, was the landlord and lived on the second floor. The top floor two-bedroom apartment was to be vacant on January 1st, and after looking at a few other rentals, I decided to take the apartment because the rent was good. Elaine helped me clean the upstairs apartment and my brothers George and John helped me with the painting. In three weeks, I was ready to move in. It was good to be back home.

12

Getting Hitched

Elaine and I had a unique relationship. From the very beginning I felt at ease when I was with her, and after our second date I was hooked. I knew she was the one for me. I had no intentions to date other girls from that point on. I had never really told her how much I loved her but I think she knew. My busy work and school schedule didn't give us the time we wanted to spend together. She understood the reasons why and she never bugged me about it. We never went to fancy places while we dated, but it didn't matter; she knew I had very little money.

Most of the time on our date we would go to the movies, or go bowling, or go for a ride. Most of our friends also had limited finances so we had no problem going out with them. We had a nice time when we went out and that's what mattered to her. She was easy to please. To make it easier for me, she insisted on going Dutch treat, paying her part of the bill. That helped me a great deal financially and meant a lot.

Before I went into the Army, I gave her a black opal ring and asked her to be my girl, to which she replied, "Does that mean that we are going steady?" I asked, "What does 'going steady' mean?" She told me that it meant we were not going to date others. I said yes. That's how much experience I had in dating girls. I don't even remember how I proposed to her at all. Did I propose to her? I don't remember.

Work at Keystone Cameras progressed as well or better than before I left for the Army. They were happy that I had come back, especially Izzy Nesson. My father had never met Elaine; my mom had met her a couple of times without my father's knowledge. Grandma (my mother's mom) met Elaine when we visited her and my aunt in New Jersey, and she liked her very much. She was thrilled that I was marrying a nice Jewish girl. Both of my older brothers married non-Jewish girls.

Two months before the wedding I told my father that I was getting married in late March. I asked him to come to our wedding. The answer was a very loud no and he went into a rage once again. He told me that I didn't know what I was doing and that I was too young, and the same garbage I'd heard a hundred times before. I told him that it would be his loss and that I was not going to ask him again, and certainly, I would not beg him to be there. I got up and left the house, not surprised, but quite mad. I decided that I was not going to loose any sleep over it and if that's how he wanted it, then it was fine with me. I had not been afraid of him after our big fight of almost two years before. Everybody else in my family was afraid of Dad, except my Grandma.

A few days before the wedding Grandma came in from New Jersey. When she found out that Dad would not come to the wedding, she got mad like I had never seen her before and she let my father have it. She told him that he was a fool for not coming to the wedding, and she told him what a great girl Elaine was. She also told Dad that if he didn't come to the wedding, she would never again speak to him and never come to his house again as long as she lived. That did it! Dad called the next day and asked where to go to get a tux. Thanks, Grandma!

It was a simple, but nice wedding with about 125 people in attendance. There was lots of tension in the air, which showed on the faces of my brothers George and especially on Johnny. At the photo session, before the ceremony, it was time for Dad to meet Elaine for the very first time. I think he smiled, but only a little. Mom also greeted Elaine as though it was the first time they met, because she didn't want Dad to know that she had already met her. That was Mom, always trying to keep the peace. It did break the tension a little, and the photo session went on without further delays. We had warned the photographer that there might be some problem with Dad and not to force the issue if he didn't want to be in the pictures. Elaine wore a beautiful gown, which she had borrowed from Linda Morgan, a very good friend of ours, who had gotten married about 6 months earlier while I was in the

Army. My brother George was the best man and Elaine's sister Elanor was the maid of honor. My brother Johnny, who was one of the ushers, was most affected by the tension and it showed on his face. I saw it when I walked down the aisle.

When I look at the wedding pictures I always laugh, because the pictures showing my family walking down the aisle looked more like a funeral than a wedding. Another memorable moment was when it was time for my father to dance with Elaine. She was a good sport and didn't allow any of my family problems to ruin her day; she just smiled and acted pleasant. I was so proud of her for not letting anything spoil the most important day of her life. We had decided to just do what we could and let whatever was going to happen, happen. Towards the end of the wedding, Dad got a little looser; he might even have smiled once or twice.

My friends and bosses from Keystone Camera were there in force. Mike Shapiro, Lou Greenberg, Earl Bornstein, and Izzy Nesson, and their wives had a great time and also had a chance to meet my family. Grandma proudly introduced Elaine to our family and friends. She was great as always; we were so glad that she was able to be there and be a part of our special day. Having our friends there too was very important for us. They were our strength during some tough times and were always very supportive. Words can't describe the love we have towards them and the gratitude I owe to each and every one of them for making us feel like part of their family. After more than 40 years, I see them almost every year and our friendships are stronger than ever.

For our honeymoon we went to Miami, Florida, for a week. Then it was back to work at Keystone. But I had plans for the very near future.

Wedding day, March 24, 1964.
Uncle Misi, cousin Tom, John, cousin Susan, a proud Grandma,
Elaine, me, Mom, a smiling Dad (surprise) and George.

Mom and Elaine.

Dad and I.

13

Starting a Business and a Family

As soon as I returned to work from my honeymoon I told my boss Lou that I'd be starting my own business and I gave him a two-week notice. I told Lou that I loved my job but I had so many ideas that I wanted to start my own refrigeration business. Lou was shocked and very surprised, but wished me good luck and told me that if I ever changed my mind I would have a job waiting for me at Keystone Camera. I thanked him for his understanding and the trust he had had in me. He said that I had brought fresh ideas to the Engineering Department and that I would be missed. That was very nice of him. I'd miss them also, but it was something I absolutely wanted to do.

With $1,500 and a lot of enthusiasm, on April 15, 1964, I started my new business on Blue Hill Avenue in Dorchester. The name I gave to the new business was State Service Company. Elaine was working for the Secret Service in Boston and we were going to live on her salary. I leased a 1,000 square foot store near our home, bought a used van and some tools and put a small ad into the local newspaper. Starting a new business was already beginning to be much harder than I expected. I only knew what I learned in school; I had no field experience and I had no clientele.

I went to see the owners of all the local restaurants and every business that had commercial refrigeration equipment within a few miles of my shop. I offered my services at a 25% lower rate than any other service company. I felt that a lower price and 24-hour service would get customers to leave their refrigeration service company and try me, but it didn't work out like that. They wanted references, but I didn't have any. After a few weeks of running around and talking to hundreds of potential customers, I still hadn't picked up any commercial business. In order to get some work, I decided to fix small and large appliances like refrigerators, freezers, washers, dryers, toasters, irons, and so on.

The first commercial service call came in as an emergency call late one evening, from a local food market on Blue Hill Avenue, whose meat cooler had stopped cooling and whose temperature alarm had sounded. Around 10:00 p.m. I received the message from my answering service. I called the storeowner, who was thrilled to hear from me. Within 12 minutes I was at the market, since I lived less than two miles away. I found a faulty low-pressure switch, and in less than 15 minutes the cooler was operational. Luckily I had the part that was needed in my truck; I tried to carry a lot of spare parts in order to save time and money for owners. The owner was pleased with the fast service and told me that he had waited over two hours for a call from his regular repair company and couldn't wait any longer, so he had called me. He couldn't let his meat spoil. I had left my card with him several weeks before. He told his friends about the great service I had provided and the reasonable fee I'd charged, which helped me in the coming months.

After five months, I stopped repairing small appliances (toasters, irons), as I picked up more and more commercial work. I worked six days a week, 12 to 14 hours a day. I was doing well with servicing refrigerators, washers, and dryers and needed extra help, so I hired my younger brother George, then, a few months later, two more service men. I also decided to sell used large appliances, and later on new ones also. We even had some of our other family members come to the shop to wash down used refrigerators and washers.

For the first two years I didn't take money out of the business and we lived off Elaine's paycheck, which enabled me to buy more tools, more trucks, and a larger shop. This was to change soon, as Elaine had became pregnant. In September 1966, she gave birth to our son Robert. We were thrilled and overjoyed to have our beautiful baby boy. Working long hours, I hardly saw my son, but the business was at a critical point and because of our limited finances, I had no other option. I refused to ask for financial help from my family and so I was on my own. Working 75 to 80 hours a week deprived me of being a part of my son's early years, but that was what it took just to survive and to make my business grow.

The next major change in the business occurred in the fourth year, when I decided to also go into air conditioning repairs. Soon after that we ventured into the installation of central air conditioning systems. I felt that the future was in air conditioning, so I guided the business towards it. In the fifth year I phased out the appliance business and expanded the air conditioning business. At first I subcontracted the sheet metal work to others. Not very far from my shop was a one-man shop. I talked with Al, the owner, and asked him to fabricate some ductwork for me, which he did at a good price. Al did good work but had limited equipment and could only do small jobs. As time went on, I wanted to do larger jobs so I bought some sheet metal equipment. I then asked Al to come and work for me. Al was in his 50s and was a very nice and honest guy. He taught us sheet metal fabrication, but he had no experience in automated fabrication equipment. That, we learned on our own!

At first we did only residential and small commercial air conditioning jobs. Months later I started to work for a few oil companies, who were doing residential air conditioning installations which they merely subcontracted out to others. The oil company sold the job and got the contract but others did the installation and service for them. I was hungry for work, so I made a deal with a few of them and started installing air conditioning systems for their accounts. At first I kept the prices low in order to get more work and to show them the quality of work we did. I did all our estimating and contract negotiations. I was also in the field doing the installation with my crews and making sure the job worked and the customer was happy. I did mostly piping, controls, and service work, while I let my brother George, along with others, do the sheet-metal work. I only did sheet metal work when we were behind schedule or short-handed.

Things were going along pretty well and the business was making progress, as we were getting ready for the birth of our second child, who arrived on September 1, 1970. I was hoping for a girl but I didn't care; we just wanted a healthy baby.

At that time some of the hospitals allowed husbands to be in the delivery room. I discussed this with Elaine, but she figured that I didn't have the stomach or the courage for that kind of adventure. That morning we took Robert to my in-laws and I took Elaine to Goddard Hospital in Stoughton, where we had an appointment with the doctor and Elaine was going to be induced. I was in the waiting room when the doctor came to see me. He told me it was time and asked if I wanted to be in the delivery room. I told him, "If you need my help I'm going," and was on my way.

After putting on protective clothing, I entered the delivery room, to the surprise of my wife. "What the heck are you doing here?" she asked me. I told her that the doctor needed my help, so I came. The nurse set up mirrors so Elaine and I could watch the birth of our baby. It was not a bad delivery, but when the baby was just a little more than half way out, I noticed that the nurse and the doctor looked at each other in a very strange and nervous way. At that moment, I knew that there was a problem, but I didn't know what it was. It didn't take long to find out. Our baby was a girl, but she did not have a right arm.

I started to cry and Elaine tried to comfort me. I should have been the strong one and I should have comforted her, but I lost it. This was so unexpected and so heartbreaking to us. The excitement, the thrill, and the joy of watching our baby being born turned into a nightmare. I was angry at the world and just could not believe it. I went back into the waiting room while they finished with Elaine and performed a quick check on our baby. A short time later the doctor came into the waiting room and talked to me about our daughter. He told me that everything else looked OK, but they would have to take a closer look the next few days. To this day, we don't have the slightest clue as to why it happened, other than that it does happen, and it happened to us.

Elaine didn't take medications, she didn't smoke, and she didn't drink. She also took good care of herself and had regular check-ups. "Looks like the baby was in a bad position and the arm didn't develop," the doctor told us. It was now time for me to gather myself and call our families and close friends. It didn't take long for them to know that something was not right. The tone of my voice told them. Needless to say, our family and friends were heartbroken for us. I was devastated. The next few days were very difficult for Elaine and me. We were looking for answers, but found none, while our lives were changed forever.

For a girl, the name we had picked was Amy Joy. While we were less than full of joy, it didn't take us long to start loving her. Because of the special circumstances, the doctor allowed Elaine to go home earlier than normal from the hospital. We lived in Holbrook, which was only a short trip. Family and friends were at our house, waiting for the homecoming of the newest member of our family. A sign was hung on the front door of our house, "Welcome home Amy Joy." It really sank in that here was our baby — we'd take care of her for better or for worse, and we'd love her just as much as we loved her 4-year old brother, Robert.

For quite some time after the birth of our Amy Joy, my business was affected. I was emotionally drained and lacked energy and enthusiasm at work. It took months for me to get back into the groove of things. Elaine and I were going to do whatever it took, and so we went about our business in an effort to raise our family while realizing we had a lot to learn about Amy's handicap. The support of our friends was overwhelming. They were always there for us and always gave us their love and support. How blessed we were to have them at such a difficult time in our life!

My focus had to get back on my business, which had taken a financial beating. I had stopped bidding on jobs for a while because I couldn't concentrate on work and I was not in a mood to see new customers. Realizing that I had to get back to work, I put my emotions aside and concentrated on getting some badly needed work in a hurry. Slowly, as weeks and months passed by, I went back to doing my job the way I did it before Amy Joy was born.

It didn't take very long for Amy Joy to become the love of our lives, and nothing has changed over the years; things just got better as years passed. One couldn't ask for a better and more loving daughter than our Amy Joy. We always wanted to have two children and had not planned on a larger family. With Robert and Amy, our family was now complete.

After a few more years of doing residential and small commercial work, I started to bid on larger commercial work. It had more risk but it was more profitable. I felt that it was the way for us to grow and make more money in the long run. Larger jobs required more equipment, more labor, and more money. I had limited money so I was forced to set up a line of credit with a local bank to finance our larger jobs. In order to get a good line of credit, the bank wanted to see a longer track record in commercial HVAC work from us. Lacking an impressive list of completed commercial jobs, the bank gave me only a small line of credit. I had to settle for only 20 percent of what I wanted. Having no other place to get more money, I had to be satisfied with that. This is the problem that you face when you are under-capitalized and starting a new business from scratch.

It took some time for me to realize that I'd made a big mistake starting the business the way I did. I lacked the needed field and office experience and didn't understand the full financial implications of operating a new business. I would have been much better off to work for an HVAC company and then become a partner, or to buy an existing business with a good reputation. Going to trade school alone was not enough.

I was young, full of vigor and ambition, and ready to work like crazy and do whatever was required. Boy, if only I had waited a few more years, and if I had just been a little less stubborn and more patient! I had full confidence in my ability but didn't realize until years later that confidence alone is not enough.

The key to a successful business is talent, financial means, and willingness to work twice the hours for a lot less. I was willing to work very hard, I thought I had some talent (maybe not enough), but had only pocket change for finances to start my new business with. Perhaps most importantly, I underestimated how things worked in the real world. I was foolish and naive to think that a bank would give me the money I asked for because I promised them that I was good for it.

Being the young fool that I was, I forged ahead through the tough times toward my long-term goal of having a successful medium-sized contracting business. It was on-the-job training at its best, and I had to learn fast. Failure was not an option to me. I was too stubborn.

At the age of one, our Amy Joy was fitted with a non-mechanical prosthetic arm. The doctor told us that fitting Amy at an early age would help her do more things and prepare her for more advanced prosthetic arms in the future. The fact was that there was very little available other than the hook, which upset me greatly.

While working long hours at my business, at home I started to look into mechanical arms and hands, but was surprised to find nothing good available at the time. Being good in electronics, I even started to tinker with mechanical controls for an artificial hand. Building and flying model airplanes, boats, and cars gave me the knowledge of how mechanical servos and controls operate. Still thinking that there must be many, or at least a few, companies out there who make mechanical prosthetics, I continued to make calls. Boy, was I wrong! I called numerous hospitals and agencies, only to hear the same thing over and over again: "No, or "We don't know anybody who does." That was very discouraging to my family and I. Finally, in late 1972 we heard that UCLA doctors were using mechanical prosthetics on children. We decided to visit UCLA and see what they were doing in that field.

In February 1973, Elaine and I, with Robert and Amy, flew to Los Angeles, California, for a week of vacation and to see the Prosthetic Department at UCLA in Westwood. My oldest brother Zoltan and Mom and Dad lived in Los Angeles, so it would also be an opportunity for them to see our kids, who had grown quite a bit. Zoltan had moved to California in the 60s and had talked Mom and Dad into moving to L.A. in 1971, for Dad's health. My father had developed breathing problems. The cold winters in Boston were tough on Dad, who was a very heavy smoker. It ruined his lungs. He had difficulty breathing and would cough like crazy, yet he refused to quit smoking until it was almost too late.

After our son Robert was born, my father had mellowed somewhat and we got along better than ever before, yet we never really got close. The memories of the past between us did not ever completely evaporate, and there was still resentment on both sides. Too bad, because he missed out on a lot of great and wonderful moments.

This was to be our first vacation since we had gotten married nine years earlier, but it almost cost the life of Amy Joy.

On Monday we left Robert with Grandma and Grandpa and we took Amy Joy to UCLA. The staff at UCLA was very friendly and cooperative and we had a profitable visit. They showed us the latest in technology and even performed a brief examination of Amy. Dr. Seraguchi, who was in charge of the prosthetic department, was just wonderful and very helpful. The visit to UCLA gave me hope and lifted my spirits. The rest of the week was to be spent visiting fun places with the kids and spending time with my family.

The following day we took the kids to Universal Studios and took the full tour, after which we were going to my folks for dinner. It was a beautiful day and we had lots of fun, especially the kids, who were overwhelmed by all the activities. They both had a wonderful time. It was around 4:30 p.m. when we headed to the last program, which was a gunfight — a shoot-out with actors acting as cowboys. We were seated two rows from the top of the bleachers. Amy was seated between Elaine and I, and Robert was sitting on the other side of me next to Mom, who was also with us. When the show ended the crowd applauded the performers. The people in the bleachers stood up, but somehow, when we stood, there was no Amy. I did hear a faint scream, and as I looked under the seat, down towards the dirt below, to my horror I saw Amy Joy on the ground under the bleachers.

I told Elaine to watch Robert as I took off after Amy down the 15 or 20 rows of bleachers. I ran like crazy, pushing people aside while I made my way down from the top. Amy was hysterical by now, screaming louder and louder as I made my way towards her as fast as possible. When I reached her, I kissed her and tried to comfort her by telling her that daddy was here and everything would be all right. I picked her up and wiped her tears away and kissed her time and time again. I almost cried myself but held back. I had to be strong for her sake and that of Elaine, Mom and Rob.

I gently carried her in my arms from under the bleachers towards where I had told Elaine to meet me. Elaine, Mom and Robert got down a short while later as I was still trying to comfort our baby. I knew she was hurt but didn't know just how badly. We asked one of the ushers if there was a first aid station around and he took us there in a hurry. Amy had fallen some 25 feet, and as she fell she hit some of the steel braces supporting the bleachers. Between the floor and the bench seats, there was no safety railing. How could they build such a large bleacher section where an innocent and young child could easily fall between the floorboards and the bench seat? Sometime later they did install a safety rail, but by then of course it was too late for our daughter.

Upon arriving at the first aid station we found a nurse on duty who almost did more harm to Amy than good. There were several large bruises on Amy's head and arm and body. After checking Amy out, she told us to put ice on the bruises on her head and she'd be just fine. I told her that we should get an ambulance and take Amy to a hospital, since she'd fallen 25 feet, but the nurse told me that I was over-reacting to Amy's crying and that there was no need for that. I was getting very frustrated with the lack of cooperation from the nurse. Being a stranger in town, I didn't even know where the nearest hospital was, but fortunately, the usher who had taken us to the first aid station gave us directions. I picked up my daughter and rushed her and my family to our rental car in the parking lot and took off for the emergency room at St. Joseph Hospital in Burbank.

It took only 15 minutes of driving but it seemed like hours, while I was praying all along that we didn't get lost. It was not a very pleasant trip and my hands shook on the steering wheel. Elaine was now holding Amy, but we still couldn't calm her down.

After a short wait in the emergency room, they gave her a full checkup and took x-rays of her head and arm. In a very short time we got the bad news. Amy's arm was broken in several places and she had a fractured skull and internal bleeding. They rushed her upstairs to the intensive care unit and hooked her up to all kinds of equipment to monitor all vital organs. Now it was time to wait and see if Amy responded to the treatment. They put her arm in a body cast and on heavy medication. We had originally planned to be at my parents' house, so I then called Dad. As I gave him the bad news about Amy's accident, I was crying. I told him that Amy was hurt, but not the full story. There was nothing he could do so there was no reason for me to frighten him. Now it was in the hands of the doctors and God.

We were told that the next 24 to 36 hours would be critical. A full-time nurse remained in Amy's room. Elaine and I also stayed with Amy, while Mom was with Robert in the waiting room. At first they didn't want us to be in Amy's room, but I insisted. Elaine and I took turns updating Mom as to Amy's condition. We didn't tell Mom how serious the injury was but I think she knew. About an hour later, Dad and Zoltan showed up at the hospital but were not allowed in to see Amy. They saw her through the window and that was bad enough. Everyone was crying; it was a horrible sight. I asked them to take Robert home with them because we were going to stay at the hospital with Amy. We just couldn't believe that this had happened to our little girl. A week that was to be filled with fun and adventure had turned into a nightmare for us.

After about 36 hours, Amy started to respond better to treatment and her color started to get back to normal. Elaine and I were helpless; we simply comforted her and told her over and over that we loved her very much and that everything would be OK real soon. We tried to put our best face forward and to act normal and not cry front of her, which took some effort on our part. We also sang some of her favorite rhymes to her.

Several days later they allowed us to take Amy home to Boston, but only with our assurance that we would take her to the doctor at once. We got back to Boston and did just that. It was a very uncomfortable and long flight back to Boston, as one can imagine. The five-hour flight felt like five days. I'm sure it broke the heart of many passengers when they saw Amy with no right arm and a body cast on the left arm. Her arm was in the air and held up by a post, which was built into the cast.

Taking care of Amy at home while she was in the body cast was a major undertaking for my wife, especially when we gave her a bath. Because of the cast, Amy couldn't do anything for herself. She couldn't play with her favorite toys or with her many friends. Our family in Boston and our friends were there once again in our time of need to help and support us. Several months later, we filed a lawsuit against Universal Studios and the bleacher manufacturer and won an out-of-court settlement. We took that money and set up a trust account for Amy.

This adventure once again affected my business, as I worked fewer hours than normal (down to only 50 or 55 hours). I wanted to be home early each day to help my wife as much I could. Once again we weathered the storm. After the body cast was removed some 8 to 9 weeks later, and after weeks of physical therapy, Amy was back to her loving self. Robert was very helpful to Elaine in taking care of Amy. He loved his sister very much and we were very proud of the way he treated Amy. We were thrilled that everything looked good, but little did we know at that time that there were more problems and more complications to follow years later, as a result of the accident.

14

Fighting the Unions

The HVAC business was once again getting back on track, as long hours of work once again were the norm for me. A big break came when an architect who liked the work I did on one of his projects introduced me to Max Wasserman. Max owned several development and construction companies in Cambridge. Max and I had a very productive meeting; he told me that he'd heard a lot of good things about me and would like to try me on one of his jobs. I told him that I would like to show him how good we were, and asked him to include us in an upcoming project. Max called me a few weeks later and told me that he was doing a remodeling job of a small office building and asked me to get the plans and give him a bid on the HVAC work. I gave him a very good price and we got the job. We did it to his liking, and even weeks ahead of schedule. I had begun to do larger and larger jobs for him when he asked me to bid on a major shopping center conversion in Cambridge Square. At first I didn't know if I should bid on such a large job, but after thinking about it for a few days I decided to bid.

We were the low bidders on the heating, ventilating and air conditioning (HVAC) work, but the bids on most trades came in over budget. Max started to squeeze the low bidders to lower their bids. I felt that my bid was as low as it could be so I didn't reduce my price, but I suggested some design changes that could save him quite a bit of money. He liked the changes I made, which also saved money on the electrical work. The job was going well at first, but soon we had more than just the job to worry about. Two months after the job started, the local sheet-metal union picketed the job and us. We were the only major subcontractor on the job that was non-union, and they gave us a lot of grief. Max had to set up a second gate for us. I wanted the job finished as soon as possible in order to end the aggravation, but the other trades held me back. Max told me to ignore them and think of it as part of doing business, but it bothered my crew and I. However, the job turned out very well, and Max was happy with our performance. I was proud of my crew, who didn't let the union trades interfere with their performance.

After we finished the Shopping Center in Cambridge Square, I had more confidence in our capabilities and I started to bid on schools and other larger jobs. The profit on the Shopping Center came in better than expected, which boosted my confidence. The job gave us an excellent reference on our resume. Things were going well, but with more business came growing pains. We needed a bigger shop and more offices in order to bid and perform the larger jobs I wanted to do.

I found and purchased a large fixer-upper building in Stoughton. Whereas in the past we had always rented our building now, after a major remodeling job, we moved into our very own building. It felt great to own our first commercial building.

As we grew, the unions harassed us time and time again. I was paying my people near and, in many cases, above union wages, and our workers didn't want to unionize. After doing more public works projects, I decided to join the piping and sheet metal unions to eliminate union picketing and harassment, and to have better access to manpower. As I found out months later, that move was a big mistake and I paid for it dearly.

The idea was to operate with the same size crews as before. Doing larger jobs required that I pull additional workers from the union hall when we needed more help in a hurry. I did not want to steal crews from our other jobs as we had very tight schedules to meet on those jobs also. All trades must maintain a project schedule, which is set by the owner or the general contractor.

Some of the workers the Sheet Metal Union sent to our jobs were a joke. They lacked the desire and motivation to give a decent day's work. With the wages we were paying them, it was very disruptive and brought down the morale of the entire crew on the job. Many of them hardly produced. Some even called the union hall and turned in pro-company employees who tried to push the job or were gung-ho company employees. We did get a few decent workers, but they were fewer than 25% of those workers from the hall.

Going union created more problems than it solved, and almost cost me my life. Jobs started to run over cost and tools were stolen off our jobs. One morning when I got to the shop I smelled gas and found a gas line going to one of the unit heaters disconnected and the valve open. I called the police department, but they said what I already knew, it was an inside job. Many of my employees had keys to our shop and knew the combination to the alarm system. Before we went union, we had about 25 employees and never a problem with stealing or performance.

As time passed, I was getting bitter and frustrated. When I questioned employees about poor performance and lost tools, I was turned into the union for worker harassment. I would send workers who didn't perform back to the union hall, only to get just as bad or worse the following day. When I complained to the union they told me that I have no right to harass my workers. With all the money we were paying these employees I had no right to question them about lost tools or poor performance!!

I lost all confidence in the union, who had no intention of helping me. We were supposed to be a team and help each other, but they didn't care about the business owner. The only thing they cared about was how much of a raise in pay they were going to get in their next union contract. I never met a more ignorant or a bigger jerk than our union business agent. He would go to our jobs and carry on union business on *my* time. Sometimes he would spend over an hour at my expense. Many times he would call our office telling my staff or me that we needed more manpower on the job. If I was in my office I would take the call and tell him to go to hell, leave my crews alone, and not to tell me how to run my business. Before going union, most jobs came in better than or close to the estimate. We were making money, which allowed us to buy our own building, more fabricating equipment, and trucks. After we went union, things started to go downhill.

While my method of estimating didn't change when I went union, we started to lose money on most jobs. As months went by, there was no improvement in the performance of our union crews other than with my original crews. The latter were performing well but they were getting heat from other union members. Not being on the job daily, I didn't get a good feel for the problems.

My loyal employees were afraid to turn in fellow workers who were not doing the job because of the intimidation they received from their union. I was getting more frustrated and bitter as things started to go from bad to worse. I decided to raise my bids on our labor cost by 15 to 20 percent, but that got us less work. In just a short time I was forced to cut our field manpower by almost 50 percent, which hurt my overhead. I was fed up with the unions, and when my union contract expired, I went back to being non-union again.

The Sheet Metal Union threatened to sue me for not negotiating with them in good faith, but I told them to go to hell. That is when things turned from bad to worse and became a nightmare. Some of my original workers stayed with me and I also hired some new employees. I decided to subcontract out some of our sheet metal work. Our sheet metal shop workers were working from 7:00 to 3:30 and the office worked from 8:00 to 4:30, but on most days I would be in my office until 8:00 or 9:00 p.m. estimating new jobs, ordering new equipment and doing many other jobs I needed to do.

One such day while working alone in my office late one evening, I heard the alarm system in the shop go off. That was surprising because I had not set the alarm system yet. I ran from the offices toward the shop in the back to see what was going on. When I opened the door to the shop, I saw a roaring fire in the back of the fabrication shop. Then I realized that it was the automatic fire alarm that had gone off, not the burglar alarm. Knowing that the fire alarm also sounded at the fire station (thank God), I grabbed one of the portable fire extinguishers off the wall and headed towards the fire in an attempt to slow down or put it out. As I ran toward the fire I saw two men running out the back door and into the back yard. Being stupid and not thinking, I ran out the side door and after them, without concern for my safety. That was a very stupid thing to do; I was an idiot!

The side and back yard had an eight-foot chain link fence. When I cut off their path from the back to the front, they turned and headed towards the back fence with me in pursuit. In the back yard we had fabricated ductwork, air conditioning equipment, and pallets of materials near the fence. They jumped on it and attempted to climb the fence. When I caught up to one of them I pulled him off the fence. He landed on top of me, knocking me to the pavement. He picked up a piece of scrap lumber that we had in the back yard and smashed me on the side of the head, knocking me out cold.

I came to sometime later in the emergency room of a nearby hospital. Fire Department paramedics had rushed me to the hospital after firefighters found me unconscious in the back yard. Fire investigators found that gasoline was poured on walls and supplies and then ignited. Just to be sure that I was OK, I was kept in the hospital for overnight observation. I couldn't wait to get out of there. I had one hell of a headache for more than a week and I was mad at the world for months.

The scars on my head healed with time, but the experience gave me nightmares for months. I could have been killed and my kids would have been without a father and my wife without a husband. I wasn't thinking prudently when I made my split-second decision not to let my life's work go up in flames. So I had tried to save the building or catch the arsonist, all the while praying that the Fire Department would get there in a hurry. Everything I owned was in that business. How could I just stand by while two bastards burned it down? I know it was union related but couldn't prove it, and I couldn't positively identify the two intruders. We never caught them.

Our shop was shut down for several months and I was forced to give out all our sheet metal fabrication to others because of the fire damage to my building. That hurt us badly financially. I wanted to get the building fixed as soon as possible and get back into production, but getting a settlement with the insurance company took many months. I had made a big mistake when I got my building insurance — I didn't get business interruption coverage. My insurance agent had never even told me about it, so I learned the hard way. Maybe that is why the insurance company took their time settling. With their delay they put more pressure on me to settle for much less than the damage actually was. After the fire, I always carried business interruption coverage, but then it was too late.

Things were never the same after that. I was afraid to stay in the office alone after dark. Who knew just how far they would go in their attempt to ruin me? I no longer enjoyed what I was doing and didn't trust anybody, not even some of my employees. The driving ambition and pride in my work was no longer there. I lost my desire and I decided to wind the business down. For years I had taken pride in and loved what I was doing. I didn't mind working 14 to 16 hour days. Also I was thinking about Amy and what we could do for her.

Our visit to UCLA, witnessing the many wonderful things they were doing for kids made me think. There was nothing comparable to that in New England. I started to think about possibly moving to California. The more I was thought about it, the more I liked the idea. It was very tempting.

In early 1977, after many discussions with Elaine, we decided to move. I couldn't focus on my job any more and couldn't get rid of my bitterness. I just didn't care anymore. I decided that the health and safety and the well being of my wife and kids were more important to me than money. In late February, I flew alone to southern California for a few days to take a look around. If I was sure about the move, I would rent an apartment or a house.

While Elaine did have some aunts and uncles living in the Los Angeles area, that was not a factor for us to move there. I did feel that the warmer climate in California would be much better for me in the HVAC business than in Boston. Also, I wasn't going to miss shoveling snow in the wintertime at 5:00 a.m.

The one major obstacle that was holding us back was the great many friends we would leave behind. We were so close to many of them. It was a very hard decision, but it was the best decision. It was time to start a new life once again, as I had done twenty years before, but this time it was different. I was married and I had the love and support of my loving wife. More than ever, I had faith in my ability, which would overcome any obstacles. I was more determined than ever before.

Part IV

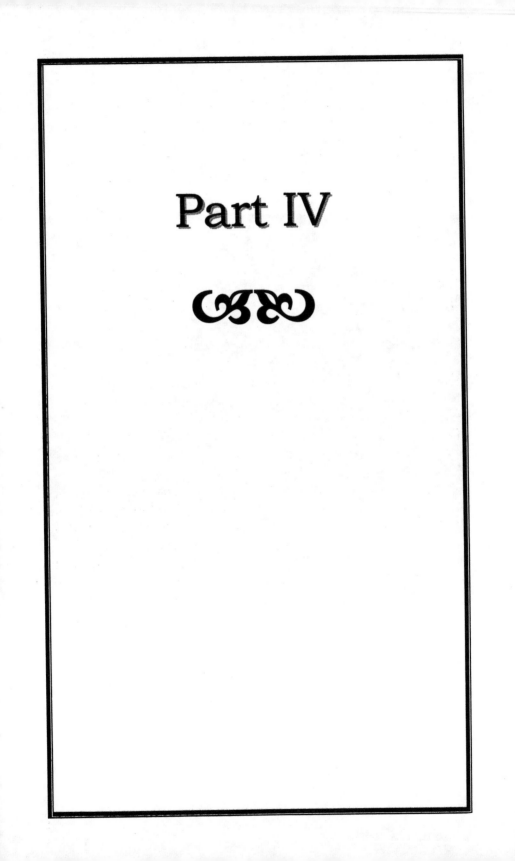

We moved into a small rented house on Allen Street in Glendale, 1977.

15

California Here We Come

On March 17, 1977, we moved to a small rented house on Allen Street in Glendale, California. I had signed a one-year lease in late February, which would give us time to see what part of California we would like. The house was right across the street from Balboa Elementary School, where our kids would be going. This was very convenient for Elaine. She could watch our kids from our front yard having recess or playing on the playgrounds. The kids only had to walk across the street to school. The house was located at the foot of the mountains on a street that was somewhat steep. After school, Robert and Amy would play or ride their bikes on the playground of the school with their new friends. We did not allow them to ride their bike on the street because of the dangerous incline.

The first few months in California, Rob had a tough time breathing. The smog affected him, while it did not affect the rest of us. We had to put him on medication. It took his body many months to adapt to the new climate and the smog.

After renting the house in Glendale, I began to look at the classified ads section of the Los Angeles Times. Finding a job for me was no problem. I was thrilled because every interview I went on resulted in a job offer. Finally, after my fourth interview I decided to take a job as an Estimator/Project Manager with a nice medium-size HVAC company in East Los Angeles. The name of the company was Los Angeles Air Conditioning. I had also an offer from one of the largest HVAC contracting firms that had their offices in Glendale. They were only three minutes from the house. However, I felt that I would do better at a smaller place where I could do both estimating and project management. It would take me 40 to 45 minutes to get to East L.A. but I felt it was worth it. It was a good decision for me. I had projects all over Southern California.

The children and I adapted quite well to our new life, but not Elaine. She missed her family in Boston and all her friends. She was lonely and at times would get depressed. Finally, after much pushing from me, she decided to volunteer at the Balboa School. That worked out great. As months went by, she gave them more of her time. She loved working with kids.

The schooling in Boston had to be better than in Glendale, because upon arriving, Robert became a good student with excellent grades. That wasn't the Robert we knew while he went to school in Boston! Later he settled down to being just an average student again.

Amy met a very nice young girl down the street from us, and in no time they became the best of friends. We met the parents, who were about our age, and we became good friends also; in fact we would babysit for their daughter, while they would do the same for ours. It worked out great. This came just at the right time, and finally Elaine had someone to talk to.

We would visit my parents, or Zoltan would bring them over to our house for a visit. Things were getting better between my dad and me, but once again we were faced with an unexpected and untimely accident. We were having my family over to our house for a 4th of July barbecue. It was our first real party since we had moved here a little over three months before. I was cooking in the back yard when my kids came to me and asked if they could go across the street to ride their bikes. I told them that they could for about fifteen minutes, at which time we would call them because food was going to be served soon. Dad decided to go and watch them while Mom was helping Elaine inside the house. Zoltan was relaxing in the back yard. While I was making hamburgers and chicken, Dad came back and took my ten-speed bike from the garage without my knowledge. He took it across the street to the school playground where my kids were riding their bikes. He had not been on a bike for 20 or 30 years, and why he decided to do it now I will never understand. He had felt much better the last few years and now I suppose he wanted to ride with Robert and Amy. I was almost ready to call the kids for lunch when I heard them running towards us in the back yard, screaming that Grandpa had gotten hurt on the bicycle down the street. Leaving the food on the fire, we started to run down the street where we saw a crowd gather at the corner. Upon arriving, we saw Dad motionless on the pavement, and a woman, who we found out later was a nurse, was trying to give CPR.

Later on we found out from the kids that Grandpa was riding my ten-speed bike with them on the playground and then decided to go around the block. The kids told him not to do it because it was dangerous, but he ignored their warning. Why he did it still puzzles us after all these years. While going down our fairly steep street, his bike picked up speed. He couldn't control the bike, and when he turned right at the next corner, he took the turn too wide and went head on into an oncoming car that could not avoid him. Paramedics who arrived in less than five minutes from a fire station a few blocks away could not revive him. They rushed him to Saint Joseph Hospital, but he was DOA. We ran back to our house. I turned off the barbecue and just left the burned food on it. We headed to Saint Joseph Hospital, hoping for a miracle that never came. There was nothing the hospital could do for Dad. Another happy occasion had turned into a tragedy. We were devastated!

Amy and Rob having fun in our pool in Burbank, 1979.

16

Back into Business

I had been working at Los Angeles Air Conditioning for two years when I decided to look for an HVAC business to buy. I decided to put an "HVAC Business Wanted" ad into the Green Sheet, which is a construction trade magazine. The Green Sheet is a must have trade publication if you bid on public works projects. I used a post office box under the name of "Mr. Stevens" and ran the ad for four weeks.

I received 10 responses and I replied to most of them. I didn't respond to a few because their reputation was something less than desirable. I was in no hurry and I wasn't going to rush into anything until I felt comfortable. I set up several meetings with prospects, but none of them interested me. Some were not the type of business I was looking for and a couple of them were on the verge of going out of business. I gave them less than a year. Both went out of business in less than 8 months. With one of them the owner exaggerated so much that it was embarrassing. Simply by looking at their operation I could tell that probably only fifteen percent of what he was saying was the truth. Nothing interested me, and I passed on all of them.

Two months later I placed a new ad in the Green Sheet just like the one I had placed before. This time I got only three responses. I talked with all three of them and made appointments with two. One of the companies was San-Val Air Conditioning in Van Nuys and the meeting was with Irv Levin, the owner. The meeting took place at 5:30 p.m. at the offices of San-Val. Irv did not want me to come while his shop was open or any of his employees were around. He was not planning on selling, but when he saw my ad he started thinking about it. I did not know Irv and did not know San-Val, so I went with an open mind. It was a good meeting and we both felt comfortable with each other. He showed me the shop, the offices, and some of the jobs they were doing. Most of their work was for general contractors doing school remodeling contracts for the Los Angeles Unified School district (LAUSD). San-Val was an HVAC sub-contractor. We talked for over an hour. I told him that I had another appointment for Saturday with another HVAC firm, but that I would call him again in a couple of weeks. I was very pleased with the meeting and thanked him for taking the time and showing me more than I expected. Irv was in his mid 60s, while I was only 38 years old, yet we clicked and both of us knew it.

My other meeting with the second HVAC contractor lasted less than twenty minutes. I did not like what I saw and there was no reason to waste my time further with that.

The following week at work, I questioned some of my suppliers about San-Val Air Conditioning. When asked why, I told them that I was bidding on a job and San-Val was also bidding, and I wanted to know my competition better. One of the salesmen I talked with named Ferrel was quite surprised because he knew San-Val well and they didn't bid on jobs like the ones our company bid on. He told me that San-Val was a good HVAC company, but 95 percent of their work was schools. He knew of Irv Levin. I tried to mislead Ferrel as to my intentions, and he played along and did not make a big deal of it. He knew Irv was around 65 years old and might be thinking about selling. Ferrel also knew that I was very energetic and might be looking for a change or even more, but he was discreet about it.

After a week of thinking about my options, I decided to have another meeting with Irv Levin. I called him and set up another appointment, and I also asked if he could make up an interim financial statement for me to review. I asked to see the financial statements of San-Val for the past three years. I called several of the general contractors regarding San-Val and got very good responses. I also called my friend Jim at Wells Fargo Bank and asked questions regarding a line of credit and receivable financing. I needed to know what my options were.

A few days later, while I was talking with my oldest brother Zoltan, I told him what I was doing. He got very interested in helping me and maybe joining me in a partnership. I told him that I would think about it and let him know. I met Irv again without his employees knowing about it, just like the last time. We discussed a sale price and other details in a probable purchase. I reviewed the financial statements as well as the jobs in progress and inventory on hand.

I asked Irv what he was asking for the business. He told me that he was thinking in the vicinity of about $275,000. Just like our previous meeting, this meeting also went really well. We set up a third meeting for a week later, when I would come back with a proposal. I asked him if it would be OK if I called his accountant, Jerome K. Richards, if I had any questions regarding the financial statements. He said no problem, and that he would call Jerome to let him know that I might be calling. I was very impressed with this and thanked Irv. He also wanted to check me out some more, and we both needed more time to think things over. I decided to call Jerome Richards and ask about how he was calculating the depreciation on the equipment and trucks and how he was handling the work in progress over and under billings. He told me that as far as Irv and he were concerned, the billings on the jobs were billed at the right rate and none of the jobs were over-billed.

I spent many hours going over all the information I had gathered and soon started to get good vibes about San-Val. But one major problem was that San-Val was not very busy at this time. The shop and most field crew workers were working only 24 hours a week. Now that I look back, that was in my favor. I felt that the chemistry between Irv and me was surprisingly strong. I was looking forward to our next meeting, which was only a few days away.

Nobody where I worked knew that I was looking for another job, or that I was contemplating buying a company. It was ironic that at about the same time, some of their key people were also thinking about starting their own company. They asked me to join them at some of their meetings. But that would have resulted in too many partners, and so I did not get very excited about it. I was flattered that they asked me, but I knew it was not for me.

Zoltan called me every other day as to what was happening. I told him that Irv and I were still talking. Zoltan wanted to be a part of the deal and I said there might be a good chance for that.

I had several options to choose from. I drafted several proposals to buy San-Val, and kept reading them over and over again. I adjusted the figures and changed things several times. Finally, I made my decision and settled on only one option. I discussed the proposal with Elaine, who left it up to me because she knew nothing about the HVAC business. She trusted my ability and told me to do what I felt was the right thing for our family.

She was always very supportive in my business ventures. Now we were once again ready to begin a major undertaking. I was cool and calm while Elaine was very nervous about the purchase. She was always nervous when we were talking about large sums of money. I was ready and wanted to get my next meeting with Irv over with as soon as possible, and see if we could make a deal. I called Irv and we agreed to move the time up for our next meeting.

Before giving Irv my proposal, I explained to him that while I liked the reputation of San-Val, I was not happy that they were doing mostly school construction. I also told him that he was always at the mercy of general contractors (GCs) who would sell him out for a buck. I told Irv that very few GCs are loyal to their subcontractors. I could change things and get other work, but that would take time.

I stated that my proposal was based on payments over time. My finances were limited and I didn't want to borrow money from a bank to finance the purchase. I told Irv what my plans were for San-Val, what I liked about San-Val and what I didn't like. I wanted to look for work other than just schools, and for San-Val to start bidding as a prime contractor and expand that part of its business.

My offer had several parts to it, some negotiable, while some were not. The offer was for $215,000 with a $10,000 deposit at the signing of the agreement and a 6-year payoff. I would assume the liabilities and assets of San-Val and would retain Irv for up to six months. The purchase date would be March 15th, 1979, but I would have to do an audit of San-Val first. If the liabilities were more than 10 percent more than the stated amount in the interim statement, then the selling price would be lowered. A similar condition applied to the assets; if the account receivables were not as stated, then the selling price would be adjusted accordingly. I also asked for two to three months to finish the audit, which would be done by an outside accountant.

After looking over the proposal, Irv came back with a counter-proposal, which was in the ballpark. He asked for $235,000, quarterly payments and a five-year payoff. He also stated that until the audit was finished, nobody at San-Val would know about the sale.

After going back and forth, we agreed on a purchase price of $225,000, a deposit of $10,000, and quarterly payments with a five-year payoff. We also agreed on how I would come to work for San-Val and how the transfer of power would take place. I was to start working at San-Val in two weeks and would act as their chief estimator. I would be making the decisions on jobs we would bid on and the bid price, but nobody other than Irv was to know that I was the new owner. We also set June 1st 1979 as the official purchase date. The following morning, I gave my two weeks notice to L.A. Air. I only told them that I had gotten a good offer to become San-Val's new chief estimator.

I had to make a decision whether I should go with Wells Fargo or Zoltan for financing help. I decided on Zoltan, which turned out to be a big mistake later. Zoltan came on board as a silent partner/investor.

Irv told his office workers and Jim Hancock, his key man, that I was coming on board on the 15th of March. Irv introduced me to everybody as the new chief estimator with full power to select jobs and to put final bids together. The first few days were very hard for me, especially when Irv went home for the day around 2:30 p.m. Irv would start early in the morning but also leave early. When Irv was gone, some of the office help would stop working and bullshit the rest of the day. Dennis, our estimator/draftsman would come out of his office shortly after Irv left. He liked cars and would talk about cars with Abby, our secretary, or anyone else who would listen to him. He would also read magazines about cars in his office when Irv was not around. I would tell them to stop the bull and that we had a lot of work to do. Our shop was working less than 24 hours a week, and it was not fair to them that the office was wasting hours each day. The office needed to work much harder, but some on our office staff did not care and did not give the extra effort that was needed. One afternoon I told our office staff that I was hired to get more work for San-Val and that I expected them to do their job, and if they had any problem with that, then take it up with Irv. I got dirty looks from them and they kept ignoring my directives, but I controlled my anger and went back in my office. Fifteen minutes later I came out and ordered them to go back to work, or go home! This got the desired result, but they were not very happy with me. They did not realize at that time that they were pissing off their new boss.

I talked with Irv later that day and told him what was going on. If the staff didn't produce more I would fire them. The following morning I had to go to a job walk at USC. A job walk is a meeting at the job-site where the work is to be performed. The project is explained, including what is up for bid and the project schedule. While I was gone, Irv talked with the staff and told them that I was hired to bid on lots of jobs and that they had to follow my orders or else. That did not go over well with the office staff. As days and weeks went by, I had to get on their case several more times. Our small office staff consisted of two full time office workers: Dennis who was Irv's estimator, and Abby who was the secretary/bookkeeper. We also had Lora, who was working 18 to 24 hours, doing purchase orders, submittals, change orders, and issuing sub-contracts. I liked Lora from the first day I met her. She worked hard and was an excellent typist.

When I came to San-Val, I let Irv stay in his office while I took a small office on the right side of the office area. That way it didn't look suspicious. I had to set my policies through Irv until the official purchase date, which was to be June 1st. Irv and I would talk daily before the office started work as to what I wanted him to do. He was no longer involved with any of the bids, but I let him do some of the buying and PR work. There was a different approach in the way Irv and I did business. Irv was much more diplomatic, while I was more energetic and forceful. He knew how to handle some of the GCs and was on very good terms with the job inspectors. I, in contrast, had no use for GCs who I regarded as crooks, and I was not going to kiss anybody's ass to get a job. I got my jobs with honest pricing and quality work. I never knowingly cheated a job just to make a few bucks more. If anything, I gave more than was required by the plans and specifications. Most architects and mechanical engineers liked me and were pleased when I was on their jobs. We made their job easy with our professionalism.

As weeks went by, it was clear that the audit was going very well and there were no surprises. Before I knew it, June 1st came around, and on that day we officially signed the purchase agreement, which had been drafted by attorneys John Garvin and Sidney Pilot a few days before. We had to make very few changes to the original draft and everything went very smoothly.

The day before the signing, Irv arranged for a special meeting for 3:00 p.m. on June 1st at our office. He directed his key outside employees to be there, as well as all the shop and office staff. Up to that moment, nobody had the slightest clue as to what was going on and what the meeting was about. Some were guessing but they weren't even close. Several of Irv's key people had been with Irv a very long time, yet they were left out of the loop. Some resented it at first. Everyone at the meeting was surprised and shocked when Irv made the announcement.

Irv spoke only briefly and told them that as of that day, I was the new owner of San-Val. He told them that he would stay for a few months to ensure a smooth transfer of power, and asked for their help and support in making it happen in an orderly fashion. I spoke for about 15 minutes. I told them that I had lots of new ideas, which would be implemented in the months to come. I also told them that we would be going after work other than just schools and we'd be doing design-build work as well. I told them that I had full knowledge of the HVAC business, both in installation and service, and that they could come to me any time with any questions or problems. I also told them that one of the first things on my agenda was to start bidding as a prime contractor and eventually do more work as a prime, while still doing a lot of work as a subcontractor.

The meeting went very well, but Dennis and Abby were a little worried about their jobs after what had transpired a few months before. Now it made sense to them as to why I was so eager to bid on more jobs, and why I didn't allow the bullshit sessions after Irv had left for home.

That night Irv and his wife Lil took Elaine and I out to a French restaurant in Sherman Oaks on Ventura Boulevard to celebrate the sale of San-Val to us. We had met Lil before; Elaine and Lil clicked from the first moment they met, just like Irv and I had clicked. We became the best of friends and were still best friends some 23 years later. We got together on a regular basis and talked on the phone 2 to 3 times a month. What wonderful friends! Our kids called them Aunt Lil and Uncle Irv. Even after Irv Levin passed away in 2001, we still talk with Lil weekly and see her regularly.

17

Transition to a New Owner

The day after I purchased San-Val, Irv called most of his GC friends as well as subcontractors, and told them that he had sold San-Val to me. One of the subs Irv called was Bob Shoup, a piping subcontractor to San-Val for many years, who came by a few days later. He introduced himself and told me that he did all the piping for San-Val. We had a very nice meeting, but I didn't like the way he was courting me for his business. He was overly nice and asked how my wonderful wife was, yet he had never met Elaine before.

One of the first things I did at San-Val was to make Jim Hancock our vice president. I put the shop and the outside crews under his control. He would have to schedule the crews for every job. I had plenty on my plate, whereas Jim knew everybody and was also Irv's right hand man. Not everybody was pleased with my decision, but it was the right decision and it had to be made. During the first few weeks at San-Val, I spent 25 to 30% of my time calling prospective new clients, asking them to put us on their bid lists for any upcoming jobs. Because San-Val did mostly schools, it was not known much outside that industry. That made my job harder, but I needed to change that, and change it fast. I did just that in a very short time. Soon the estimating department was overloaded with new jobs to bid on and my hard work started to pay off. We were especially eager to bid on jobs that started right away. We needed work for both our shop and for our field people. I used the Green Sheet to look for upcoming work and spent long days at my desk, but this was nothing new to me. The second and third week produced some new jobs, and we were off to bigger and better things. I know Irv was impressed with the way I handled the staff and bids. He was all smiles as he told some manufacturer's reps that he wished he had known me years earlier. I had Irv do PR work, calling suppliers for bids, and I bounced ideas off him as I was thinking down the road to bigger and larger jobs.

It soon became evident that my selections of jobs to bid on were very different from that of Irv's. In my second week at San-Val, I decided to bid on an HVAC installation job at the VA Hospital in Long Beach.

It was the first time in the history of San-Val that we bid on a job like that as a prime bidder. We were the low bidder and finished our contract four weeks ahead of schedule. The fourth week at San-Val I completed our second prime bid, this time at the Duarte Middle School. It was an HVAC remodeling job and was perfect for our set-up. We got the contract in a very close bid. This was just the beginning; I wanted to increase our prime bidding to 25 percent within two years. That required more bonding power and a bigger line of credit from our bank. It would also require time and a much stronger financial statement.

We also bid a lot of schools as a subcontractor and picked up our largest job ever, doing the HVAC work at the Westlake School. Our contract was for $845,000 and was five percent larger than our previous largest job at UC Irvine (University of California at Irvine), which they had done in 1971.

Things started to move for San-Val in the right direction, and in no time the shop was back to working forty hours a week once again. There were smiles on the faces of our workers. Lots of high fives were given in a short period of time as we picked up good jobs as a subcontractor at Lakewood YMCA, Oak Park High School, Pacific Telephone, and Berkeley Hall School. We also picked up jobs as a prime at Loyola Marymount University, El Camino College, and the Arco Refinery in Carson.

It was a relentless bidding schedule, which was resented by Dennis, our sheet metal take-off estimator. He wasn't happy that I had taken away all the spare hours he had had each day prior to my coming to San-Val. I told him that we were more than capable of handling the larger load, and if he had a problem with that, then I would get someone else to do his job.

Irv and I went out to meet most of the GCs he had worked with over the years. Some of them I knew already and had called as soon as I went to San-Val. Some of the GCs we met did not impress me, nor did I like the way they spoke to me. When someone tells me that they will give me the last look on a job, that is a red flag, and does not go well with me. I was not going to change my bid just because someone else had a lower price. I told Irv that the price we quote is our price and it was not negotiable.

Before I came to San-Val, Irv had been bidding jobs early to his GC friends, and most would give him feedback as to the other HVAC prices they received and from whom. Irv would call them back fifteen minutes before bid time and check the prices again, then lower his bid to meet or beat the competition on jobs he wanted badly. That was not going to work for me, and soon it became apparent to most GCs. It came time to bid on a school job, the first since I came to San-Val. I waited to release my bid and it was the same price for all of them. A few of the GCs called back a few minutes later, saying I was high and needed to drop my price by $8,000, but I told Irv that our price was firm. One of his friends called and told us that we were $13,000 too high, but that was a lie, which we found out later. We didn't get the job, but I wasn't about to cut my price 8 to 9 percent in order to get it.

Some of Irv's friends resented my bidding methods and gave Irv a hard time about it, which made me very upset. It was my doing, and if someone had something to say, they should have spoken to me, not Irv. They talked to Irv because he was the boss at that time. Irv would try to smooth things over with them, as that was his style. He was good at negotiations but went about it in a different way, and sometimes the wrong way. Irv did not want his friends to use other subcontractors and sometimes lowered the price more than he should have. To do a job for nothing is only the last resort, as far as I was concerned, unless we wanted to get in with an owner or needed the work very badly. As time went on and we finished work that Irv got before I came to San-Val, I found that some GCs took advantage of Irv.

On one of the jobs that was under contract with Argo Construction of Sherman Oaks, San-Val made a big mistake in its bid. Argo asked us to bid the job, but they never called Irv back that his bid was 20 to 25 percent lower than everybody else. They had five other HVAC bids, yet they never called Irv to check his prices. What a friend! No wonder we got the job. Later we found out that the underground piping, which was shown on the plot plan, was also part of the HVAC contract, but our estimator didn't realize it and that part of the work had been left out of our bid. When we got the call from Argo Construction that the job was ready for the underground installation, we said, "What underground piping?" We had no choice but to do it and eat the cost. When I asked them why they didn't call Irv to check his price, they just gave me some stupid excuses. From that point on they never received another bid from us, which later proved very costly for them.

What got me really upset was the fact that out of the seven GC bidders on the job, we only bid Argo. We were free to bid to any of the other general contractors, but Irv decided against it. We were the HVAC subcontractor to Argo. They asked us to bid the job and they were Irv's friends. Irv always gave them the best prices and they knew it. Our costly mistake gave them a big edge in getting the job against the other GCs. We lost about $25,000 on that job. I know that Irv felt real bad about it and was angry with Argo for what they pulled on him. With friends like that, who needs enemies?

As I told Irv time and time again, as long as we bid the jobs right, there was no reason for us to cut our price at bid time. We didn't need to get every job and we'd get our share of the work at the right price. Our prices were very competitive against qualified HVAC contractors but we couldn't compete against small non-union shops. Taking on work and liability for very little is foolish and we'd do it only when San-Val was hurting for work. There had to be a very good reason for us to bid on a job at cost or near cost. I tried to bid only jobs that we had a good chance to get. The GCs that Irv used to deal with were upset with me for not negotiating my prices with them. They liked the work we did and knew that having San-Val on the job meant having no problem with the HVAC portion of the job. If they used the low bidder and the low bidder was not experienced in school construction, then it would be a nightmare for them. It would require a lot of extra supervision on the part of the GC. The contractors were looking to get one of the best HVAC subcontractors at the lowest price, at our expense.

There were several GCs that were honest. They did not try to beat our price down, while there were others who always squeezed you to lower your price on every job. They were always looking for an edge at your expense. They didn't care about anybody but themselves and were the dirt of the industry.

Irv was a member of the Building Industry Association (BIA), which had an awards dinner meeting each year, where the best subcontractors in each trade would be recognized in public and presented with a very nice plaque. Most years San-Val was voted the best HVAC contractor of the year. The numerous awards Irv deservedly received were proudly displayed on the walls of the offices of San-Val. We belonged to the BIA for a while longer, but resigned as our operation changed and the course we chose dictated that action.

It was always a pleasure to bid and work with people like Steed Bros., C.W. Driver, Hayward Construction, Holwick Constructors, CMC, Western Alta, and Newberg Construction. There were times when these GCs received lower HVAC bids than ours, yet they used us on the job because they felt that it was well worth it. We always appreciated it and we always gave them the best prices when we bid. We took pride in the work we did and always worked well with the owner, architect, engineer, and the prime contractor. We were a good team player and that is why they asked us time and time again to bid on new jobs with them.

I kept a close eye on most of the GCs we worked for, how they ran their jobs, as well as how they paid us every month. It didn't take long for me to figure out how most of the school contractors operated. Once I knew that, I would bid accordingly. Some, like Harris Levin Construction (Irv's buddy), became the first casualty. Harris Levin (no relationship to Irv) had the worst project coordination of any GC we knew. His superintendent would show up on a job once in a while and had very little idea how to run the job and how to schedule the many trades on the job. We would lose money on most of his jobs, and to make things worse, he would not pay us in a timely manner.

Under California state law, the general contractor must pay his subcontractors within a few days. The law varies from state to state and could be from five to ten days. The one good thing on a public works job is that the payment bond the low bidder needs to post on the job protects you. As long as you have your paperwork in order and you are performing on the job, then you have many remedies.

Knowing the law, I used it time and time again to protect us and to get our money from those who tried to cheat us. I had my first confrontation (but not the last) with Harris Levin on one of the jobs we were doing for him on a school-remodeling project with the Los Angeles Unified School District (LAUSD). We had over $15,000 due from him for the previous month's work, which we knew the inspector had approved. We always verified our pay request with the inspector prior to submitting it to the general contractor at the end of the month. When it was time for us to receive our money, he kept telling us that he had not received his payment from LAUSD yet. However, we called LAUSD and were told that he had been paid, and on what dates. I sent a registered demand-for-payment letter to Harris with a copy to LAUSD, the State Contractors License Board, and his bonding company.

In that letter we told him that he was not complying with the law, was paying us late, and in many cases much less than was approved by LAUSD. It was a very strong letter, but I was mad as hell and fed up with the lies we had received from his office. He never returned the many calls I made to him. Harris used our money and that of other subcontractors, and made us and others wait in some cases for months to get paid. In the letter we advised him that if we did not get all the money that was due to us within 48 hours after receipt of my registered letter, we would file with LAUSD for direct payment and would also file a claim with his bonding company.

Being only a few miles from us, Harris received the demand letter the following day and hit the roof. He called my office and asked to speak to me. I wasn't going to hide from him, as he had from me, and I was ready to take his call. I had met him in person only a few times and he didn't impress me from day one. As soon as I picked up the phone, he started to scream and swear at me as loud as he could. He told me that after all the business he had given us, how dare I do that to him. After listening to him nonstop for about a minute, I told him to shut up and listen to me, but he kept on yelling at me, so I hung up. He called back within seconds and started at me again, only to make me hang up again; this was repeated two more times. Finally, when he called back the fifth time, he sounded more human, but I'd had enough. I told him that he better listen to me and listen real good. I told him that I was not Irv and I didn't take shit from anybody and especially not from him. I told him that I was not just some dumb kid and that I wanted my money as a cashier's check on my desk within the given time stated in my letter and that it was not negotiable. I told him that it was his move and that there was nothing else to discuss, and hung up on him.

The following day he sent over a check, but the check was not a cashier's check and it was not for the full amount that was due to me. I refused to take the check, which was $2,100 less than was due me. I told Harris' man that I wanted the full amount that was due me and we would only take a cashier's check. I told him to tell Harris to stop messing with me or else. I also told him to tell Harris that he had less than 24 hours left to get that cashier's check over to me. The man left and within fifteen minutes Harris called and started to scream, at which time I hung up on him. I did the same thing four more times as soon as we knew it was Harris. He was pissed, but so was I. The following day, we had our cashier's check for the full amount.

The following month he tried to screw me again, at which time I filed for direct payment with the LAUSD. I wasn't going to do this every month, and after providing the LAUSD with all the documents, the school board approved the request. This killed Harris, as it was now public knowledge that a subcontractor had filed and received direct payment from LAUSD against him.

Irv loved how I had handled Harris and he told some of his GC friends about it. They got a chuckle out of it. Irv finally realized that some of his GC friends, like Harris Levin, had been taking advantage of him, but in his later years Irv didn't care. He knew that he'd be retiring in a few years so he did not want to make waves.

I got several calls the following week from other subs on the job. They wanted to know what I did because they had also not gotten paid for months, and when they did get paid, it was only part of what was owed to them. I told them how I did it and most filed for direct payment on the job.

A few months later a plumbing contractor friend of Irv's and San-Val called and wanted to see me about a problem he had. His name was Joe Volkmar and he owned Consolidated Mechanical in Glendale. He told me on the phone that he had a problem with Harris Levin also and was having a hard time getting money out of him. I told Joe to come by and bring his job folder. After I reviewed the file it was clear that Harris was also screwing Joe, but Joe didn't have the knowledge as to how to fight him. That would soon change. I told Joe what options he had and helped him get his money. I told him what to do and how to do it. Joe was impressed and thanked me over and over. I told Joe to stick to what I told him and he would get his money in a week or two. Five days later Joe called and told me that Harris had paid him in full, and how thankful he was for my help. I was happy for him and glad that the letter worked again.

As time went on, Joe and I and our wives became the best of friends; we got especially close after I retired from the construction business. Today, some twenty years later, we are still best friends and are still getting together at least once a month.

The troubles for Harris Levin didn't end there. He was always in hot water with LAUSD and his sub-contractors. He was always months behind schedule on every job and finally, on May 6, 1991, the Board of Education of the City of Los Angeles terminated his contracts on the Castelar Elementary School and on the Loreto Street Elementary School. The firing was the result of failure to provide sufficient staffing and supervision, failing to make sufficient progress towards completion, and prevailing wage violation. Harris Levin was also banned from bidding on any LAUSD projects for a period of five years. It was about time! I was jubilant when I heard of it the following day. Nobody shed tears for him, and most of us wished that it had happened years sooner. But he was not the only rotten contractor on LAUSD projects.

Inexperienced contractors by the dozens were eager to get into the school remodeling business, but as most found out, it was a costly mistake. Lawsuits and termination of contracts were commonplace on the school board agendas. Criminal charges have been filed against many contractors, prime and subcontractors, for their failure to pay the required prevailing wage on public works projects. No wonder they got the jobs. Honest and good contractors who played by the rules had had no chance against crooks like them. The bad contractors learned the hard way. Some were banned from bidding to LAUSD and some were jailed for falsifying certified payroll records.

18

The Early Years at San-Val

It was 1979 and in less than six months, we were bidding on six times as many jobs as before I came to San-Val, and were getting our share of the work. It was now time to bid more work as a GC, but lack of bonding power held me back.

Irv had very little bonding capability, but he did not need it so he never went after it. I called our agent Marc C. Leahy for a meeting and explained to him my situation and asked him if his bonding company (Fairmont Insurance Company) would triple our bonding power and also give us a better rate. I gave him up-to-date financial data and told him that I needed to know in less than a week as I was also getting quotes from other bonding companies.

In the Green Sheet there was an insurance company that was doing a lot of advertising for insurance and bonding, so I decided to call them a few days later.

I made an appointment with Mr. Archie Stahr who was the owner of AB Stahr Insurance Company. When we met I showed him our operation, and we talked at length about what I had in mind for San-Val in the coming months and years.

We had a productive meeting; he told me that he knew San-Val because several of his customers were GCs and San-Val had worked for them for years. He also saw San-Val doing lots of bidding direct to owners as a prime contractor.

I gave him up-to-date financial data and also told him that I needed to know in less than a week. I also told Archie that if we got our bonding from him, then he would get all our insurance business, including health insurance.

About a week or so later, I got my quotes from both bonding agents, and it was no contest. Archie went to bat for me and got me a good package. Not as good as I wanted, but it was close, and he told me that once we showed them how good we were, then they would increase our bonding limits. I took him at his word and it was the beginning of a great relationship between our two companies, which grew tenfold over the years. We did everything we told him we would do, and he went to bat for us time and time again.

Our bidding began to focus more on prime bidding. I was also calling on lots of owners and other school districts to get on their bid lists for upcoming jobs. My hard work paid off, and in less than two months we were getting invited to bid on jobs at USC, Cal State Universities, and UCLA.

The following month or two we were also on the bid-list for Claremont College, Glendale College, Burbank USD (Unified School District), Covina USD, Glendale USD, J.P.L., Rockwell, Northrop, Arco Refinery, Pacific Telephone, Eastern Airlines, LA Times, Weber Aircraft, Children's Hospital, Cedar Medical Center, and many others.

It was very important to me that we didn't work for just a few school districts. If we were good enough to have done several hundred jobs for Los Angeles USD, then the other school districts had no problem with us. One of the contacts that paid off well was with Weber Aircraft, who asked us to do a small emergency job for them. We did, and that got us in for several future jobs.

One of those jobs included a major "design-build" large office building near Burbank Airport. It was a big HVAC design-build job, the largest design-build job San-Val or I had ever done. The job went very well, and so we had another good job reference.

We were hiring new field employees to handle the many new jobs we got, but I wanted to keep the office staff small. I had a talk with Lora and asked for more hours from her as we needed more help, but I didn't want to hire another part-time worker. I asked her to work 36 to 40 hours a week, and after a little pleading and begging from me, she said she would give me 32 to 35 hours a week. I was thrilled. She was a great worker, all business and fast and accurate. After she said yes, I decided to give her more money also, which was a pleasant surprise to her. After it was no longer a secret that I was officially the owner of San-Val, Irv set up a meeting and introduced me to the vice president of his bank, Mr. James Talon of California 1st Bank in Van Nuys. It was a lunch meeting that proved to be very fruitful.

Irv had a small line-of-credit with the bank, had been with them for many years, and had a good relationship with them. He told Jim how I had more than doubled our backlog of work and that the jobs were much more profitable.

He also told Jim about how I had already taken on some of the GCs, and Jim got a kick out of the Harris Levin episode. I told Jim that in the months to come I might need to increase our line of credit because we were doing more and larger jobs. Our financial statement was going to be better than the year before and that we should be making close to a $40,000 profit for the year, and that we should more than double that in following year.

He was a little skeptical, but I had a feeling that California 1st Bank wanted to work with San-Val and me. A short time later, they changed their name to Union Bank. The Bank of Tokyo owned them at one time, and I think they are still owned by them today. I opened a personal checking account with them also, which I still have more than 23 years later.

Our fiscal year ended up 10 to 15 percent better than I originally estimated in late July. We more than doubled our profit from the year before, which was good news, but later became bad news for me also.

A few days after I received my financial statement from my accountant, I called Jim and set up a meeting with him at my office. His office was only five minutes from us. That made it very convenient for us when we were going to the bank. We never had to stand in line at the teller's window, as Jim or someone else would take our deposits and we would be out of the bank in less than 20 seconds.

When Jim came to the shop, I showed him some of the changes we had made. I also showed him some of the new and larger contracts we were doing, before sitting down for some important business. I told him that we wanted to increase our line of credit and wanted to set up receivable financing. It was a very productive 30-minute meeting; we eventually got most of what we asked for, but we were required to do interim statements. When we purchased new trucks, they were also financed by California 1st Bank.

I sent Zoltan a copy of the financial statement, as was required by our agreement, and sent a note with it recommending that we only take out 10 to 15 percent of the profit from the business, because otherwise I would have a major problem with the bank.

I told him that it would be best if we didn't take out any money the first three years because we needed it to grow our business. We had talked about that prior to his investing in San-Val, and he agreed, but now he changed his mind.

He wanted to take out all or most of the profit and we had a major argument over it. I tried to talk him out of it, but could not, even though I sent him a letter explaining in detail why we needed to keep the money in the business.

On purpose, I had taken a very small paycheck. I worked 65 to 75 hours a week for half of what I paid Jim Hancock or the others, and they worked only 40 hours. I wanted to make sure that we had money in the bank to pay our workers and suppliers.

Nothing that I did changed Zoltan's mind. I was furious with him. Finally, I came to the conclusion that we could not operate under those conditions because it would lead San-Val and I to financial ruin. Either he had to buy me out, or me him.

I had a long-term vision for San-Val. Zoltan was only looking at the present moment. Had I known that, I wouldn't have bought new trucks and additional equipment just a couple of months before! This would put me in a very bad position with the bank.

I wanted to increase my line of credit, but this would kill that opportunity. After several sleepless nights, I called him and told him that if he insisted on this course, I had no choice but to break up our partnership. I paid him off over a period of time, as per an agreement we both had signed.

The next few months were devastating to San-Val and me. I took money out of the business as well as my own to pay Zoltan off, and it showed on our next interim financial statement. I didn't even dare go to the bank and ask for more money. I was forced to ask some of my non public works owners if I could get my money faster, as I was in a bind. I also had to give a good discount to Weber Aircraft to get paid twice a month, but it was a big job and I had no other choice. This was also embarrassing as hell. I was unprepared because I had never expected this to happen, but over the long term it was for the best, because it gave me more freedom and after that I did not have to account to anybody.

Paying off Zoltan affected my financial statement badly as well as our capabilities regarding the size of jobs we could bid on. I explained it to the bank and they understood my position, but now they wanted quarterly interim statements, which we provided.

I refocused and would not let it interfere with my objectives, but it took me over a year to get out of the mess. I was not a very happy person as I went to work to dig myself out of the hole. It wasn't easy, but I was determined to succeed and I was not going to just give up.

By this time Irv had retired, but we would talk on the phone every few weeks and I kept him abreast and informed as to how things were going with the business. Irv never knew that Zoltan was a silent partner and I didn't bring up my fight with Zoltan when I talked with him. Though I was angry and very bitter, I tried to focus on the future. Irv remained thrilled to see some of the new contacts and the progress we had made in such a short time.

In early 1980, I saw a big job that was open to bidding at the Jet Propulsion Laboratory (JPL) in Pasadena. I took out plans for it, but it was too big a job for me to bid as a prime contractor.

After looking over the blueprints and bid documents very carefully, I decided to do something San-Val never had done before. I decided to bid the entire mechanical and electrical sections of the specifications as a package.

I called my friend Bill Treder of Beling Electric and told him what I wanted to do. Beling Electric had worked at JPL in the past as a prime electrical and as a subcontractor to me, and I knew that they were an outstanding electrical contractor.

The package I decided to bid included the plumbing, heating and air conditioning, fire sprinkler, electrical work, and the automation control portion of the project. I saw that the bid list included Steed Bros. and a couple of other GCs we knew.

I called Justin Brown, the chief estimator from Steed Bros. and a friend of mine, and told him that we were bidding it as a package deal and that they would be getting the best price from us.

We were also going to bid just the HVAC work to Steed Bros. alone. He was happy that we were bidding because it was a very big mechanical job and it required a good HVAC contractor.

The funny thing with Beling Electric was that they didn't like to bid to other contractors. All their work was directly with owners and they were very happy with that arrangement.

One day, several months before, I was bidding on a job at JPL and needed an electrical contractor who was familiar with the requirements at JPL. I called someone at the JPL contract branch that I knew and asked if he could give me the names of a couple of good electrical contractors who worked at JPL.

He told me that Beling Electric was very good and I should ask for Bill Treder. I called Bill and asked him if he would bid a job to us that were bidding at JPL.

He told me that they didn't work for any contractors. They only bid as a prime bidder. They had had bad experiences with GCs in the past — most of them didn't know how to run their job. Beling had gotten screwed by GCs in the past and wanted no part of them ever again.

I told him that I didn't operate like that. We met at his office where I'd brought the bid drawings we were bidding at JPL. I also brought information about San-Val. I told him that I felt the same way about most GCs and that was why we were bidding more and more jobs as a prime contractor. He seemed impressed by my presentation.

I told him to call any of the other subcontractors I'd used in the past and I gave him over 50 names and phone numbers for references. If he didn't like what he heard, he could tell me to get lost!

I was looking for a good electrical contractor and I went after Bill without hesitation. He also wanted a list of owners for references, so I gave him that also. He called me a few days later and told me that he was going to bid the job to me. He would try me out.

We got the job and it was the start of a long-term relationship with Bill that lasted until I retired from the construction business in 1994. We had mutual respect for each other. We were both good contractors, we both were very honest, and our word was as good as gold!

I decided to do all the estimating and bid the upcoming job at JPL by myself. The project was an addition to a chiller plant for Building-230 and the plans were complicated. I wanted no mistakes, as it was to be by far the largest single contract that San-Val ever bid on.

I got quotes from two good piping contractors on the piping portion of the bid. I wanted to make sure that we got an honest piping bid from Shoup Mechanical and for that reason I asked for a bid from another good piping sub Martin Mechanical..

They were both good piping contractors and I knew that both could do this big job. I had to be competitive and had to cover all my angles because I wanted this job real bad.

About 30 minutes before bid-time, I called Steed Bros. and gave Justin Brown our bid-price on the HVAC portion of the contract, and told him that I should have the package bid price in a few minutes.

A few days before the bid, I had mailed the scope of work we were going to bid to Steed Bros. and the two other GCs. The morning of the bid we called them to make sure they each got our bid package and told them that we'd have the price by 1:45 p.m.

I answered all their questions and wished them good luck. I looked over my bid and the bids of my subcontractors several times to make sure we covered everything and nothing was missed.

About 25 minutes before bid-time I called Steed Bros. and gave them my package price. Five minutes later I called the two other GCs and gave them our price, which was about three percent higher than what we gave Steed Bros.

Just as I hung up on the last GC a very nervous Justin Brown called me and told me to check my price because our bid was quite a bit lower than the totals of the other bidders he had up to that point. I told him that I'd call him back in a few minutes. Then I called my major subs to have them check their prices quickly. I told them not to change anything if their price was good. I checked over my bid and it looked OK. I called my subs again and they told me that all was good and we could go with their prices.

I called Justin Brown back and told him that our bid was good and to go with it. I also told him that he'd better get the job because the other two GCs were quoted three percent more!

A few minutes later Justin called me back to tell me that they just received two more electrical bids and our bid looked perfect. I was relieved, thanked him for the call, and wished him good luck again.

We were already doing a job at JPL so I had one of my workers go to the bid opening and told him to call us with the bid results and look at who each general contractor carried for the mechanical trades.

166 / A Light In The Distance

About 2:35 p.m. I got the call for which we were nervously waiting. Steed Bros. was the low bidder and they carried San-Val for all the mechanical trades, which was our full bid package. I gave out a loud YES to the office staff, who rushed into my office because they knew why Joe had called us from JPL.

Within ten minutes Justin Brown called me to let us know that they got the job and we'd be their sub on the job. He used our package bid and thanked me for the good price and for staying with the original price. I thanked him and then called my major subs to give them the good news.

A few months later we started the job, and it proceeded well, ahead of schedule and under budget. Our crews worked great with Steed Bros., as they normally do.

The owner added a bunch of change orders, which made the job even better, even though it created a little confusion near the end. Lora in our office handled all change order paperwork and was very efficient with it.

Within the first five months we received many approved billable change orders and we got a bunch more a few months later, at which time Lora came and told me that there was a problem with some of the change orders.

The way the change orders were handled was confusing at times because they were not approved in number order and we think they were funded from different accounts.

It seemed to Lora that Steed Bros. had given us about $16,500 more than we were due. They had included in the last group of change orders two that were already approved and given to us two months earlier.

I told Lora to check our files to make sure, and if that was the case, then I'd call Steed Bros. and thank them for the bonus. Lora came back and told me that Steed Bros. had indeed made a big mistake, and she showed me where the problem was.

I called Justin Brown at Steed Bros. and as a joke, I thanked him for the generous bonus we had received from them on the JPL job. He didn't know what the heck I was talking about, at which time I told him what had happened with the change order overpayment.

He told me that we'd probably made a mistake, but I told him that the mistake was on their end; however, we'd be more than happy to take their money and put it to good use.

I told him that it was about time they gave us a nice bonus. He told me that he would check into it and call me in a couple of days. He did, and told me that they had screwed up and would never have found it on their own, and he thanked me for our honesty.

He told me that many others would have just kept the money without saying anything to anybody. I told him that San-Val didn't work that way and he thanked me several more times.

When the job was near completion and the only trades on the job were San-Val and our subs, Justin called me to ask if it was OK for him to pull his superintendent off the job.

Justin told me that his superintendent had nothing more to do and they had another big job that was ready to start and he needed him on it. I told him that our people did not need a baby-sitter and we could finish our work without having anybody from Steed Bros. on the job. It would also save Steed Bros. seven weeks of payroll.

He thanked me and pulled his man off the job. He asked us to keep an eye on things, which we did. I had no problem with it and I would have done the same thing if I were in his shoes.

A week or so later Justin called me that and told me the owner wanted a fairly good sized change order carried out and asked if I could bid the entire change order, including the roofing and painting. I said, "Of course." He gave me the drawings and a few days later we gave him the price, which included several trades that were not our own.

We handled everything, and everybody was happy. It was good for both of us, and besides, JPL knew the situation. Steed Bros. didn't add supervision to the change order, which saved money for JPL. It was good for everybody and because JPL knew us well, they never hesitated.

Our best friends, Lil and Irv Levin in a 1984 photo.
(former owner of San-Val Heating and Air Conditioning).

19

More Success and a Defense of Our Rights

About the same time as the JPL job we were doing several other good-sized jobs, but we still did fine with scheduling our manpower. A good friend of ours, Larry Polizzi, a Partner in Holwick Constructors, then called me about a large medical center they were going to bid on in Thousand Oaks. He asked me if I would bid on the HVAC work to them. I told Larry that I would love to and asked him to send me the drawings and specs. We gave Larry a good price. They were the low bidders and Larry carried my price.

A few days later Larry called and told me that the project had come in over budget. He asked me to look at the HVAC system and let them know if there was a way to make it less costly. I took the drawings home to see what I could do. I came up with a new design that would save lots of money on the HVAC, electrical and structural steel. Before I gave this back to Larry, I decided to call Bryant Matosian, the mechanical engineer on the job, and get his blessing. I did not want to do something behind his back, and that we had told the owner that the design was great, but money talks and the job was over budget. The owner had asked us to cut a lot from the job and I asked Bryant if he had any cost-cutting ideas, and I told him what I had in mind. He thought my idea was great and told me to propose it to the GC.

A couple of days later I sent Larry a proposal for the new design. He took it to the owner for review. The owner liked the design and the price, but he told Larry that I would need to sit down with the mechanical engineer and get his approval! Larry didn't know that I had already talked with Brian. We got the contract.

The contract called for a design-build HVAC system with all the equipment, ductwork, piping and controls, but did not include the tenant work. I had to give them a unit price, by square foot area, for the tenant work. By the time the primary HVAC system was installed, many of the suites in the building were being leased. A few of the doctors wanted to use their own HVAC people in order to save money. This is where Larry came to our defense and helped us a great deal. He told the doctors that until the primary HVAC system was finished and approved, nobody other than San-Val could work on it or attach anything to it. He also stated that as long as union mechanical trades were on the job, no non-union mechanical trades would be allowed. He told the owner that he couldn't allow labor problems on the job because he needed the work to be completed by the given date. Once the present contract for the entire building was 100 percent completed and approved by the owner, then they could do whatever they wanted.

That was great for us because we picked up most of the tenant work, which was very profitable. We gave the tenants an excellent job for a fair price. I called Larry and thanked him. He told me that I deserved all the tenant work because it was I who saved the project for the owner with the redesign, and so I had earned all the extras. That is why we liked to work with Holwick Constructors and GCs like them. They protected their subs on the job. Thanks, Larry!

Later in 1980, we were called by Gust K. Newberg Construction to bid on the San Fernando Courthouse HVAC system, which was a very big job. I didn't like the list of GC bidders, and to estimate the job for only 1 GC out of 11 would be foolish, lowering the odds of getting the job. I talked with Bill, the estimator at Newberg, and asked him if they were going for the job. He told me yes and that they wanted to use us. Bill felt that they had a good shot at getting the job. I told him to send me the drawings and we would bid the job to them only. It was a major estimating job and I worked hard on it. At the same time I squeezed my suppliers for the best price. We had worked for Newberg Construction before and knew them as an outstanding contractor. Odds or not, Newberg got the job and we got the HVAC portion of the work. We finished the $1,445,000 contract, the largest job of San-Val to that date, without a problem and on time. This wasn't going to be the last big job with Newberg, as they called us to bid several much bigger jobs in later years.

We had barely started the courthouse job when our old friend, Steed Bros., called us and told me about a job they were bidding at UCLA. The job was the Wooden Recreation & Sports Center, which was to be the home of the UCLA Bruins. Steed Bros. got the job and they carried San-Val in their bid, yet I think there was a lower price out there for the HVAC portion of the contract. However, Steed Bros. never asked us to lower our price, but carried us because they wanted the best HVAC contractor on this very large job. Thanks, Justin! This job was also more than $1.4 million dollars and we did it perfectly. We did a lot of work over the coming years at UCLA, and were complimented several times on the great job we had done on the Sports Center. That complex was used for gymnastics and other events in the 1984 Olympics. All these jobs looked great on our resume.

We also bid on lots of smaller jobs in order to fill the gaps in scheduling. I also decided to stop bidding to many GCs, and started to increase our prime bidding. At first, most of the work we were bidding as a prime contractor was HVAC-related. Under our C-20 license we were allowed to use other trades on the job, as long as most of their work was supplemental and incidental to the HVAC systems we were installing. Doing more and more prime bidding required that we find a few good carpenters who would do our miscellaneous construction work. After using several small carpenters on many different jobs, I finally found a good small GC out of Long Beach. He went under the name of JAC Construction and his name was John Watson. I asked him if he would bid to us and he told me he would. After just a few jobs, John Watson and I became close, and as time went on I used his company only for all our concrete and carpentry needs. He did good work and was easy to work with. Some time later I talked him into coming to work for San-Val. I wanted to set up our own in-house construction department. John Watson would be put in charge of it.

Things were going well until we bid on a major HVAC project for the Walnut Unified School District. I called some of my best subcontractors and asked them to bid the job to me. It was a big contract that had to be completed in just 70 days, but I knew we could do it. I bid the job by myself, as I wanted no mistakes on it. We were thrilled to be the low bidder and to get the job for several reasons. It was a very close bid between the four lowest bidders, the job had a good engineer, and it had to be completed while school was shut down for the summer. When you do a large project like this in only 70 days, you can make good money — that is if you bid it right! We were all excited, and told our suppliers to get their submittals in as soon as possible, as this would be a very fast job and we had no time to waste.

Our joy did not last long. A few days later we got the bad news from the engineer on the job that the second bidder, Shirley Bros., had filed a protest of our bid with the school board and asked that our bid be rejected because we were not properly licensed for the project. The day after the bid, without anybody's knowledge, Shirley Bros. had gone to the State Contractors License Board, showed them the drawings with all the electrical work, drywall, roofing, painting etc., and asked them what kind of a license was required for the GC. The reply was that it required a B-1 license, and Shirley Bros. got a letter from a deputy the same day stating that fact. Shirley Bros. then hired an attorney and filed a protest against our bid with the Walnut School Board, making the letter from the State Contractors License Board part of their case, that a B-1 license was required for the job, and since San-Val didn't have one, that therefore they should be disqualified.

We were not the only C-20 contractor who bid the job. The contract required a C-20 or a B-1 license. There were two or three C-20s and several GCs with a B-1 license in the bidding. We were not going to walk away without a fight. Now it was time to make a stand and defend our rights, and not allow some jerk to steal away our job. When I called the school board they told me that they were looking into the matter and that we should be hearing from them in a few days. I had no choice but to prepare for an all-out defense.

If I lost this job, that would set a precedent, and other GCs would use it to kick us or other C-20 subs off future jobs. I called my attorney, Larry Levine, to prepare for a lawsuit if I lost the job. I also called a good friend, Gerson Ribnick, who was a contract law specialist in Los Angeles and had helped write much of the construction licensing laws in the state of California. I told him about the project and asked for his advice. He told me that I had every right to bid on the job and be awarded it, but that we might have to go to court over it. I hired him as a consultant and he was very helpful in our defense.

A few days later I was notified that a school board meeting would be held and our case was on the agenda. I was told to bring with me whatever evidence I had in our defense. I knew that this would not be an easy case to win, and so I dedicated a few days to preparing for the fight. I got several calls from friends, some of who were GCs. They had heard what Shirley Bros. was doing to me and came to my defense. They told me that I had every right to bid and asked if they could be of help. One of the calls came from Steed Bros., who had also bid the job. I told them that a letter to that effect would be nice and I would very much appreciate it. I also called some of my other GC friends, owners, engineers and architects for references, and within three days we received over 45 letters in our support. I was moved by this and I used it in my defense. I put together a binder in which I defended my case, point by point. I didn't know what to expect, so I had with me numerous documents, contracts, and law books.

I was more than ready, but I was furious with Shirley Bros. for what they were trying to do to us and for the additional cost to defend our rights. I knew that most GCs were hurting for work, as there were very few jobs out there to bid on. The mark-ups on jobs were small because of the tough competition. I was comfortable with my bid and knew if everything went well, we would make a little profit on the job. It was a struggle to get any job, let alone one that would show a profit. For some contractors, it was much harder; they had to lay off most of their workers for months, and in some cases for a few years. We had laid off some workers and were going to lay off more in the months to come.

The day of reckoning arrived and the school board meeting was called to order. Several of my subcontractors were there, as they also had a stake in the outcome. After routine school board business was finished, it was time for the protest to be heard. The president of the school board read the protest and gave us instructions as to how the hearing would be held, and the time limits that would be allowed for each side. First, Shirley Bros. was given 15 minutes to present their case. Their attorney stated that this was a clear case of a mistake on the part of the engineer who wrote the specs that called for a C-20 or a B-1 license for the prime bidder. He told the board that they had in their possession indisputable evidence that the project required a B-1 license and they would be inviting trouble if they allowed specialty subs to do a project of this magnitude, which was well over 1 million dollars.

He then went into the details of the project. His presentation was good, but his tone got me very upset. He told the school board that the electrical work was over $300,000 and besides that, the job required new electrical service to the school. A great deal of underground work, concrete work, drywall work, roofing and painting were also involved, he told the board. His point was that the job required the experience of a qualified general contractor, meaning Shirley Bros., to ensure that the job would be done on time and in a professional manner. When his time was up, he wanted to go on, but they told him to sit down. He had overwhelmed them with information and could have spoken for an hour or more. This attorney was very good and forceful, and had the State Contractors License Board on his side.

Now it was our turn. I decided to speak first for about 10 minutes, and then Mr. Ribnick and Mr. Levine would have a few minutes each. I started out by stating that if I seemed emotional and bitter, that was correct, because I had just had to listen to 15 minutes of bullshit and lies. That got a chuckle or two from several members on the school board and applause from my supporters. I laid out my defense step by step, picking up confidence as I went on. I gave each member on the board a copy of my binder folder, which had clearly labeled tabs. I explained in short detail each section of the book and why each section was important. Within the documents I had also highlighted all the important lines with a yellow marker, clearly showing the critical information that was part of my defense.

Tab one was a copy of the bid document. It clearly showed that the invitation to bid required the bidder to have a C-20 or a B-1 license, a bid bond and later a performance and payment bond. (Clearly we were in compliance.)

Tab two was a copy of the construction law section which clearly stated that a specialty contractor could bid a project as a prime as long as the work of the other trades was incidental to the work of the specialty contractor. The law did not care if the electrical work was $500 or $300,000, as long as it was incidental to that of the specialty contractor. This is where I scored big. I explained to the board members what "incidental work" meant on this job. For one example, I told them that the only reason there was an electrical contractor on the job was because we needed to power the new air conditioning system that we were installing. I made it very clear that if there was no new HVAC system installed, none of these contractors would be needed on the job.

Tab three was probably the biggest and best-documented section of our defense. I wanted the school board to know the qualifications of San-Val. I told them that we were one of the largest, if not the largest, school contractor in the field of HVAC, and had been in business since 1954. In our documents I listed the over 40 school districts we had worked with in the past, including their own, the Walnut Unified School District, along with the name of the director of each of the construction departments and their phone numbers. I listed the names and phone numbers of over 75 engineers and architects as references as well as a list of work we had done in the past 25 years. The several hundred school jobs we listed had to impress them.

In the next section, tab four, I had enclosed the 29 letters we received from GCs and subs supporting us. I also enclosed the 16 letters we received from architects and engineers supporting our qualifications. I read the letter from Steed Bros, who was one of the B-1 GCs who had bid this job, coming in third. I told the board that I had gotten an unsolicited call from Steed Bros., as well as from over a dozen others, who were outraged at the dirty tactics used by one of their own. I also told the board that Shirley Bros. had misled the State Contractors License Board. They didn't tell the state that every trade was supplemental and incidental to the work of the HVAC contractor.

Tab five was the winner. I explained why a highly qualified HVAC contractor like San-Val was the best for this job and would benefit the district the most. I told the board that in our bid, we used only the most qualified subcontractors. We didn't use some of the lower bids on the electrical and roofing portions of the job because, when we asked for school references, those subs were not able or willing to provide any, yet those same subs were used by Shirley Bros. I told the board that we wanted to use only the best and we were willing to risk losing the job because of it. We felt that this job was not a job for newcomers to school construction.

With five minutes remaining, I turned the mike over to Gerson Ribnick, who covered the intent of the construction law, then to Larry Levine to quickly explain the legal issues. To my amazement, we finished our presentation in the fifteen minutes allowed.

At that point the board members made some comments and thanked both parties for providing useful information that would help them make their decision.

A couple of the board members asked us a few questions, at which time one of the members on the right side of the Board made a motion, which was seconded very quickly. He recommended that San-Val be awarded the construction contract as they were the low bidders, and that San-Val was more than qualified and would serve the district the best. At that point the attorney for Shirley Bros. jumped up to the mike and asked to be recognized. He was told by the president of the board to be seated but he kept asking for a point of order, time and time again, and was told to sit down over and over. Just then a very angry board member loudly called on the president of the board to be heard. He was recognized, and in a stern tone he told the school board president that he had a motion on the floor that had been seconded, and he asked for a vote on that motion.

It was "all in favor" of the motion, which drew cheers and loud applause from those in attendance. The president then told me that the contact was ours and they were pleased to have us on their project. I was also congratulated on the binder that I had submitted; he told me that they had never seen a more professional presentation. I thanked him and the board and told them that they would not be disappointed in our performance. An angry and defeated Shirley Bros. team stormed out of the school board meeting. We won! The bastards lost!

I was mobbed by my supporters and was congratulated by well wishers. The icing on the cake was when most of the members of the school board came up to congratulate me. The hard work put into the defense had paid off. The engineer called me the following day and told me that he was thrilled to have us on the job because we had worked with him on many other jobs in the past and he'd never had a problem with us. I told him that because we'd lost time due to the protest we would need their cooperation in getting the submittals approved as soon as possible!

While the contract was typed and while we posted our performance and payment bonds, our submittals had already been sent to the district and the engineer for expedited approval. We gambled that everything would be approved as submitted and had already issued purchase orders to several suppliers. Time was of the essence. The protest had stolen sixteen days from the schedule, but by the opening day of school, our work had to be 100% completed. We had several buildings to do at the same time, and coordination of trades and the availability of materials were critical if we were to meet the deadline.

We got our contract and started our work the next day. Everything went as planned and we finished our job on time and on budget, to the delight of the engineer and the school district! I was relieved, since our reputation was on the line. Sam's Electric, the electrical contractor on the project, did a magnificent job, as I knew they would. That is why I used them and paid more for their services. Good subs make you look good, while bad subs cause you nightmares.

We were hurting for more space because we were doing larger and larger jobs. I also wanted to set up our own piping department but did not have the room in Van Nuys. We needed a larger shop, more offices, a bigger yard and a larger storage area. I started to look around for a new shop closer to freeways and closer to downtown Los Angeles. I wanted to find a new shop before our lease was up for renewal. After three to four months of looking, I found a larger shop in Burbank and negotiated a five-year lease with an option for five more years. It was now time to set up our own in-house piping, and a construction department also.

A few weeks after our fight with Shirley Bros. over the Walnut School project, I decided to change the name of San-Val Air Conditioning Inc. to San-Val Engineering Inc., and to get a B-1 license. I did that to eliminate any possible problems on future jobs. That way I could bid on any HVAC job or a B-1 construction project. That was one of my best and most important decisions. I decided to take a crash course for a B-1 license. I studied hard at night and I was determined to get it on my first try. I filled out my application and submitted it to the State Contractors License Board with all the back-up documentation.

Several months later I was notified to take the test for my B-1 license. I felt comfortable in both of the tests, the trade and the law, so I wasn't surprised when I got the notification that I passed, and got my B-1 license. As years went by, we bid and were successful on a great many jobs where the HVAC work was only 15 to 20 percent of the total job. We were even called by owners to bid on projects where there was no HVAC work involved, because we did good work and were well liked.

However, my troubles with GCs were not over yet. For many months after I purchased San-Val, I kept an eye on how the generals performed on jobs we did and how they treated us. During those months I decided to raise my prices 10 to 25 percent to those who ran their jobs poorly, while giving the best prices to those who treated us fairly and ran their jobs in a professional manner. On any given job, we might have three different prices out there. Some of the GCs were no longer getting quotes from us and they were not very happy.

Several months later on a major job, we quoted only four GCs and didn't bid to the other seven, one of which was Argo Construction. Steed Bros. beat Argo by only $500; we had the best HVAC price out there and we got the job. All four GCs listed us in their bid, which is public knowledge as the bids are opened in public. Argo would have been the low bidder if they had had our price. A few hours after the bids were opened, Argo Construction called me and asked how come we hadn't bid to them. I told them that they would never get another bid from us after the screwing they had given us the year before. I also told them that there would be many more times when they'd lose jobs because they wouldn't have our bid. As far as I was concerned, they were history and they could go to hell.

A few days later, we received a nasty letter from Argo. They told us that we were throwing away a friendship that had given San-Val a lot of work over the years. I took that letter and put it on our copier machine. I put my hand under the sheet with my middle finger extended, then made a copy. It came out great as it clearly showed the finger and there was no doubt what my message was for them. I mailed it back; our staff thought it was a hilarious response. Needless to say, Argo never called us again. When Irv found out what I did to Argo, he got a big kick out it. Irv supported me 100% and that made me feel real good.

The problem with many GCs was that they only cared about themselves and didn't care if the subcontractors made or lost money on their job. There was no loyalty to subs from most GCs, and that is why I decided to stop bidding to many of them. The worse the economy got, the worse it was to bid on public works projects. As months and years went by, I realized who were the butchers of the industry and who were the decent ones. There was no reason to bid to the butchers; you only helped them with your bid. In most cases we would bid to less than half of the bidders on a job, but we had very little choice. That did make it much harder for us to get jobs. If one of your GCs didn't get the job, then you had no chance at all, and if they did, San-Val had to have the low HVAC bid.

By fiscal 1981 (in less than 3 years), our revenues had more than doubled to $6.6 million in sales, and we ended 1981 with a healthy profit. I gave Christmas bonuses to most of my employees, some of them over $10,000. That year I also started our first annual Christmas party at Sorrentino's Restaurant on Pass Avenue in Burbank. Over 120 San-Val employees and guests were treated to a sit-down dinner, dancing, and trivia games with cash prizes. It cost me a pretty dollar but it was worth it. Our workers deserved to be treated to a feast. We also invited some of our engineer friends and some owners. We had a great time and so we did it every year for about ten years. We certainly knew how to throw a great party!

Our piping department was now doing over 75% of our piping work with our goal of 100% within the next 12 months. That would never materialize, as major problems were on the horizon between the Pipe Fitters Union and me. Those damn unions wanted to bust my balls again!

Myself, Elaine, her parents Pauline and Abe Dores in Las Vegas, 1980.

Elaine with Amy and Robert, overlooking Avalon Harbor in 1980.

Part V

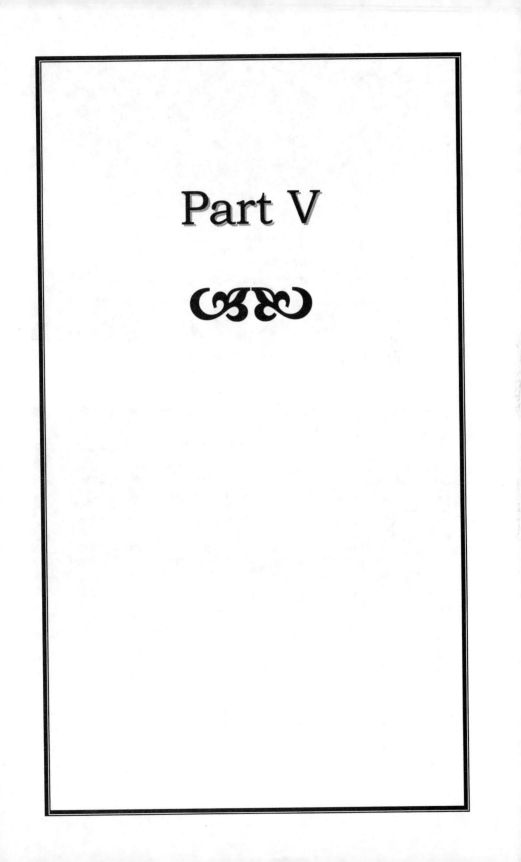

Mom's 80th birthday party in 1982 saw us serenading her slightly off key!
Me, Laszlo, Zoltan, Mom, George, John.

Mom at the party in 1982 with her sister Baba on the left
and her brother Armin on the right.

20

Troubles Start

Starting in 1982, we were bidding on dozens of heat reduction jobs each year for the LAUSD and other school districts as a general contractor. Many GCs and subcontractors were hurting, but we kept our head above water while things got real tight. We were very competitive and got our share of work, but at the same time the private sector was cutting back on expansion and new construction. The high interest rates stopped most of the large private projects. Because of that, many small contractors, who had never bid a school project before, were now bidding them for lack of any other work. Many didn't realize how hard it was to do a school project, and lost large sums of money on their jobs due to their low bids. Dealing with LAUSD was getting harder as the years went by.

The new GCs were also using unqualified subs, many of whom went belly-up before they finished their contract. The poor workmanship and the length of time it took them to complete the projects frustrated the school district. Most good contractors couldn't even come close to the low bidder, and many of them gave up bidding projects for a long time because it was a waste of money and time. We were getting beat by 15 to 20% on most jobs, and we knew that they couldn't do it for those prices. They couldn't possibly make money or at minimum, break even. We knew these jobs better than most because we had done so many of them, and for many years. On several of those jobs, the bonding companies had to take over the job because the contractor went bankrupt. We were called in by several bonding companies to finish the jobs. Many contractors also failed to pay the prevailing wages as was required by the contract documents. Dozens of GCs and subs were fined for their failures to pay the specified wages, and some were jailed for falsifying certified payroll records.

Jobs were harder to get, profits were squeezed, and competition was ugly. We were bidding against companies we never heard of before, and they were beating us badly on most jobs. Because we had to lay off 25 to 40% of our workforce, our overhead increased, which hurt the bottom line. We had to bid ten or more jobs to get just one, and even then at very little, if any, profit. In late 1982 we were called by the Northrop Corporation to bid on a major HVAC project at their new computer facility in Pico Rivera. Jim Beecher of Beecher and Associates had recommended San-Val to Northrop. The owner had purchased the HVAC equipment direct from Beecher and Associates but needed a good HVAC contractor to install it. I had worked for Jim Beecher on several other jobs in the past, and they loved our work. I looked at the job but was terrified by the 45-day completion schedule and a $2,000 per day penalty if the contract was not finished on time. The computer center had to be completed on schedule because Northrop had gotten the B-2 stealth bomber contract and the design was going to be done at this new facility.

Northrop purchased an old Ford plant in Pico Rivera and converted it to their use. Most of the Ford buildings were leveled and the computer center had to be the first thing ready. I decided to bid the project anyway and felt comfortable with the bid. It was a major piping job in a tall building requiring special equipment and a large crew working lots of overtime. Our crews began working 12 to 14 hour days with time-and-a-half overtime pay after 8 hours a day. We were also working on Saturdays and Sundays at double-time pay. Soon we ran into trouble because we needed to pull extra manpower each day from the union hall, but most of those pipefitters were useless. They didn't know how to silver solder for DX piping. Before bidding the job, I talked with Jim, my business agent from the union, and asked him if there was any problem in getting 16 to 20 DX pipefitters for an upcoming job that I was bidding on the end of the week. Jim told me that he could give me 30 of them if I needed it. What a liar!

We delivered our equipment and materials and started our job on the scheduled day. The first day we put only six pipefitters on the job to do layout. We would start the job with an additional 10 to 12 more the following day, and more as days went by. My job superintendent Bob would call the union hall and order whatever manpower he needed. I was busy bidding other jobs and let my crew run the job with supervision from Jim Hancock from our office. We were behind schedule because we couldn't get good pipefitters from the union, so I asked a friend of mine, Joe Volkmar, if he could help me out on the job for a few weeks. He told me he would and I had him work with my crews. Bob, my job superintendent, was screwing me on the job. He became friendly with the electrical foreman on the job and would take two or three-hour lunch breaks with him while 6 to 10 pipefitters were standing around doing nothing. They were waiting for orders as to what to do next. I didn't find out about this problem for a couple of weeks, when I got some feedback from Joe Volkmar and one of my sheetmetal workers. They told me that hardly any work was being done on the piping, and most of the pipefitters were just walking around aimlessly. I went to the job unannounced the following day around 1:00 p.m. and could not find Bob. I asked several of the workers, but nobody gave me an honest answer. Finally I found out that Bob had left for lunch about 11:45 and hadn't returned yet. The pipefitters that were hired from the hall were sitting and waiting for him while tons of work had to be done. Only 8 of my pipefitters were actually working, and I was fuming! And those that were sitting or walking around couldn't care less about the job and were milking it, while making a ton of money. I ordered them back to work and directed traffic while I waited for Bob to return from lunch.

Finally, about 2:45, Bob showed up, and he was shocked to see me. I asked him what the hell was going on. He started to give me some bullshit, but I had heard and seen enough. He was making over $2,400 a week with the overtime. I fired him on the spot. I stayed on the job for the rest of the day and fired eight other pipefitters within a short time. They had no clue as to how to silver solder DX piping. I was mad as hell! I called the union hall and requested 12 other pipefitters, and advised the hall that they better know how to solder or I'd send them home in 15 minutes. I asked Joe Volkmar if he would run the job for me. He agreed and I gave him full authority to hire and fire people as he saw fit. The job had to be done on time and there was no time extension allowed.

The following day the union sent Bob and most of the others I had fired back to my job. I got the call from Joe Volkmar just after 7:00

a.m. and he told me what was happening. I directed Joe and my own staff to kick them off the job, and then I called the Union Hall. They started to give me a hard time, saying I had no right to fire people like that and they must be put back to work, and that they had to be paid for showing up. To all of this I stated, "When hell freezes over." I also told my business agent Jim to go to hell; no union would tell me whom we were going to hire or fire. The men would not be allowed on the job and would not be paid a penny, and if they didn't like it then it was just too bad, but this was MY company! The union threatened to remove all union pipefitters from the job, to which I replied with another "Go to hell," and hung up on them. I didn't give a damn, and prepared to change course on the job.

I called a few HVAC and piping contractor friends and told them that I was in trouble on a job and needed some manpower, and asked if they could spare some pipefitters for a few weeks. Soon I got commitments from several of them for the following day. After spending an hour on the phone, I rushed from the office to the job to get a handle on this disaster. We had to work longer hours and pay lots of overtime. We hired union and non-union pipefitters, which is allowed if the union can't provide qualified manpower. I had plumbers and pipefitters on the job who did good work, but we were way behind schedule. I checked the work done to date and found so much poor workmanship that we had to remove, then replace, most of the work that had been installed by some of the crews. The work of my regular crews was good, but that of the others was terrible and I didn't want to take a chance. We did it over, just to be sure. Jim, the union business agent, was at the job every day giving our people a hard time, but I told Joe and everybody else to ignore him and not to talk to him; to tell him to call the office if he had a problem. He did call our office four and five times a day but I refused to talk to him. He spent most of his time watching what our people were doing.

Two weeks later the air conditioning equipment arrived and we scheduled our crews to rig them on to the roof with a helicopter. Because I needed the pipefitters working on piping, I used mostly union sheetmetal workers to do the rigging of the equipment into place. When Jim, the business agent, saw that I had only one pipefitter doing rigging with three sheetmetal workers on the ground, he went crazy. He ran to the rigging area and wouldn't allow them to rig the units. Big Joe C., our sheetmetal foreman on the job, had had enough of Jim. He grabbed him and physically removed him from the area, and threatened to hurt him if he came back. Joe was a member of our Local 108 Sheet Metal Union.

When I heard about this, I got mad as hell at our piping union. We were doing 40 to 45% of our piping and giving the rest of the piping work out to Shoup Mechanical, A.R. Merante Mechanical, or Martin Mechanical. As far as I was concerned, I could give out 100% of the piping work and the union could go to hell. I didn't need these bastards; it was over with them. Their ego and greed for power was too much for me to take. I decided then to shut down my piping department as soon as the job was finished, or shortly after.

In spite of all our troubles, we finished the job the morning of the last day of our contract, but it cost us about $65,000 out of pocket. We should have made $32,000 on the job. It was a disaster financially, thanks to our business agent and our piping union. When the job was finished, I fired all my pipefitters that were on the Northrop job, and as soon as my other jobs were finished, I fired the rest of them. I hated to do it to some of them, but I had very little choice. From that point on, all of our piping work went to others!

I sent out a letter explaining my situation to fourteen piping contractors, advising them that we were no longer doing any of our own piping and were looking for some good subs to take over that portion of our work. Offers came within days, requesting to be put on our bid-list, as our reputation was second to none. Everybody loved to work for us. We were good to our subs, and we always supported them if the owner or engineer tried to screw them. I wish I had done it months earlier.

1983 continued the downward trend for San-Val, and dozens of other good and honest contractors. Regardless of what we bid, there were 15 to 20 bidders on every job, most of them being new contractors who had never done public works jobs. Jobs were coming in well below owners' and architects' estimates, to the joy of owners, but soon that joy turned to frustration. We were lucky if we finished better than sixth, even if we had no profit built into our bids. Architects and engineers told us horror stories, as one contractor after another would go out of business or just walk away from the job. They underbid jobs drastically and used unqualified residential subcontractors for major

188 / A Light In The Distance
trades like plumbing, HVAC and electrical, which later came back to

trades like plumbing, HVAC and electrical, which later came back to haunt them. Bonding companies had a nightmare on their hands.

Things went from bad to worse when some of my key employees turned against me.

We had very little work on hand and I was forced to lay off about half of our shop and field crews. Even the ones that were working worked only 24 hours a week. One day I got a call from Gust K. Newberg Construction, asking me to bid to them the Olive View Medical Center reconstruction project, which was bidding in about a month or so. I told them that I would pick up the drawings and give them a bid. I felt good because it was a much bigger job, and good GCs like Gust K. Newberg would never take bids from untested contractors. We would have to compete against only 4 to 6 contractors, all of them large contractors, which would give us a good chance at the job.

My joy of possibly getting a very nice job turned into disappointment after I took a good look at the drawings. The job was much too big for us, and I couldn't risk bidding it. It would require 50 to 100 sheetmetal men on the job for more than a year, and I wasn't comfortable with bidding that big a job. The job was tempting because Newberg was going for it and when they went for a job they normally got it. I spent three days putting together a preliminary rough estimate on what looked like an $18 to 20 million dollar job. After sleepless nights and much heavy thinking, I walked away from it. I called Bill at Gust Newberg Construction and told them that the job was too big for us and I'd send back the drawings the next day. They were very disappointed and tried to change my mind, but I stuck to my decision, although it was a very hard one to make.

We all have to know our limits and stay within that limit, or risk losing everything because of bad judgement. No one knows your business and your financial capabilities better than you do. Should something go bad on a job that size, it could wipe us out in a hurry. A lifetime of work could be down the drain. Once I made the decision, I felt comfortable with it, but it angered some of my key employees. When our shop and field people found out that we were not bidding the job, there was anger towards me, especially from Jim Hancock and Harry Smith, our shop foreman. They came into my office and told me that I didn't care about our workers' welfare and that I was selfish. They felt that we could do the job and it could give us a great two year backlog of work. After listening to them for 10 minutes, I had had enough and I told them that I had made my decision and the matter was closed.

The next day or two there was lots of talking behind my back, and very little work was done in the office and in our shop. I called Jim and Harry into my office and gave them a proposal. I told them how we could bid the Olive View job, and I laid out my plan.

If they wanted me to bid the job and they felt we should because we could do it, then each of us should put in one million dollars and we'd bid. We would split the profits three ways or we would split the losses three ways. They had only three options: put up the money, shut up, or get another job; but they'd better never again question how I ran my business. This was my company, my money, and it was my decision as to what job we bid or didn't bid, and that was not negotiable. They stormed out of my office and didn't talk to me for days. A week or so later, Jim came into my office and told me he had gotten another job, and he was giving me his two-week notice. I said fine and wished him good luck. I wasn't going to beg him or anybody else to stay. They had their own lives, and our door worked both ways.

As I expected, Gust Newberg got the job, and the low HVAC bid went for a little more than $16 million dollars. My bid would have been over $18 million for sure and we would have lost the job, but I felt that the low bidder was very low. Later on I found out that the next bidder was more than $1 million dollars higher than the low bidder. I had a hunch that the low bidder was going to have to work miracles in order to make money on that job.

In 1984, we got a call from a company out of Texas named TRANS-VAC Systems. I was in the office and took the call. I found out that they had the contract to do the design and installation of the laundry system at Olive View Medical Center and were looking for a good local mechanical company to receive and install their system. I told him that he should talk to the mechanical contractor already on the job because they could save him money. He told me that they had and had gotten an absurd quote from them. Gust Newberg Construction had given him my name, and they had heard a lot of great things about San-Val and me. I told him that I'd think about it and get back to him in a day or so because I wanted to check them out first. He felt that was fair and thanked me for my time.

The following day I called the offices of Gust Newberg and wanted to know, from Bill, what this was all about. He told me that TRANS-VAC was a very big manufacturer of stainless steel laundry equipment, and they were good people. He told me he recommended that we do the job because we would give them a fair price and a quality job. He also told me that if we wanted it, Newberg would pay us directly if we didn't feel comfortable with TRANS-VAC. A few hours later I called TRANS-VAC and told them to send me the drawings and I would give them a price in 7 to 10 days after receipt of the bid drawings. A week or so after I received the drawings, I mailed a quote for the work, but my price wasn't going to be cheap. I wasn't very comfortable with the bid, so I had added 25 percent to the cost of my labor. I did this because we had never done anything like this before, and this was unfamiliar specialty equipment to me and to San-Val.

A week or so later I received a call from TRANS-VAC thanking me for my quote and asking if there was room to negotiate the price. They told me that while the price we quoted was much better than the one they received from my competition, it was still higher than the estimate they had used in their bid. I told him that San-Val had never installed this kind of equipment before and I had to cover myself, so I had added extra hours to my bid to protect myself. I made him an offer: give me the contract for the full amount of the money, and if the job came in better than I quoted, I'd deduct the $6,500 extra that I had added to the labor. He told me that he would talk to his boss and get back to me.

The following morning Bill from Newberg called to tell me that TRANS-VAC had informed them about my proposal. Bill had told them to take me up on my offer because they were never going to find a more honest person than me or a better company than San-Val. I thanked Bill. A few days later we got a contract with a not-to-exceed price and a thank you note for the professional manner with which we'd quoted the job.

A few months later we got a call that the equipment would be delivered on several large trucks, and that they'd need us to receive the equipment and start installation of it as soon as possible. Our crews received the equipment and started the installation. I was afraid that the prefabricated ductwork would not fit properly and we would have to stop installation to fabricate some of the stainless steel ductwork ourselves. I was pleasantly surprised. The plans had been good and almost everything fitted perfectly. We had to make up very few fittings and that was mostly because the original building drawings were not accurate. Tons of new materials and equipment arrived weekly, and I decided to go to the job to check out the unique installation we were doing at the Olive View Medical Center. After being satisfied that things were going well on our portion of the job, I decided to talk to Newberg's superintendent and also to take a look around and see the mechanical work that was being installed by the low bidder. I didn't count, but it sure looked to me like they had over 120 sheetmetal men, plus about 35 to 40 pipefitters on the many floors on which they were working.

A couple of months later when we finished our installation, I went to the job again and checked our work and what remained to be done. Out of curiosity, I checked again on the progress of the building, and it seemed to me that they had more sheetmetal workers than two months earlier, which was not a very good sign. We found out later that they lost about two million dollars and went out of business. Their estimate was wrong and they had underbid the job by over $2 million dollars. I felt sorry for them, but I was glad it wasn't San-Val. Our original labor estimate on the laundry equipment installation turned out to be more than we needed, and when I billed the final monthly pay request, I deducted more than the $6,500 I had told them we would deduct from our contract. We had made good money and we treated them fairly, and above all else, we did a good job. Thanks, Ray and crew. A week after we billed the job, we received our final payment with a big thank-you.

The week after Jim gave me his two-week notice I had been thinking about a replacement for him. Should I hire an outsider or should I replace Jim from within? I decided not to rush into it and that I would pull double duty until I made up my mind. On his last day Jim came to my office and asked to speak to me. He was in tears and told me that the other job offer wasn't what it seemed, and that he would like to stay if I let him. I told Jim that he could stay under one condition only. San-Val had only one boss and it was me. Jim agreed and stayed with San-Val to the end. The economy was still in turmoil, and we lost about $92,000 for the year, as it was very difficult to get profitable work through the end of 1984.

ASSI was formed to distribute my TITLE-24 software in the 80's.

21

Business Organizations and
Computers in Their Infancy

Title 24 was a new law, for California only. It forced architects and engineers to design a more energy-efficient building. If the design did not comply with the guidelines set by the state, then the building permit was denied. Title 24 saved energy because it reduced the amount of glass used on most construction, required more shading devices, and forced us to use better insulation in walls and ceilings.

Most engineers hated Title 24 because it required a lot more work in the design, and the calculations in many cases took days, especially on a large job. At times, you had to recalculate the building several times, because it failed to comply with the new Title 24 state mandates. It was due to the new Title 24 law that I ended up getting more into the world of computers.

I began by thinking that perhaps a computer could help with these time-consuming calculations, but there were no computer programs available on the market at that time. Computers had just started to surface and they were not yet a household name. Very few engineers had computers or knew what computers did, and hardly anyone used them for personal applications. Most of the computers on the market were Radio Shack Models II, III and IV, and used a single floppy disk because there were no hard drives available. I had a Radio Shack Model IV, which had a single 48K floppy drive. Can you believe that? We used a dot-matrix printer and we were in heaven.

It seems so long ago, though it really was not. I paid three times as much for my very plain Radio Shack Model IV computer (48K), no hard drive, no software, in 1983, than I paid for a new 1.4 GHz Pentium 4, 30 GB hard drive computer in late 2001, which also came with a CD burner, CD-ROM drive, 512MB RAM, sound card, modem and more. This is one of the very few products that gets better and cheaper each year. No one foresaw what the personal computer would be capable of doing in just 10 to 15 years. We all knew about the IBM mainframes, which cost millions of dollars, but that was not an option for people like me. Today PCs can perform more calculations than the mainframes did not that many years before.

There was hardly any computer software at that time to choose from. The first two software programs that I purchased were for wordprocessing and a spreadsheet. I still remember the VisiCalc program, which at that time was good, but compared to what we have now, on a scale of 1 to 100, it was only a five. Still, with VisiCalc I wasted no time in designing spreadsheets for estimating in my business, which immediately started saving me lots of time.

I attended one of the first, if not the first, computer exhibitions at the Los Angeles Convention Center, and was wandering around looking at new computers and gadgets. I stopped at an Eagle display booth and asked questions. The salesman behind the counter introduced himself as Jake Metzler. Of all the people I met at the exhibition, he was one of the few who knew what he was talking about. He told me about the products he was selling and showed me the advantages of his computers over some of the others in the hall. He had an answer to every question I asked. I told him that I would call him when I was ready for a new computer, which might be very soon. I was impressed by the Eagle computer and its features. If I bought a new computer in less than two weeks, could I get it at the show price? Jake said yes, if I bought it within 15 days.

Most of the other salesmen had very little knowledge of the products they were selling. At one of the booths, the salesman knew less about his product than I did. He had to go to his manager for every answer to the questions I asked. The sad part was that the manager did not know his product that well either. I went to only a few other booths, and then I went home with a lot more knowledge about the computer industry, and a better vision as to what computers would be doing in the coming years. I had learned more from Jake Metzler at the Eagle booth than all the others in the hall combined.

A week later I called Jake and I told him I was ready to buy one of his computers. They ran on the CPM operating system, and came in two models, a single or dual floppy drive. Being smart, I purchased the dual drive machine. The nice feature of the Eagle was that it had a one-piece construction, which included the keyboard. It came with simple but very good wordprocessing software called "Spellbinder." The keyboard had dedicated keys, located where we have our F1 to F12 keys now. One key was for "open a file," one was for "save a file," another for "print," and so on. It was so simple that I learned the software in a few minutes. The wordprocessing software with the dedicated function keys so impressed me that I decided to buy another one the following week for Georgia, my secretary. Jake gave it to me for the same price, which was very nice of him. That started a long and fantastic relationship, which lasted for many years.

Because we did a lot of typing of letters and proposals for the many jobs we were doing, a computer would help Georgia be more efficient, making our office more productive and saving us money.

However, Georgia wasn't very happy with me. She did not want the computer and was happy using just her IBM typewriter. I showed her how simple it was to use, but that didn't help a bit. She had made up her mind and that was it. At that point, I had to put my foot down. I told her that we would be using computers in our office; computers were here to stay; we would use them, and that was final! She had no choice in the matter, as I was the boss. As days went by, Georgia realized that there was nothing to be afraid of. Soon the computer became her best friend.

Some months later, I needed the services of Jake and his company again. His business was called Computer Challenge and they were located in El Monte. It was a fairly new and a small company, with only two people. One was Jake, who was the hardware specialist, and the other was his partner Isaac Behar, who was the software specialist. Both were very smart in their specialty. Over all the years we did business with them, I was satisfied with every single transaction.

Although I had designed the outline for a new Title 24 computer program, I was not a programmer; for that I turned to my very talented programming friend, Isaac Behar of Computer Challenge. I asked him to design software for Title 24. After just a few months and some more minor software modifications, the product was ready for beta testing. The new software performed Title 24 calculations in less than ten minutes, which included the input time. Prior to my software, everyone had to do it by hand, which took from 3 to 8 hours for each calculation. After doing 15 to 20 different job calculations, I was ready to have others try it. I gave a copy of my program to a good friend of mine, Joe Nishimura, and asked him to try it for his next Title 24 project. Joe was not a computer wizard, but his son Chris was. Chris learned my software in just minutes and he loved it. Joe was ready to use it on their jobs.

Now it was time to market the product. I set up a separate company and called it ASSI (Applied Support Systems Inc.). We sold the software for $199, and for those that did not want to own a computer or did not want to buy the software, we did the calculations for them for a fee. The final calculations went into a professionally bound report. The plan reviewers at City Hall in several cities were so impressed with our reports and the capabilities of our software that many purchased it to use it for checking other Title 24 submittals. The first software was written for the Radio Shack models and for those computers that were running in CPM, which was the standard operating system at the time. Almost a year later, the IBM format MS-DOS became the standard of the industry with 128K floppies, and we modified the software accordingly. The operating system was so simple and the program was very fast, and besides, I never had to restart my computer because the computer had crashed! The MS-DOS operating system was less likely to crash than the newer operating systems like the Windows-98 and even later operating systems. The reason for that was the simplicity in MS-DOS. My Title 24 software was a hit with engineers, architects and contractors. And so I'd developed another aspect to my business.

When you are in business, it is always a good idea to belong to a contractor's association, which promotes your business. You have very little free time when you own your own business, but it's important to take few hours a month to attend their meetings, especially if you are a union contractor. The cost of belonging to an association is well worth it; you will get it back many times over. You meet your competition, you make contacts, and you learn more about your business. Meetings are normally a social event with dinner and a guest speaker. I was always very involved with the industry because I wanted to improve it and make it stronger, which would benefit us all. When you belong to a trade association, you learn about legislative updates and new technology. It is also a lobbying organization. You make contacts, meet new suppliers, and most importantly, you make new friends. Many of the new friends I met came in very handy as years passed.

One of the best and most professional organizations I ever joined was the Los Angeles-based local ASHRAE, which stands for American Society of Heating, Refrigeration and Air-Conditioning Engineers Inc. — "An international membership organization of engineers who create the worlds we live in." The Association's membership included professional engineers, HVAC contractors, architects, and manufacturer's reps. The inclusion of all elements of the Industry made ASHRAE a much more diversified organization. This was a very large group with a strong and dedicated membership. I had the pleasure of meeting some of the best engineers our industry ever had. Many of them wrote books, codes and laws. I was only an Associate Member because I was not a professional engineer, but even with that handicap, I was a very active member. I was not afraid to give my point of view and did not hesitate to enter into group discussions on topics of importance. I was also a guest speaker at several of the meetings.

Of all the speeches I made at an Association meeting, I think that my best lecture was on "Title 24, Energy Conservation Calculations." Because I had developed new software that would reduce such calculations to just a few minutes, they had asked me to be the speaker on this very important and timely issue.

I had my portable Eagle computer (it wasn't that portable, about 30 pounds) with me, to use for a software demonstration. After the meeting was over, dozens of contractors and engineers stayed and wanted to see the computer program close-up. Most of them were quite impressed. However, some were worried because they did not own a computer, and felt that buying one, just for a few Title 24 calculations a year, was not worth the cost. However, my Title 24 program was very easy to learn since it was menu driven. I must have sold 30 to 40 software programs because of that lecture. Some engineers and contractors bought a computer only because they wanted to use this software.

As years passed, I was nominated for and then elected to serve on the board of directors of our local ASHRAE in the early 90s. I was honored to serve on the board and grateful for their trust. My reputation and the reputation of San-Val in the industry were well known; I didn't have to hide from any engineer or sales rep. If you want to succeed in the industry, then it's very important that you be a team player.

An engineer can make your life miserable and a bad relationship can cost you a great deal of money on a job. Treat engineers with the respect they deserve and remember that we all make mistakes. When I had a problem on a job, I learned to work out the problem directly with the engineer and not to embarrass them in front of an owner or an architect. Most projects are hard enough; we can use all the help we can get on every job. A friendly engineer on the job will save you money. On the other hand, if an engineer is a jerk, and tries to make you eat all his or her mistakes then, nail them. But before you do that, be sure that you document things really well. There is no better friend than a well-documented job. The cost of writing letters and sending copies to third parties is necessary in the construction industry. It can save you a lot of money and on a major project, it can save your business. Trust yourself and only those you know. In all my 31 years in the industry, I never knowingly hurt any engineer unless I was screwed by them, and only then did I take action.

For several years I have been a member of our local SMACNA (Sheet Metal and Air Conditioning Contractors' National Association), which is also a great organization. It is "An international trade association dedicated to providing product services, and representation to enhance members' businesses, markets and profitability." In just a few years, I was also nominated for and elected to serve on the Board of Directors of SMACNA. While I was a member of this organization, I met many of my competition and I became friends with a number of them. In subsequent years, many of them worked for me as a subcontractor on some of our major projects.

22

A Friend Who Turned Out to be a Crook

As a member of ACSMA, I met Wayne McNulty, who owned Crown Heating and Air Conditioning Inc. Most of the work his company did was HVAC service and small HVAC installations. We became friends. His work was mostly residential and light commercial HVAC work, whereas we were doing large commercial and lots of government work. School and hospital construction work was our specialty, while Crown did none of that, so our businesses did not compete. Wayne and his wife Mary would play cards with Elaine and me at their house or ours. We socialized on a regular basis.

At the end of 1985, my five-year lease on our building on Isabel Street in Burbank was up for renewal. Six or seven month's prior to that, I had asked my landlord if he would sell me the building. I wanted to make more offices and tear down the building in the back, but he didn't want to sell. I got along well with my landlord, a very nice older man. He wanted to keep the buildings in the family and give them to his children. I understood, and started to look for a building that we could own in Burbank or Glendale.

I had a hard time finding a building at a reasonable price. Most of the places had very little storage area or little parking or both, yet they asked high prices for them. One day while we were playing cards with the McNultys, I mentioned the crazy prices they were asking in Burbank for a 10,000 sq./ft building. Wayne told me about the industrial park Crown was in and said the prices there were very reasonable. He told me about the building belonging to McNulty

Construction, which was going to be available the middle of December 1985. (Wayne owned Crown, and was a part owner of McNulty Construction.) He said he could get me a good deal on a lease. It was about the right size with a great backyard.

A few weeks later we were at their house, again playing cards, and after about an hour he asked Elaine and me to take a ride with him to Monrovia. We drove to the Duarte Industrial Park and he took us inside the offices and warehouse of McNulty Construction. The offices were very nice and spacious. In the warehouse behind McNulty Construction was Crown's sheet metal fabricating shop and warehouse. It was across from the Crown offices, about a hundred yards away. It was a weird set-up, but didn't bother me. He told me that he was thinking about retiring and maybe I would also be interested in Crown. He would give me a good deal. That should have been a warning. But Wayne was a friend, and he wouldn't lie to me. Would he?

A few more months went by and I still could not find any buildings in the Burbank or Glendale area that suited our needs. One day in November, Wayne came to me with a proposition that included the McNulty Construction building and the sale of Crown. I told Wayne to send me the last three years of Crown's financial statements. At first he was very secretive about showing me Crown's finances before we had an agreement. Finally, he told me that I could go to his office and look at them there, but that he wouldn't let them leave his office. A few days later I went and looked at them. It was not a properly set-up financial statement, and I had a hard time making sense out of it. It was not prepared by a certified public accountant, nor even a good public accountant. I looked at the assets and liabilities, with emphasis on current receivables. I asked for details on the current receivables and was assured that they were all good, and current.

After thinking things over, in late November 1985, I made an offer to Wayne for Crown. In order to protect myself, I made the September 30th financial statement part of the agreement. After first making several counter-proposals in which he wanted more, but which I refused, he accepted my offer. The agreement called for payments over a given time and interest of ten percent per annum on the outstanding amount. Wayne owed 90 percent of Crown and his son

Richard owned 10 percent, but Wayne did all the negotiating and it was clear that he was running the show.

Then I made a very big mistake. I had the attorneys draw up the sale agreement but I did not ask for an audit to verify assets and liabilities. I took Wayne's word that the September financial statement was accurate and that there were no surprises outstanding. After all, I had known him and his wife for several years. He would not screw me out of my money. How stupid I was! This was business, but I let our friendship blind me. I gave notice to my landlord and in late December 1985, we moved into the old McNulty Construction building in Monrovia. On February 11, 1986 we signed the purchase agreement and I became the owner of Crown. Most of Crown's sheet metal equipment was old, so we just sold it and used our own equipment from Burbank, which was very good. I also purchased a computerized plasma-cutting system, which was state-of-the-art. Now it was time to combine the manpower and run two companies.

For the first eight months, I let Crown operate as before, so I could get a better feel as to how they operated. I was very busy bidding and doing LAUSD jobs, and I thought that things would be OK at Crown. I did make it clear to the Crown estimators that I wanted to see the bids on jobs over $10,000, and I also wanted to see monthly reports on jobs in progress. I was too busy running San-Val and consequently spent very little time, if any, looking into the operation of Crown. It took me much longer than I anticipated to look into my new company. Crown's bookkeeping was atrocious and I had a hard time sorting things out. I directed their two bookkeepers to adapt a new bookkeeping procedure, but they lacked experience and had no clue as to how to keep books for a business. Their boss (Wayne) had not known any better either. After a few more weeks I found things were just as bad as before; nothing had changed. It was very frustrating to me that my orders were ignored and changes were not instituted. At that point I had Luz, my bookkeeper at San-Val, also take over the bookkeeping chores on the Crown side. We set up a computerized program for them, just like we had used for many years for San-Val. That is when trouble started to surface. The cash flow at Crown wasn't what it was supposed to be, and I had to transfer a lot of money to Crown to pay their bills. They were not collecting on several large receivables. I hit the roof, and started to look into the problems personally.

I couldn't find records of billings for several jobs that were shown on the financial statement. When I asked the Crown bookkeepers about it, they told me to talk to Wayne. They refused to tell me anything about those jobs and why we could not collect. Wayne was no longer working for me because I no longer needed his services, so I had to call him at home and ask him to come to the office. The following day I confronted Wayne about the problem receivables and asked him why we hadn't collected on them. Wayne acted surprised that the monies had not been collected. He told me that he would look into it and would get back to me in a few days. Two or three weeks went by and there was no response from Wayne, and he didn't return my calls either.

It was now over a year since I had purchased Crown, and time to get things resolved without further delay. I called Ruth, one of the Crown bookkeepers, into my office and demanded answers. I needed the facts on several outstanding receivables and it was time to tell me the truth. Both bookkeepers had been loyal to Wayne and had not reported any problems to me. I reminded Ruth that she now worked for me, not Wayne. Finally, Ruth told me the truth, and it was ugly.

Among other things, Wayne McNulty had overstated the amount of accounts receivable on the Crown balance sheet in the approximate amount of $209,114. He had falsely stated that there were insurance deposits of $58,815 on the financial statement, whereas in fact this insurance deposit had no cash value of any kind. A full year had passed before I learned the truth! How could he do that to me? What a lying bastard! At first I was only angry with Wayne for his lies and for trying to cheat me out of a lot of money, but later I got mad at most of the Crown staff. Over the prior months I had asked several of them to give me the facts, but none of them had come forward and given me a hint, yet they all knew. Boy, was I in a mess! In reality, I had no one to blame but myself, for trusting a friend.

There were several major problems, all of which created a financial hardship for me. All of a sudden, the net worth of Crown was only about half of what was shown on the September 30, 1985 Financial Statement. This was fraud, and I wasted no time in confronting Wayne with my findings. When I presented the facts to him, he gave me a story that he was not aware that those receivables were on the financial statement and that he knew nothing about the problem. That was a big lie, because he knew everything that went on at Crown. A few days later, I gave Wayne a written proposal intended to fix things.

In the proposal, I gave Wayne two options, either of which would have solved the problem. The first option was to have him remove the problem receivables from the purchase price I paid for Crown and adjust the sale amount accordingly. Wayne could collect and keep whatever monies he could collect from those accounts. The second option was to deduct $150,000 from the sale amount and then we'd try to collect some money on the bad debt.

Wayne wanted no part of my proposal, either option, and resisted any change to the original agreement. It was my problem and no adjustment to the sale price would be made. I told him we would see about that. I talked with his son Richard, who felt really bad, but could not do anything. While he agreed with me, he told me that he couldn't turn against his father. He was in the middle of a war and wanted no part of it. He was a good kid and I felt sorry for him, but Wayne was screwing me and something had to be done.

In writing I notified Wayne McNulty and his son Richard that from this point forward I would not make any further payments to them until adjustment was made to the sale price of Crown. The next payment was due in a few days but I wasn't going to pay it. I was ready to make a stand and I was ready to nail the bastard to the wall. When Wayne called me about not getting his payment I told him that none was coming until I recovered all the monies he owed, and if he didn't like it he could go to hell. Then I hung up on him.

Several weeks later I received a letter from a Mr. Kenneth Holland, Wayne's attorney, stating that Wayne was threatening to sue me for non-payment. I called Kenneth and gave him the facts, which Wayne had never done. He told me that he would talk to Wayne and see what we could work out. A few days later he called and told me that Wayne would not negotiate. He didn't agree with Wayne, but it was out of his hands. I decided to stay the course.

Now it was time to clean house. I fired half the office staff of Crown, including Richard McNulty and Al Montante, the Wayne's son-in-law, who worked as an estimator. I was fed up with the McNulty family.

Whereas Richard had signed a covenant not to compete agreement when I purchased Crown, I now signed an agreement in May 1987, allowing him to work for another HVAC contractor. I had nothing against Richard and didn't want to penalize him for his father's actions.

Wayne now sued me, and I hired Robert L. Bacon of the Law Offices of Bacon & Hamilton in West Covina to defend me. I counter-sued Wayne McNulty for fraud. As it turned out, I made no further payment to Wayne or Richard until the cases were settled, which took several years.

On November 21, 1988, we filed our counter suit against Wayne McNulty, Richard McNulty and the McNulty Family Trust for fraud in the sale of Crown Heating and Air Conditioning. Our suit had three key elements.

Element one: McNulty knew that C. F. Opel Inc., a creditor of Crown for the amount of approximately $91,114, was in serious financial difficulty. The collectability of the amount billed by Crown was in grave doubt and that should have been disclosed to me.

Element two: The insurance deposit listed on the financial statement, dated September 30, 1985, included an insurance policy on the life of McNulty claiming to have a cash surrender value of $58,815. In fact it had no cash value of any kind, as loans against it obtained by Wayne McNulty were equal to or greater than the projected cash value of the policy.

Element three: The accounts receivable from Excell Electric in the approximate sum of $118,000 that was included in the accounts receivable figure of $501,230 was not an account receivable from a bona fide customer of Crown. It was in fact the amount of money lent by Crown and/or McNulty to Excell Electric, an unincorporated association composed of Al Montante, Wayne McNulty, Richard McNulty and one Scott Williams. This company was known by McNulty to be in serious financial difficulties. While this amount had been outstanding for years, it was shown on the accounts receivables as current.

Besides damages, we also sought punitive damages and reimbursement for the cost of our suit. In addition, we sued to restrain Wayne McNulty or Richard McNulty from transferring, selling or in any way negotiating my promissory note.

Wayne called me a few months later and offered to settle, but his offer was a joke and I told him to shove it. I was bitter and mad. It was time to get after others who owed us money. In late 1988, I hired the firm of Crawford & Banks and we filed suit against C.F. Opel and also against Excell Electric. We had three lawsuits going at the same time, all related to the Crown purchase. What a mess!

A few weeks before we deposed Wayne, I had lunch with a friend of Wayne's who had done business with Wayne and knew him better than I did and for a much longer time. The friend (who I won't name here) knew that I had purchased Crown from Wayne. He also knew that I had problems with Crown and that I had stopped paying Wayne on the outstanding amount owed. He asked how things were going between Wayne and me, and if we had settled the issues yet. I told him that we were in court and doing depositions, and we'd be deposing Wayne in a couple of weeks. I told him how Wayne had cheated me with the sale of Crown, and he said that he wasn't surprised. Wayne was not a very honest man and had screwed people before. This friend was very honest and would not lie to me about Wayne, and I really appreciated the information he provided me.

He told me that Wayne was a smooth operator, always looking for an angle to make money on other people's money. I heard details about some of the shady things Wayne had done and how he had screwed others, especially one of the partners at McNulty Construction. I asked for more but my friend told me that I should talk to the guy involved, but he refused to give me his name or his telephone number. He did tell me that this man had a small construction company in Monrovia and gave me the name of the street, but not the address. He felt that he'd already given me more information than he should have, and that I needed to do the rest on my own.

The following day I drove up and down on the street and found only one construction company. I stopped by but the place was closed. I took down the name and the full address and called later in the day, but got only the answering machine, so I left a short message. No one returned my call, so I called early next morning and finally got hold of the owner (who I will also not name). I said that a mutual friend of both of us had said that I should talk to him regarding Wayne McNulty. I asked him if he knew Wayne and if he had been a partner at McNulty Construction a few years before. He said yes.

At first he didn't want to talk to me. I asked him to listen to me for just two minutes, and if he then did not want to get involved, I would understand and would never bother him again. I told him that Wayne had fucked me on the Crown deal and I wanted to nail him. I told him that with his help I would have a better shot at it. I asked if I could talk with him for fifteen minutes at his convenience, at any time. He told me to come over and he would give me fifteen minutes. Within five minutes I was in his office.

In the first few minutes I told him about myself, and how Wayne McNulty had screwed me. Then I asked him what had happened between him and Wayne. He started to tell me things about Wayne, how he operated, and how he always tried to take advantage of people. He had nothing good to say about the man, and he was glad that someone was taking Wayne on. This man had heart problems, probably because of his episode with Wayne, and did not want to risk his health and his life in taking him on. He was a very nice guy and a gentleman, who had been screwed, like me, by a smooth-talking bastard.

He told me about how McNulty Construction got started and what his role had been. He had been a friend of Dennis Tierney, who was Wayne's son-in-law. Dennis and he had both worked at the same concrete construction company. Dennis was a project manager, while this man was an estimator. They decided to go into their own concrete construction business. Wayne, Dennis, and this man became partners. Wayne provided some financing for the company and became the president. And so the company started, but soon things began to unravel. Starting a business is always difficult, but they worked hard, bid on lots of jobs, and were low bidders on several projects. When it came time to sign contracts, Wayne refused; he did not want his name on any contracts at that time.

Shortly after the business started, Wayne purchased a new Cadillac automobile without the other partners' knowledge, and paid for it out of McNulty Construction funds. Dennis was upset but did not confront

Wayne. However his partner did. Wayne told him that it was none of his business and if he didn't like it, he should leave the company.

Shortly after that episode the partner confronted Wayne again as to why the contracts were not signed, to which Wayne replied that the bids were wrong and he would not sign such contracts. Tension started to build, and shortly after that, Wayne convinced Dennis that they did not need a third partner. Wayne broke up the partnership. The partner had no choice, and because the company at that time had few assets, they paid him off with very little money. After the partnership was broken up, Wayne began to sign the contracts, and they were on their way.

But, they soon got their asses kicked. They did not know how to run a construction company and went broke. That was this man's only reward; he saw McNulty Construction go bankrupt. He had lost his shirt dealing with Wayne McNulty. We talked for a half-hour or so, and at times he got a little emotional and I saw tears in his eyes. I thanked him for the information and said I knew that some of this was very difficult for him. I knew how he felt, and I told him that I was going to get the bastard even if it took several years.

I had only a few days to prepare for the deposition of this crook. I called Robert Bacon, my attorney, and told him that I had information that would get McNulty, and that I would write out most of the questions. It was my opportunity to turn the tables on Wayne, and I planned things carefully. It was my hope to trap him into lies that he wouldn't be able to get out of. I worked on it for a few nights and I typed up the questions and numbered each of them. I told Robert that I'd be in his office fifteen minutes before the deposition to go over with him what I had in mind.

I told Robert that after he'd conducted routine questioning, he should switch to my questions. I also came up with a system as to how we were going to jump among the questions and how to take a break if I felt we needed to talk. On a small piece of paper I would write the number of the question I wanted Robert to ask next. If I wanted a break, I would push a paper saying "break" in front of him. Depending on Wayne's answers, I would jump around in the questioning. I wanted to make sure that he did not suspect anything.

I was a little nervous when we first went into the conference room, but Wayne looked at ease. He was smiling, but not for long. Robert started to ask routine questions as to his ownership of Crown and how the purchase agreement was reached, and so on. After about thirty minutes, it was time to begin with the questions that I had listed. I just sat there, next to Robert and across from Wayne and his attorney, and listened to Wayne's answers. At some points I put a little slip next to Robert with a number on it, which meant that he needed to jump to that numbered question. Wayne saw what I was doing, but couldn't figure it out. He stared hard at me, but I just sat there and smiled. He had no idea what was to come, and we took him by surprise.

We trapped him into lies time and time again. We asked Wayne about his involvement with Excell Electric, and the life insurance policy; he tried to talk his way around it but we did not let him. Finally it was time to ask him about the McNulty Construction fiasco. At first he did not give direct answers and kept saying he didn't remember, but Robert hammered away. Wayne started to get real nervous and was sweating, while I just stared at him and kept pushing the numbers toward Robert. The pressure on Wayne showed, and his answers got all mixed up. They took time out to regroup, but it didn't help; we were relentless to the end.

At the conclusion of the deposition, an angry Wayne McNulty stormed out of the room without even saying good-by to his attorney. I just smiled. Robert looked at me and also grinned, and that moment was worth a million dollars to me. We had him where we wanted him, and we hadn't allowed him to wiggle out of it. We got him on all points, and that made me feel real good. The hard work that went into this deposition was worth it, and I was more confident than ever in my case against Wayne McNulty.

As months went by, we made headway against C. F. Opel and Excell Electric. On February 23, 1989, we received an offer from C.F. Opel to settle our case against them for 75 percent of the balance due Crown. This would bring our loss from $172,238 to only $43,059. We also had spent an additional $13,621 in litigation fees. I decided to take the offer and go on with other important matters. We also got Excell, but they had few assets and we were able to recover very little. We also got a promissory note for some more money, which was to be paid to us over a period of time. We settled with Excell, and now it was time to concentrate on Wayne. A few weeks after we settled our case against Scott Williams and Excell Electric, Scott called me and wanted to talk to me. I told him to come to my office.

This was the first time I met Scott, who owned Excell. He was a nice young man. He told me that the mess was the McNulty family's doing. He told me how they had come to him to bid this big job and how they had cut his price to below cost, yet they had no idea how to estimate electrical work. He told me that he had no hard feelings against me and he understood why I had to sue him. At the end of our meeting I felt really bad for Scott. The McNultys had also screwed him and he lost everything in the partnership fiasco. He was out-hustled by Wayne and his family. I told Scott that I would like to help him.

I told him that if he wanted to do electrical work for San-Val, I would be happy to use him on smaller jobs and help him get back on his feet. I told him that I was going after Wayne, and Scott offered to testify against Wayne if I asked him to do so, because Wayne had ruined him. In just a short time Excell Electric started to do work for San-Val, and they did a fine job. I could not use him on big jobs but tried to give him as much small work as I could.

A few weeks after we deposed Wayne, he offered me a settlement. It was nowhere near what I asked for, and I told him to get lost. He called a few more times to settle but each offer was only a little better than his previous one. As the court date approached, I made a last ditch effort to settle the case. By this time we had settled with C.F. Opel and Excell Electric, so I knew what my losses were against Wayne. I put a proposal to his attorney for a $110,000 deduction from the purchase price, and for both sides to pay their own legal fees. My offer also included interest payment on the reduced purchase price. I felt it was a fair offer because I wanted to stop the mounting legal costs. I wanted the Crown mess behind me. By this time I was so busy with San-Val, the sooner I settled with Wayne, the better it would be for me. I gave them 48 hours to accept my offer, after which time it would be removed and we would go to superior court, the following Monday morning.

They ignored my proposal; we were on our way to court. I was more than nervous as I drove to the courthouse, and kept going over important things in my head. I arrived twenty minutes early and was sitting on a bench just outside our courtroom. Robert Bacon wasn't there yet, and a few minutes later Wayne McNulty showed up with his attorney, Kenneth Holland. As they walked past me, Wayne made some remark about whether I was going to try the case myself, to which I replied, "Yes if I have to."

A few minutes later Wayne came over and wanted to talk. How stupid we were to spend huge sums of money for attorneys, and why didn't we settle the case before we spent a lot more. I told him that he had had the opportunity to settle for several years, but he was too stupid to admit that he'd lied and cheated me out of a lot of money. He asked me what would it take to settle the case, and offered $100,000. I told him to get lost, because it was not even close.

He left and talked with Kenneth for a minute or two, then came back and told me that he accepted my offer of a week earlier for $110,000. I told him to forget it because that offer had expired several days ago, as was stated in my proposal. Now it would cost him a lot more. At that point I became very angry and told Wayne that I had a final proposal for a settlement, which was good for three minutes only, after which time he could go fuck himself and no more deals would be offered, and we'd let the court decide the case.

I made my last offer, which was much more than the $110,000 I would have taken a week before, plus I offered no back interest payment and I added on my legal costs. It was take it or leave it, and I gave him the three minutes to make up his mind, which was not negotiable.

Just as he left and went back to talk to Kenneth, Robert Bacon showed up and asked me what the heck was going on. He had seen Wayne talking to me and he was a little puzzled as to why I would talk with the opponents without him being present. I told him what had transpired during the past ten minutes or so, and what my final offer for settlement was. At that point I looked at my watch, and when it reached a minute to go on my deadline, I called out loudly "You have one minute left on my offer." I saw Kenneth trying to convince Wayne to settle, and with about twenty seconds to go, Kenneth came over and told Robert that Wayne had agreed to the terms.

It was time to go into the courtroom, but the two attorneys went to see the judge and asked for a little time because there was a settlement offer and the case could be settled before the trial started. The judge gave us a half-hour to settle. At that point of time, Robert and I went into a small conference room and I dictated the terms of the settlement, which Robert quickly put into legal terms. The terms were very harsh and I told Robert that no part of that agreement could be altered.

They did try to modify a few items, but my answer was that nothing would be changed, and that was final! Take it or leave it! Fifteen minutes later Wayne signed the agreement, at which time I also signed it. I made him sign first, and I read the agreement over one more time, just to make sure, before signing it myself. It was a great moment! Robert could not believe it! Wayne could have settled for less than half of that years earlier, but he thought he would outsmart me and would win because he had never lost before. The news spread quickly and congratulations came into my office by the dozens. The nightmare was over. We had nailed his balls to the wall, to the delight of many that were his victims.

Normally I don't let my emotions show, but this time I didn't hold back. I was ecstatic. It was a great relief that it was over and we won, but it was even sweeter because we had settled on my terms; not his. We had a strong case and I'm sure we would have won, but now I could close a sad chapter with Crown. I never spoke with Wayne McNulty again.

Myself, George, Zoltan, Laszlo and John in 1989.

23

Dealing with the Los Angeles Unified School District

In late 1986, I received a call from By Kimball, who was the head of the Construction Branch at the Los Angeles Unified School District (LAUSD). He asked if I could make it to an important meeting in his office the following day. I arrived on time and was told to go right into his office by his secretary Ms. Grigsby. In the office were By Kimball, Samuel Moore, the head of Architectural & Engineering Services of LAUSD, and another gentleman, Mr. Wilbur Green, whom I'd never met before. Wilbur Green was from a program management team (PMT). Later on in the meeting I found out that he was representing Morrison Knudsen, a very large construction consortium in Los Angeles. They had been brought on board as a PMT by the LAUSD. I was very surprised.

By Kimball laid out a plan by LAUSD whereby they had hired a PMT to manage the many new projects that were coming out to bid in the next several months. The purpose of the PMT was to expedite the many new "Air Conditioning Projects at Year Round Schools" and to complete those jobs on a fast-track basis. LAUSD felt that the PMT would bring expertise in processing paperwork and at the same time save the district a lot of money by providing better monitoring of change orders and time extensions. Supposedly, they would introduce timesaving procedures. They would also review plans and specifications to make sure they were complete. The PMT had an engineering staff that would ensure the designs were appropriate for each school. This would save on costly change orders.

By Kimball then turned the meeting over to the PMT, who gave some details as to what they had in mind. I was told that over seventy schools were involved and for control purposes, certain projects were to be combined with others projects in the same area. The bid packages were in the range of $200,000 to $2,000,000 and were competitively bid with a "B" license requirement. When I looked at the details, I was shocked and very surprised, and I just chuckled. The preliminary plans called for completion of the jobs in as short as 45 to 60 days. Having more experience than any other contractor in work like that at LAUSD, I knew that their schedules were only a pipe dream. The projects could not be done in the specified time frame; I voiced my concerns and questioned the sanity of those who had come up with the master plan. I asked many questions, some not very flattering.

The first question I asked was, "How can we complete any job in 45 to 60 days at LAUSD when it takes 90 to 150 days or longer to approve a change order?" The PMT responded quite forcefully that these jobs would not be run like any other LAUSD jobs. That is why they had hired the PMT. Change orders would be approved within ten days and RFIs (request for information) and RFPs (request for prices) would be expedited like we'd never seen before. I questioned how change orders could be approved in ten days when they also had to be approved by the school board. He replied that the PMT knew how to expedite jobs, and their engineers and project managers would review the plans. I was also told that there should not be many change orders on the jobs, and the allocated time period had more than enough days in it. Wilbur told me that I should not concern myself with the allowed time. What a dreamer!

At one point I got a little upset because the PMT talked like they were experts in air conditioning jobs at LAUSD and had done hundreds of jobs like these for LAUSD and other school districts. The fact was that they had never done a school-remodeling job in their life, nor did they truly understand what it took to do a job like this in just 45 to 60 days. I flat out told them that I did know what it took to get jobs done faster and I gave them several good suggestions. I also told them that their plan could not and would not work, and it would end up costing them a fortune in contract delays. By Kimball told me that the school board wanted the PMTs and they felt it will help them save a ton of money because that is what the PMTs told them. What fools! Stupidity at its best!

The following day By Kimball called me and thanked me for my time and suggestions and he told me that he understood my concerns, but people above him were pushing things through. He told me that he also had reservations, but he hoped for the best, and he asked if we would bid on those jobs, to which I replied that we certainly would. It was a sad day for contractors, architects and engineers when LAUSD hired the PMT, and it started one of the worst periods in LAUSD construction history.

Within just a few weeks several of these air conditioning jobs came out to bid at LAUSD. I was shocked to see the very short completion times and, to top it off, they had put a $500 per day penalty into the bid documents if the contractor didn't finish the job on time. Boy, did the short completion schedule and the high penalty clause scare off a lot of people! I had to think about it myself for a couple of days, but decided to bid anyway. If there was one company that could do it, it would be San-Val, and I was ready for the challenge!

Getting subs to bid the jobs to us under the terms of the contract was very difficult. Most of the subs wanted no part of the $500 per day penalty clause either, and many told me that I was a fool for taking on such a gamble. I called some of my best subs and told them to bid the jobs to me and that we would protect them. They trusted me and knew that my word was as good as gold, and most of them told me that they would bid the jobs to me only, as long as we protected them. I agreed and decided to bid the jobs carefully and to cover ourselves and take no chances. Soon it was time to bid the first four jobs and we were the low bidder on three of them. On some of the jobs we were the only bidders, but because the jobs came in within budget the contract was awarded. Because many jobs were put out to bid in a week, we decided to bid only selected projects. Some of the jobs were impossible to bid because we couldn't get enough good subs to bid the jobs to us. I refused to bid these fast-track jobs with inexperienced subs. I would rather not bid the job, or rather come in high with my bid, than to be the low bidder with less than the best subs on my jobs.

All of us who bid the early PMT jobs took a big gamble because of the involvement of the PMT. In just a few weeks San-Val bid over 20 of those jobs and was low on about half of them.

Around that time I had been talking to Joe Volkmar. I mentioned before how Joe had helped me through a tough stretch on my Northrop job in 1982.

Joe was an excellent plumbing contractor, and we were happy whenever Joe was a subcontractor on our jobs. He got along well with engineers and plumbing inspectors. Joe was the only contractor to whom I would give a contract on a handshake. Our word was always good on the many jobs we did together. Although Joe's plumbing business (Consolidated Mechanical) was small, he knew his trade like no other. His shop was in Glendale, only 15 minutes from our shop. He worked very hard, he was very honest, and he wasn't afraid to get his hands dirty. My kind of guy!

He asked how we were doing with our bids. I told him that we were doing pretty well and as soon as we got our new higher bonding limits, we'd do even better. I was in the middle of getting my bonding limits raised.

All public works jobs over $25,000 had to be bonded and it's not easy to get a high bonding limit from insurance companies. Your bonding limit is based on your financial condition, liquid assets, past experience, and organization.

The trouble was that the jobs came out for bidding in bunches and that screwed up my bonding. I told Joe how I had just sold most of the stocks I owned and one of my rental properties and was putting the money into the business. That would help me get more bonding. I also told him that I had gotten my line of credit raised by Union Bank to one million dollars. That would also help. These opportunities might never come again. It was a big risk to put all my money into the business, but I felt it was well worth it. My wife Elaine was very concerned, but I had tried to explain the opportunities, while hiding from her the real risks and the involvement of the PMTs. I was so confident that it was the right road to take that I didn't hesitate for a moment. In the long run it worked out for the best.

A few weeks later I was in my office when Joe stopped by to drop off submittals to Lora and asked me how we were doing with our bids with LAUSD. I told Joe that we had picked up a bunch of LAUSD jobs, but we had stopped bidding for a few weeks. We would bid more after we finished some of the jobs and got our backlog down a bit to free up our bonding limit. Joe stayed only a couple of minutes because he knew that I was busy and he never tried to bother anybody who was busy. He left and I went back to work.

About forty-five minutes later he was back. He came right into my office while I was on the phone and threw a check in the amount of $100,000 on my desk. He told me to go bid more LAUSD jobs, said good-bye and walked out. I put my caller on hold and went after Joe, who was already in the parking lot. What was this all about? Joe again told me to bid more of the jobs and then just got into his truck. I couldn't believe it! He had just left a check there, no receipt required. What a fool, or perhaps what a friend!

A little less than three months later, I sent Joe two checks. One was for $100,000 for the loan, and the other was for the interest. The fool (or friend) sent back the second check with a note saying that it was too much. He told me that his bank did not charge him that much interest and he wouldn't take a penny more than the bank charged him. I could have killed him! I made money on the loan he gave me, yet he would not accept any part of the profit I made. Thanks, Joe! I owe you.

Some of the jobs went fairly smoothly but the paperwork more than doubled. Nothing was simple, which provoked many angry letters from me to LAUSD and the PMT. I tried to document all contract delays on their part. When we didn't get replies to RFIs or RFPs within a few days, I fired off letters to the district and their agents. I put them on notice that they were holding up my jobs and we'd hold them fully liable for delays in the completion of our contracts. I had to document everything to defend myself against that $500 per day contract delay fee. I did not like the idea of spending so much time writing letters, but the risks were too high.

San-Val had never been charged penalties for delay of contract in its history, and I wasn't about to start now. The introduction of PMTs didn't expedite the jobs, they hindered them. Every job meeting was like going to war. The constant addition of layers of paperwork and change orders formed a bog of bureaucracy and incompetence. The PMTs had no clue how to estimate a change order, yet they constantly pressured the contractor to lower his prices. As I knew all along, the experiment was a total disaster, and a year later, as I had predicted months before, the PMT's contract was terminated.

On March 14th, 1988, we received a letter from Jules Cabeen, Program Manager from Morrison Knudsen (the PMT), notifying us that their contract had not been renewed by LAUSD and after March 31, 1988, they would be off all jobs. It was great news and we were overjoyed, but our happiness didn't last long. Hundreds of boxes and folders were dropped off at LAUSD. They contained change order requests and other important documents. It became the job of LAUSD to sort things out and process paperwork. It took months, and the frustration of LAUSD's staff was evident, who had been left with the monumental task to figure out where everything was. It was a mess like no one had ever seen before. Jobs got delayed, tempers flared, and taxpayers got screwed again.

Three weeks later, LAUSD hired several new PMTs to run new jobs that were coming out to bid. What fools! Didn't they learn from their previous mistakes? The hourly billing rate for a construction manager was close to $100 per hour, yet they blasted us for charging $42 per hour for a tradesman. They charged more to the district for their clerks and secretaries than we did for our foreman on the job. What shameless jerks! The multimillion dollar PMT contracts blew my mind. I was not aware of the amount they charged the district until we requested copies of their contracts in a lawsuit at a later time. I wish I'd had that information a few years before when we were trying to get our change orders approved by the PMTs. They sold LAUSD a bunch of horse manure and nothing more. The cost to LAUSD ran into the millions.

Each PMT was worse than the last. Each tried to outdo the other and show LAUSD how tough they were. Their attempt to impress LAUSD soon backfired, as architects and engineers also started to write nasty letters to LAUSD. Complaints mounted as jobs went from bad to worse. Each PMT tried to show the district how they saved money by beating contractors down on change orders. The presence of a PMT generally makes for an adversarial relationship between the project's various parties. All communication between the contractor and the architect or engineer is channeled via the PMT, so normal give-and-take between the two is impossible, which impacts the project.

LAUSD didn't understand the risk when they hired the PMTs, and they paid for it dearly.

In 1988, we continued to bid more LAUSD jobs and got many of them. We had a chance to work under several of the newly hired PMTs. LAUSD hadn't learn their lesson from the previous year's fiasco as they let the new kids on the block dictate the terms of the contract. I decided to take a stand and not let the PMT ruin my jobs. One of the projects where I decided to do this was the 15th Street School, which was one of several projects coordinated by the new PMT. Our change orders were rejected time and time again. The additional layer of bureaucracy slowed the job to a crawl, and I finally hit the roof. I demanded an urgent meeting with Dr. Mel Ross, Director of the LAUSD Construction Branch, and asked him to have the inspector, supervising inspector, and the PMT also present. The purpose of the meeting was to settle disputes on our outstanding change orders, many of which were over 60 days old. A few days later we had our meeting in Mel's offices.

As usual, I came prepared; I showed Mel all our outstanding change orders on the job and asked him why they had been rejected. With each change order we had supplied all backup information and the costs were fully itemized line by line. On the first rejected change order, the PMT said that the price was out of line by almost 50%. Until a revised and much lower price was submitted, there would be no approval. At that point I demanded to know where in hell we had charged more than we should have. I was getting angry, and my voice was raised to a much higher level. I went down the change order line by line asking, "Which line is overpriced?" There was no response, and that is when Mel finally got into the game. He was also getting more then a little upset with the proceedings.

He took my change order, looked it over for a few minutes, and then directed a question to the project coordinator for the PMT. He asked for the PMTs estimate on the change order so he could compare the two. He wanted to see where San-Val had overcharged. But no estimate had been done by the PMT. Mel asked, "How can you say with such authority that the change order is priced wrong, and under what criterion are you asking San-Val to cut prices by 50%?" Mel also asked on what proof they had forced the job to a halt. There had been hardly any work done on the job for several months. The project coordinator just stared at Mel, but couldn't produce a good reason for the delays, whereupon Mel got even more angry and asked both the inspector and the supervising inspector if they had looked at the change orders. Did they feel the estimates were really out of line? Both looked; the inspector then checked his notebook and stated that the change orders, as far as they were concerned, were more than fair. They told Mel that they had talked to the architect, who also agreed with them.

As a matter of fact, the architect's estimate was 18 to 35% higher on most of the change orders. But that did not matter to the PMT. The PMT was in charge on the project and the role of the architect/engineer (A/E) was negligent in the eyes of the PMT, even though the A/E had all the liability on the job.

The bottom line was that the PMT could not show one single item on the several change orders that was out of line.

An angry Mel asked the PMT if they had talked to the A/E regarding the change orders. The answer was no, to which Mel shouted "Why the hell didn't you call the architect if you are that stupid and could not price or evaluate the change order?" There was only silence. Mel then ordered the inspector to review, in consultation with the architect and engineers, all outstanding change orders and report back to him within 48 hours. At that point Mel ordered the PMT out of the office and had a good talk with the inspectors. He ordered them to report any future delays by the PMT directly to him. Mel turned to me and apologized, and told me that he would review everything and that we should hear from his office soon. A few days later we got the call and were directed verbally to proceed with all the change orders as submitted, and formal change orders would follow very soon. Normally I would not take a verbal approval, but because this came from Dr. Ross himself, we started on them at once.

In about a week we received written authorization, just as Mel had promised. The sad part was that he was one of the very few who was not afraid to override the PMTs and to give them a good lecture. Dr. Ross knew construction and at times he was very tough, but he was always fair. He looked out for the district but would not screw the contractor when LAUSD or their agents screwed up. He was honest and tried very hard to push the jobs and the PMTs. A few days later we had a new project manager from the PMT and things improved a little, but mostly because for every delay, the letters I sent out to the PMT and inspector were also copied to Dr. Ross.

When the job was over, we filed a claim against LAUSD for delay of contract. The claim was at first denied, which forced me to sue. We won. Never before in our 35 or more years of doing business with LAUSD had we needed to file a claim. But these were not normal times at LAUSD, and my hand was forced. The delays cost me a lot of money and I wasn't going to pay for their stupidity and ignorance.

I handled the filing and negotiated the claim myself for the 15th Street School. We settled on May 6, 1991 for 211 days at $200 per day for a $42,200 settlement in reverse liquidated damages. Bridge Street Elementary School followed it for $32,000, and that was just the beginning. Projects are priced and bid very competitively, and there is no cushion built into them to absorb losses that are caused by others.

The PMTs were out to screw several other good contractors besides us. But they picked on the wrong company when they picked on San-Val.

It was a sad day for decent contractors, when on Jan 31, 1989, By Kimball retired as the head of the Construction Branch at LAUSD. Of all the years that we worked at LAUSD and the hundreds of jobs we performed on, we never had a fight with him. He had integrity, he was honest, and he had the respect of others. He was very knowledgeable with all phases of construction, but did not hesitate to ask for advice from others. It didn't take long after his departure for LAUSD to realize how valuable he'd been over the years.

A less talented team of managers and department heads took over a formerly smooth-running construction branch team. Ignorance ruled, while integrity was a lost word, and big egos with lack of experience took charge. What a mess, what a fiasco! Buddies of bureaucrats, regardless of their qualifications or talent, replaced hard-working, decent administrators and department heads. Good people like Dr. Mel Ross, Director of the Construction Branch, Supervising Inspectors Tom Whiteside and Bill Floyd, Change Order Coordinator Walter Jones, and many others worked hard to keep things moving, but they lacked authority, and their efforts were in vain. Higher-ups with little or no management experience ignored their good advice and dictated their own course of actions, regardless of the consequences. As time went on, Dr. Ross retired, but I think he may have been forced to by the new administration. It was sad to see good and honest people leave and be replaced by less talented personnel.

Just as I had done for years before, I continued to write letters making suggestions to LAUSD regarding better construction practices, HVAC design improvements, and money-saving bidding procedures. Numerous times, I had been consulted by the LAUSD Personnel Commission to help assist in the evaluation of candidates in their personnel selection process. On a regular basis Mr. Harold Mason, Chief Mechanical Engineer, or Mr. Al Tomei, School Facilities Planner, would call me and ask for my input on more advanced or more complicated HVAC designs. I provided a written opinion in response to each request. I never requested a penny for my services, nor was I promised anything in return. We worked for LAUSD for more than thirty years, so I knew a lot of people there and they knew my qualifications. I felt it was my duty to help them. My advice and suggestions were implemented on score of projects. It was very upsetting to watch things go bad.

Soon, bloated project management teams took full control of projects, overshadowing LAUSD personnel, some of whom were highly motivated and experienced. Friction was visible all around. Good and highly knowledgeable inspectors and A/Es were playing second fiddle to the new kids on the block. The many new jobs required LAUSD to hire additional inspectors, whose lack of experience added to the horror. New projects were overloaded with unqualified personnel who were slow to process requests for information (RFIs), requests for price (RFPs), and change orders. That caused jobs to be delayed by months, and in some cases by over a year.

LAUSD and the PMTs didn't check the plans and specs properly for errors and omissions. Many of the jobs were poorly designed, and it was obvious that whoever had checked the drawings and the design had no idea as to what they were looking at, otherwise the jobs would never be allowed out for bidding. New A/Es were hired to design the many projects LAUSD wanted to do in the coming years, but many of them had no previous experience with LAUSD and the paperwork that would be required. Boy, did the mountain of paperwork surprise them! For some, just one job with LAUSD was more than they could take. Many would never do another job for LAUSD again.

On many jobs and in many cases, changes were made to drawings months after the job started, at the request of the principal or teachers. Those changes should have been discussed prior to letting the plans out for bids. The changes delayed some jobs over a year. Politics had a lot to do with it. Some principals in tough neighborhoods were catered to, and LAUSD went out of their way to please them, even if it delayed the job by more than a year.

The huge amount of money that was wasted on those changes and the added cost due to delay of contracts was very costly to taxpayers. The tab ran into millions, besides the millions that were wasted on the PMTs. A good common sense approach and professionalism had been replaced with stupidity and ignorance. The uncontrollable egos on the part of project managers and administrators were more important than the successful completion of a project. Time and time again I tried to give advice to LAUSD on bidding and contract procedures that could save them a lot of time and money, but soon that effort got me into hot water.

One day my office received a call from LAUSD that my presence was requested, along with my change order administrator, Lora, at the construction branch. Lora and I went to the meeting and sat down at the conference table. In the room were more than a dozen key executives from the PMTs and six to eight top administrators from LAUSD. To the best of my knowledge, I was the only contractor present. Doug Brown, who had replaced By Kimball, chaired the meeting and sat at the end of the table smoking a cigar. Before I sat down, I greeted Doug, but he ignored my greeting. I was a bit surprised, but in a minute or so it became apparent that he was more than a little pissed at me.

Doug Brown started the meeting by blasting me in front of everybody. Pointing a finger at me, he told me in a harsh and threatening tone to mind my own fucking business and to stop telling LAUSD how to run their business. Boy was I shocked! Lora looked at me in disbelief, shaken by Doug's harsh tone. Doug was referring to some of the unsolicited suggestions I had made in the weeks and months prior to this meeting.

Some suggestions had to do with the role the PMTs played in the management of fast-track projects, which, instead of a "fast track," were crawling at a snail's pace at best. I was one of the very few who constantly voiced my concerns and was not afraid to speak my mind.

It was obvious that I had gotten him mad, because for the first minute or so of this very important meeting I was the target, and he really let me have it! I just sat there and took the verbal abuse, but I wanted to see what would develop from that point on. I wasn't going to walk out of the room and I wondered what else would happen. I had no clue as to the purpose of the meeting, but I knew that problems on all jobs were plentiful, regardless of who was the contractor on the job.

After he took his frustration out on me, he turned to the rest and said, "What in hell is going on and why are the jobs months behind schedule and what can we do about them?" He wanted to know why new jobs were coming in way above budget. Why all the change orders and why all the delays? Doug sounded very frustrated, but I wasn't sure if he really was angry or just putting on a good show. He wanted answers and solutions, and he wanted them now! Some of the men gave bullshit excuses, but no one made constructive remarks; most of the others just stared, afraid to open their mouths — a bunch of overpaid chickens sitting there afraid to say something wrong or stupid. However, I wasn't going to just sit there and say nothing, because I had plenty to say.

When no one else spoke up, I did. I told Doug and the others in attendance things they did not want to hear. I made it clear that if they did not change their idiotic procedures, the district would end up paying tens of millions in damages to dozens of contractors. I again suggested timesaving procedures to process change orders. I told them that jobs were coming in over budget because they had too many jobs bidding in a very short time. I stated further that good qualified contractors could only bid on so many of those projects. Contractors were raising their prices because there was little competition.

I told Doug that the change order process with LAUSD was a nightmare, and no other school district made the process as cumbersome. I also warned them of the lawsuits that would surely follow, because no contractor could absorb the financial burden caused by the PMTs and LAUSD. I was quite sure that I did not make any new friends at the meeting. I just told the truth, but I also wondered why I was the only contractor present. Perhaps the rap had been just for show, while they really wanted my input? But it proved to be just more talk with little or no results. Things did not improve and if anything, got worse.

I had my battles with the PMT, but some of the architects were also openly fighting with them. In a way I was glad that it was not just San-Val. But I did not expect one of them to be Martinez Architects, nor did I expect them to be so forceful.

There were several architects giving hell to the PMTs. We knew they would, because they are their own people. Incompetent managers do not easily boss them around. Over the years we'd had the pleasure of working with Martinez Architects on many multi-million dollar projects. We found them to be one of the best in their field. We respected them, and they respected San-Val and me. Our teamwork produced some great projects. When the A/E and the contractor work in total harmony, the jobs get done faster, the quality of work is always at its best, and the owner benefits. It's a win-win situation.

On three of the jobs with LAUSD, the Bridge Street Elementary School, Broadway Elementary School, and the Breed Street Schools, there was constant fighting between the PMT and us. I felt that the architect's responsibilities were taken over by the PMTs. When they told the architect how to design, they stepped over the line, and then some. I wasn't totally surprised when we received a copy of a blistering letter that Norberto R. Martinez, AIA, sent to Robert E. Donald, Deputy Director of Building Services at LAUSD. Copies of that letter were also sent to all administrators in the chain-of-command at LAUSD.

In that letter dated June 26, 1989 he informed LAUSD that as of that date, they would no longer recognize the PMTs participation in any of their jobs. "It is both unacceptable and intolerable to Martinez Architects to have the PMTs hounding every decision or clarification that comes up — making mountains out of molehills. The PMTs have not helped LAUSD to accomplish the original goal of expediting construction. In truth, we feel they are interfering between the architect and contractor, creating an unnecessary amount of paperwork, as well as animosity among all parties involved."

San-Val had been saying that for two years, but nobody listened. They had made us out to be the bad guys. The two-page letter went right to the point and was right on. It was well written and long overdue. I'm sure that they were not the only A/Es that sent letters like that to LAUSD.

Because Martinez refused to take orders from the PMTs, we also bypassed the PMTs and dealt direct with the A/E on minor problems. Things started to speed up. We still had a project manager from LAUSD on the job that handled the change orders, and so on, but a layer of bureaucracy had been removed and paperwork was also reduced. Thanks, Norberto! It takes a lot of patience to deal with districts like LAUSD. Other projects of similar size with other districts were completed in half the time it took at LAUSD, saving a lot of money.

We did more of those PMT jobs than any other contractor who worked for the LAUSD. I believe that the next three contractors' total was close to what San-Val did alone. They also had their fights with the PMTs. Most of them would call and ask me if I had any problem with those "idiots" on any of my jobs. They told me that the PMTs were driving them crazy. Many of those good contractors had worked for LAUSD for ten or twenty years or more. We were all in the same boat, trying to go on, hoping that sense and logic would soon follow and praying that the PMTs would be history once again. It didn't come soon enough for many honest contractors.

As years went by, our sheet metal department became less profitable because the HVAC work was less than 15% of our total work. Our shop had fabricated less than 200,000 pounds of sheet metal a year for the past three or four years. That made our shop very expensive to operate. Our sheet metal shop made our overhead very high and so we were losing a lot of work because I was stubborn and had wanted to keep it. As I looked for a new building for San-Val, I decided that our sheet metal department was not going to be part of that move. I had a lot of friends in the industry and so we had no problem lining up good HVAC subcontractors for future jobs.

As we did with the piping department earlier, we replaced our sheet metal division with a few qualified HVAC subs. Offers poured in. I decided on just a few like MES, Circulating Air, Strategic Air, Air Flow Sheet Metal, and Ideal Heating. They all knew how to do public works jobs and they gave me very competitive prices. I was not going to use just one HVAC contractor. I would not have as much flexibility as when we did the metal work ourselves, but I would be more competitive. I also would not need a 20,000 square foot or larger building. Now, I could look for a building only half the size, with a location closer to our core business area.

Finding a suitable building was harder than expected. Finally, after several months of looking in October, 1988, I found a piece of property in Los Angeles near the Glendale line. Five small and very old buildings located on nearly an acre of land. I couldn't use the buildings, but bought it for land value only. I paid $692,000 for it, which was a lot of money, but the location was fantastic.

I leveled all the buildings and erected three stand-alone buildings. The sizes of the buildings were 5,200 sq/ft, 5,530 sq/ft and 11,200 sq/ft. I wanted to rent out the two smaller buildings and keep the larger one for us. Prior to the completion of construction, I advertised the two smaller buildings for lease with a realtor. A few weeks later I received an offer to buy the smaller building. At first I said, "Not for sale," but the buyer would not accept my answer and told the realtor to talk to me again. At that point I told the realtor that I would listen to an offer but it better be very good. After some back and forth offers, I accepted $520,000, which was very close to what I wanted. The buyer was a local garment manufacturer who needed a larger building.

After designing the buildings it took me months to get our building permits. Dealing with the city of Los Angeles was more than frustrating. It was a nightmare! We leveled the existing buildings, which were falling apart, replacing them with a beautiful complex, but they wanted more and more, which added to our costs. I would never build another building in Los Angeles. The permit fees were absurd! The final project was a success and I was looking forward to occupying our new building for 10 to 15 years. We moved into our spacious, spanking-new building in September 1990. Within a few months we leased out the other building to another garment manufacturer.

On February 28, 1990, after more than thirty-five years in the HVAC business, I phased out our HVAC business and began to subcontract that portion of our work out. I sold Crown Heating and Air Conditioning Inc. and, at a private sale, sold all our sheet metal equipment. I also sold all the equipment and tools for our piping department, which we had shut down some time earlier.

Once I made my decisions, some of my office and field workers were very upset with me. However, it was a business decision, and had to be made by me alone. One of the workers I had to let go was my sheet metal estimator, Rich Richardson, who was very upset over losing his job. He took it personally and took revenge against San-Val and me years later. Being an owner, you have to make tough decisions, and sometimes they are unpopular decisions.

I don't take pride in letting people go. Running the business forced my hand. It's your duty to do the best for the company as a whole. You must keep your personal feelings out of it and make a business decision, for nobody knows your business as well as you do. An employee has no financial risk in the company and he or she can leave the company at any time if a better opportunity arises. It's their right and their choice, but when an owner lets someone go, it can get very personal. Unfortunately, sometimes employees blame you for the ills of the world. I always treated my people with respect and paid them well. But sometimes, regardless of what you do for them, they feel it's not enough. They feel they deserve much more. Some just can't be satisfied.

Two years after I purchased San-Val, I started to give out bonuses at Christmas time to our employees. Some years it was only a few thousand dollars, but some years when we did well, it exceeded $80,000, and one year much more. That was great for the staff, yet some did not even say thank you. That really pissed me off. I noted that and the following year they got nothing. Some members of our staff and crews were mad as hell at me, but I did not care. Some years when we did not make money, I was forced to cut way back on the bonuses, and they were mad at me again. They wanted that big bonus every year, regardless how San-Val did. There were many that thanked me several times for the bonus and sent a nice note to my house, and that made me feel good. I did not have to give bonuses, but I did because I felt it was the right thing to do. I wanted my workers to share in our successes.

One of my key employees, John Watson, gave me a hard time with the bonus, but in the opposite way, to my surprise. He refused a bonus, which was quite large. He felt that I paid him well and he was more than compensated for the work he did for San-Val. I told him that he did more for San-Val than any other employee, and he deserved the large bonus, which was well into five figures. He didn't want to take the money, so I told him that I would fire his ass if he didn't take it (I wasn't really going to). I told John that if he did not want the money, then give it to his two beautiful twin daughters. Finally, he took the money. He earned it. I loved John because he was my most honest, loyal, and non-demanding worker. He had had his own business for many years, so he understood the agony of being the boss. Even though he had had only a few employees, he understood the risks and the responsibilities that went with being a boss.

San-Val building under construction June 1990.

The finished product. The new San-Val Engineering, Inc. building
11,200 sg.ft completed in September 1990.

Part VI

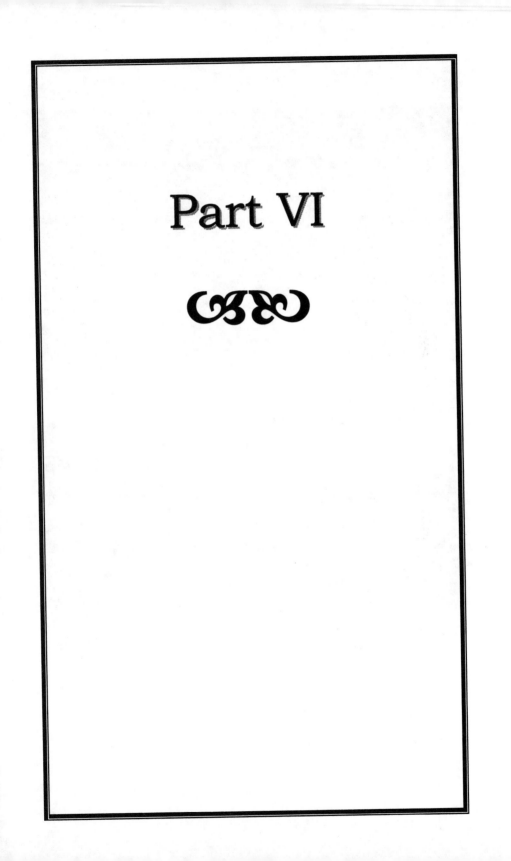

In August 1990, Amy decided to go to France for a year.

24

Difficult Times Ahead

Family problems at home started to interfere with my daily work. We had some medical problems with my daughter Amy, and shortly after that Elaine became very ill. In August 1990, Amy decided to go to France for a year as an exchange student. She was almost twenty years old at the time. She went against our advice; she had made up her mind. Only days before leaving for France she had minor surgery. That did not help matters and complicated things. At first Amy was miserable in France. Almost every night she would call and cry to Elaine about it.

I would come home and see Elaine sitting on the sofa crying too. I knew that she wasn't feeling well, but this was more than that. I confronted her and she told me that Amy had called. This went on for several weeks, and one night when Amy called, I told her that she had gone to France against our advice and if she was so miserable, then she should get her ass on an airplane and come home. She should not make everybody at home miserable also. We did not want to hear any more about her problems. That finally did the trick. As a matter of fact, in a very short time Amy started to like it there. By the time her time was up in June of 1991, she loved France so much that she did not want to come home.

But Elaine's health and her overall condition started to deteriorate even more. She was working as a volunteer at Muir Jr. High School in Burbank, but had to quit because she could not even pick up or hold a book. The smallest task had become a monumental chore. At first, her right leg tingled and hurt. Soon, several other parts of her body rebelled and her condition became very grave. As time went on, she lost the feeling in her arms and legs. I had to dress her in the morning and undress her at bedtime. She couldn't use her arms. She stopped driving because she could not push the gas or brake pedals. Months later she could not lift anything heavier than a few ounces. She could not even pick up a glass of water or open the refrigerator door. Soon she could not even flush the toilet. She could not cook anymore or cut her own food. She had to be taken care of like a baby.

Her body would jump an inch or two while sleeping as if getting an electric shock treatment. If someone welcomed her with a hug, her body would start shaking like crazy. We could not allow anybody to touch her. No one was allowed to hug her, or even shake her hand. It was a hell of a way to live and an agonizing experience for me to watch the love of my life suffer like that. I had to be strong and do her chores: from cooking to cleaning up, to taking her from doctor to doctor, and in-between I also had to run San-Val. I had to try to keep things from her in order to protect her as much as I could.

I was devastated to see Elaine suffer like that, but I could not do anything to stop her suffering. Soon she went into a depression, and that was even worse.

Elaine didn't tell Amy much because she did not want Amy to worry. Amy knew that Mom was hurting badly, but did not know how badly. Elaine was not a complainer. She kept her problems between just the two of us. It was a very difficult time for all of us, and the worst part was that specialist after specialist could not help her. We tried every possible treatment out of desperation, including acupuncture and non-traditional treatment. All to no avail. Physical therapy was the best medicine for her and she went several times a week. She was losing a lot of weight and looked like an 80-year-old woman — all bones and skin. She was only fifty years old. I forced her to drink high protein liquids (like Ensure) to put some weight back on her. After years of physical therapy and medications, her problems eventually started to improve. The side effects were sometimes more harmful than the cure.

While taking care of my wife, I also had to take care of business. We were bidding on a lot of work in a very competitive market. San-Val was low bidder and received a $3,169,000 contract from the LAUSD for the Venice High School modernization in October 1991. The completion date was fourteen months from the time of the contract, but due to delays and change orders, it took over 28 months.

The delays were caused by 39 change orders. We sued LAUSD for delay of contract and finally settled the claim in October 1995 for $60,000. I didn't get my money on the suit until after I retired from construction. It took us sixteen months to get paid on the claim. It's a shame that you have to spend so much of your time documenting contract delays, but if you don't, your chances of getting liquidated damages is slim to none.

For more than forty years, San-Val performed well on every job, and our reputation for honesty and integrity was never compromised. We did an honest job for an honest price. We never knowingly screwed anybody just to make a few bucks more, even when we were losing our shirt. As a matter of fact, we went out of our way to do more and to make the owner and the A/E happy. That is how San-Val operated, and we took pride in it! We did over $100 million dollars worth of contracts over those forty years, and we were proud of every one of those jobs.

In May of 1986, I bid and was awarded a complicated job for the General Services Administration (GSA) in San Francisco. It was a major remodeling work on the HVAC system at the Hawthorne Federal Building in Hawthorne, California. The building was a large multi-story office building and was fully occupied.

At that time, the Federal Building in the city of Hawthorne had an old style "constant volume" HVAC system. Constant volume systems are not energy efficient. In order to improve energy efficiency, the GSA decided to retrofit the building with a new "Variable Air Volume" (VAV) system. VAV systems are much more energy-and cost-efficient than constant volume systems, but the comfort level is not as high.

All of the existing fiberglass ductwork had to be removed and replaced with new galvanized steel ductwork. We were also to install new variable air volume boxes and new electronic speed controllers for the existing large 60 horsepower air handler motors. All the existing HVAC equipment was to remain, as well as the registers, grills and the last piece of flexible ducts going to them. The work was to be performed at night, and the HVAC system had to be fully operational each morning by the time employees came to work. Whatever ductwork or equipment we had removed each night, the new ductwork and new equipment had to be installed and made operational by the morning. It was a complicated job, because you had to work over existing furniture and t-bar ceilings and had to do the work in small sections. If the air conditioning was not working, there was no way to open the windows.

Before bid-time, there was a job-walk, during which the GSA personnel and building maintenance people showed us the job and the working conditions.

One of the people who was doing most of the talking and giving contractors instructions was Richard Broadrick, who became the contracting officer on the job, out of the L.A. offices of the GSA. Before bid-time I went back three more times to get more familiar with the working conditions. The job had a two-year time frame and I wanted to make sure that I knew what I was getting into. It was a tricky job, but it wasn't complicated.

We had done many much more complicated jobs than this. In order to make sure that I gave the best possible price, I waited to release my bid until only a few minutes before bid opening. It was a public bid opening and I decided to have one of my employees fly to San Francisco. He took the bid with him and I would give him the final price a few minutes before bid-time.

Boy, was I surprised when less than five minutes after the bids were opened, I received the call from my employee! He told me that we were the low bidder. I was also told that we were the *only* one who bid the job. That scared me a little, but I was not really surprised. Of the half a dozen or so contractors who had walked the job, all had complained that the job couldn't be done over existing desks, filing cabinets, T-bar ceilings, and so on. They didn't think the HVAC system could be kept fully operational on each day of the contract. They were so scared of the working conditions that they passed on the job. I had also voiced those concerns, but we were told that there was no place to move the tenants, and that was how we had to bid the job.

Because I had done many other jobs for the GSA in the past years, the L.A. office of the GSA gave San Francisco good recommendations regarding San-Val. Within sixty days after we bid the job, the GSA awarded the contract to us in the amount of $1,898,000.

After the GSA gave us our contract, they hired PAE, a Los Angeles mechanical engineering firm, as the project manager and inspector for the job. They were to report directly to the GSA in San Francisco. As mentioned, Richard Broadrick was the contracting officer for the GSA. In years past we had worked with PAE on other jobs; I believe that we had also worked with Broadrick before.

After signing our contract and posting our performance and payment bonds, we started at once on submittals and shop drawings. We found problems with the duct design, but could not talk with the design engineer (Brockmeier) because the GSA had fired them before it let the job for bids. Later on we found out that Victor Tablante, a design engineer for the GSA, had finished the design and let the project out for bids.

After we submitted the shop drawing for the ductwork, we received it back as "disapproved." I called and asked why Tablante had rejected our shop drawings. He said that most of our duct sizes were undersized and needed to be revised and enlarged. I tried to explain to him that the bid drawings were wrong because portions of the high velocity ductwork were sized for low pressure, which would screw up the controls on the VAV boxes. In order for the VAV boxes to work properly, we needed to maintain proper velocity in the high-pressure side of the design.

Boy, I should have realized at that point that Victor Tablante had no idea what I was talking about. He didn't have a clue about high velocity systems design or VAV systems. At first I didn't want to believe it, but soon I was convinced that he didn't understand high velocity systems, pressure drops, and lots of other things, yet he was a design engineer for the GSA. He told me to send him charts and curves and to send the shop drawings back. A few weeks later we got it back "approved."

Then he also rejected the VAV boxes we selected. I had to argue with him for weeks. I told him to please call Krueger Manufacturing Company (who made the boxes) and talk to their engineers, and see if our selection was right or wrong. I also told him that if he wanted to change the VAV boxes to a different selection, then he should just mark up the shop drawings accordingly, but I warned him it wouldn't work. If they didn't work, I told him that the GSA would be fully liable for replacing them. Tablante's lack of understanding or experience delayed getting the shop drawings back to us.

I had to call time and time again, and also sent several letters stating that we could not start the job if our equipment and shop drawings were not approved in a timely manner. It took us more than two months to get approval, and it should have taken less than two weeks. Most engineers would have approved it in less than a week. And after all that, the final shop drawings were approved the way we originally submitted them! I was getting very frustrated because it was costing us money out of pocket.

Shortly after our piping contractor started their portion of the work, they notified the inspector that some of the existing pipes had asbestos coverings, which were not shown on the drawings. After testing confirmed that it was asbestos, the GSA directed us to give them a price for removing it. Shortly after, we were issued a change order for removing the asbestos. We hired a well-known certified and bonded asbestos removal company, and they performed the work.

As the job went on, the GSA began getting complaints from tenants that the HVAC system was not working properly — they claimed they were not getting enough air circulation in the rooms. The building maintenance people let my foreman know of the complaints. Our people checked out any complaint as soon as we got to the job and took care of it at once, if it had anything to do with our work. But the problem was not with the HVAC system we installed. It was with the design and the new CFMs, which regulate the amount of air sent to the room. The building also had problems with their existing chillers and their air compressor. That caused many complaints, but it was also not part of the scope of our work. All equipment was existing and had nothing to do with our contract.

The complaints were mostly about airflow. Up to now they had had a constant volume system, which is the best money can buy, but it's very costly to operate. The new design changed it to a variable volume system, which cut the air change by 60 to 70%. This made the room feel stuffy. When you take the best system money can buy away from tenants and give them lesser quality, they are not going to be very happy.

When the thermostat reaches the desired temperature in a room, a VAV box cuts back the airflow to a minimum setting. The tenants didn't care about saving 40% in energy. They only knew that they had been much more comfortable before we did our work. We tried to explain the principles of their new VAV system. We told them that we had to comply with plans and specs. That was what the GSA had designed, and that was what our contract forced us to do. The maintenance people understood it, but wanted no part of the fight.

The maintenance people wanted to be the nice guys — they were going to have to live with the system for years to come. During our contract, we wasted hundreds of hours of our time talking to tenants, without compensation. There was no comparison between the new and the old systems. It's like driving a Cadillac and then a Chevy Nova. How would you feel? I know that I would be pissed! This project was performed to save energy, not to provide the same comfort levels to tenants.

One day in early 1988, out of the blue, we were requested to issue a price for removing two existing sixty horsepower motors on the roof fans and replacing them with new 100 horsepower motors. We did not ask for this — it was the GSA's idea in order to make the tenants happy. After the change order was approved, we requested the appropriate CFM and RPM settings for the new motors. We needed to order larger pulleys for the new motors. We never got the new CFM or RPM settings from PAE or the GSA, so after waiting for more than a month, I directed my HVAC Estimator, Rich Richardson, to select and order the proper pulleys. By this time the contract was nearing its completion, with more than 95% of the work done.

After the new motors were installed and started, one of the huge fan's blower wheels was damaged because it could not take the higher RPM. The original as-built drawing showed the roof fan as Class-II, but weeks later we found out from the factory that built the units that it was only a Class-I fan. It could not take the 100 horsepower motor, or the higher RPM setting. The fan housing and the blower wheel was existing; we had only replaced the motor and pulley. Apparently someone hadn't done their homework, but I don't know who. That was the GSA's problem.

After the damage was done to the roof fan, Victor Tablante and a Mr. Heaky came from San Francisco to correct the problem. A few days later we heard rumors and allegations of defective work by San-Val, but nothing from the GSA directly. At the next job meeting a few days later, we were told that the people from the GSA in San Francisco were not here to point fingers, but to come up with solutions.

25

Preliminaries to Battle

By December 2, 1988, the job was substantially complete. In spite of this, and without consulting Richard Broadrick, the GSA abruptly ordered San-Val to stop all work. A short time later, we were ordered off the job until further notice. We sent a notice to all subcontractors advising them not to go back to the job until notified. At the beginning, we thought that they were going to evaluate and redesign part of the HVAC system, and so we were not concerned. The job was on hold and I put our people on other jobs, but I was not worried. We had done nothing wrong and there had been no punch-list given to us to correct any deficiencies, as required by the contract.

When a job is completed, but before the owner accepts the job, a punch-list is given to the contractor. The architect, the engineer, and sometimes the inspector, do up the punch-list. The contractor must make any corrections needed. This is standard procedure on every job, public or private, and is part of the bid documents. Many times, a value is placed on the amount of the punch-list and that amount is withheld from payments until the corrective work is completed.

Shortly after we were ordered off the Hawthorne Federal Building job, two gentlemen from the Inspector General's offices came to our office and wanted to see our files. We were not advised in advance that they were coming, and I was a little shocked by how they flashed their badges and demanded to see our project files. For a few seconds it was like a flashback to Hungary in August 1950, when two men had come to our home, flashed their badges, and told my mom that the government was taking over our business. But now I lived in the USA and here we had no dictatorship. This is America, and there was nothing to worry about here, because there are laws to protect our rights. How stupid and misguided I was!

I told my secretary Georgia to give them the files, and whatever else they needed. They asked for a space to look them over and we put them into the take-off room at a spare desk. Later they asked if they could copy a few of the papers and I told them that they could copy whatever they wanted. I had no idea what they were looking for, but we had nothing to hide. During their stay they were friendly. They said they needed to review some of our files, but gave no other hints. I did not even consider calling my attorney to find out if they could just demand to see our job files without a court order. Perhaps it was a mistake on my part, but that is something I will never know. They stayed for several hours and took copies of some of our documents with them. When they were finished, they thanked us.

After a time, the GSA hired a small local contractor, a Mr. Britton of Mount Air, to check out and calibrate the VAV system. This contractor tried to tackle a job they were not qualified to do. I don't know what they were paid, but it was a waste of taxpayer's money.

Britton had no experience in calibrating this kind of a system so he requested help from AirCon, our control subcontractor on the job. Cliff Bailey of AirCon told Britton that he had a contract with San-Val and he should call San-Val for help because San-Val knew how to calibrate a VAV system. The next day Cliff called me and asked me what the heck was going on at Hawthorne. I told him the truth, that I had no idea, but that the GSA seemed to be trying to figure out what was wrong with the system.

Britton then called the manufacturer of the VAV boxes, but they told him to get a qualified control contractor or the company that installed the system. Britton still didn't call us.

At one of our ASHRAE meetings, one well-known local engineer came over to me and asked if we were doing a job at the Hawthorne Federal Building. I was a little surprised by the question, but answered yes. I knew this engineer well; San-Val had done dozens of jobs with their office and they were a good-sized engineering firm. "Was there a problem on the job?" he asked. I told him that the GSA had ordered us off the job and we really didn't know what was going on. He told me that the GSA had requested his firm's services, but they had turned them down because something smelled fishy.

A week or so later I got a call from another local engineering firm. They asked a similar question and told me that the GSA wanted to hire them to do an evaluation of the installed HVAC system because there seemed to be poor workmanship on the job. When the engineer asked who the contractor was, the GSA told him it was San-Val. The engineer then told them that San-Val was the best contractor they had ever worked with, and that their work and cooperation on a job was second to none. He also declined the job offer from the GSA.

I felt a little puzzled and embarrassed hearing about this, because during the past two years, neither the GSA nor PAE had ever notified San-Val that there was poor workmanship on any portion of the job. Every time a floor was turned over as completed, all work had been inspected and signed off by the contracting officer of the GSA and PAE. We had also been paid fully for the work completed, less the retention, as per the contract.

After the GSA were turned down by numerous A/E's, they hired MB&A, an HVAC engineering company from Burbank. MB&A was to check out the project and give the GSA an as-built drawing of the installed work. They were also requested to provide solutions for the problems at the Hawthorne Federal Building.

If there was any engineering company in California who could have nailed our ass to the wall, it was MB&A. Of all the engineers we had ever worked with, MB&A's were the only ones who we had made look bad in front of owners. We did two jobs with them, and on both jobs we had some problems. They had every reason to get back at us and this was a perfect opportunity.

On one of the jobs we did with MB&A, the Burbank Main Library, we were doing a major installation of a new HVAC system. The work included the removal of all existing HVAC systems and their replacement with a new chiller, multi-zone air handlers, cooling towers, pumps, and all associated piping and ductwork. The equipment, other than the cooling tower, was to be located in the existing mechanical room. The work had to be completed in a very short time and we were not going to remove the old equipment until the new system was in transit to the job. Because of the time restraints,

244 / A Light In The Distance

we selected the specified units to save time. We got the equipment approved, and then we ordered the units on an expedited delivery schedule, as required by the contract.

It was a great design and everything looked good, but the selected Trane equipment proved to be too large and would not fit as shown on the drawing even though we used the specified equipment. We did not find out about the problem until after we demolished the existing equipment, ductwork and piping, and were ready to start pouring concrete pads for the new air handlers and chiller. We gutted the room and while where we were doing our layout, we found the problem. It was an honest mistake by the engineer, as there were several components to the large multi-zone air handlers. Somehow they got the wrong information from the manufacturer. The equipment was on its way and it was too late to change it now.

In order to install the equipment, we had to move things around. This required additional ductwork, piping, and money. Because the job had no money left for change orders, the city of Burbank got very upset with MB&A. We were caught in the middle of a dispute between the owner and the engineer. In the end, the city let MB&A go and asked me to redesign the project and make the equipment fit with the least cost to them. We did just that, to the satisfaction of the city and the library.

On the other job with MB&A, when we were working for the LAUSD, we did a job using electronic speed controllers, and the design was flawed. It was a complicated modernization of an existing HVAC system, and in addition, someone had overlooked the need for a speed controller on the return fan. It is customary for most manufacturers to help select the equipment for an engineer, but something went wrong and the wrong application was used. We helped in the redesign and the job was completed, but MB&A looked bad in the eyes of LAUSD.

Now, after several months of reviewing the GSA job, the original drawings, and the as-built drawings, MB&A recommended that San-Val be allowed to complete the job and a punch-list be compiled and given to us, as required by the contract.

The GSA was furious and ordered MB&A to modify their reports, but MB&A refused to issue a report which was not based on fact. The GSA would not accept MB&A's conclusions and recommendations, and terminated MB&A's contract. The GSA also and refused to pay their $16,000 invoice for work performed to that date. The GSA wanted to dictate the text of the report, but MB&A was not going to be bullied, not even with the threat of non-payment. A bunch of bureaucrats who had no idea as to how to fix the job wanted to control MB&A, and when that failed, they fired them. What bastards!

With no love between MB&A and us, MB&A still refused to give a phony report just to make a few bucks. They could have buried us, yet they refused. Their honesty and integrity cost them $16,000 or more out-of-pocket. I salute Dave Lowe and the staff at MB&A for their honesty and integrity. Thanks, Dave!

For eighteen months the GSA investigated, hired and fired people because they disagreed with GSA personnel as to what was required to make the HVAC system work at the Hawthorne Federal Building. My letters and calls to Broadrick, the contracting officer, were ignored. We also heard rumors that the job would be redesigned and bid again. I did not know what to think, so we just waited for directives from the GSA, which never came.

Approximately nine months later, in August 1989, our contract was terminated by the GSA, without due notice, and without allowing us to finish our work. I finally got hold of Broadrick, who told me that I should call the GSA in San Francisco. He did not know what was going on, and told me that he had also been left out of the loop. He apologized for not calling back and not responding to my many letters, but also told me that he was just following orders. I called the GSA in San Francisco and was told that they were redesigning the job and they would let me know when it was done. I said fine. I did not realize that beneath what turned out to be lies, something horrible was brewing.

There are several hundred mechanical engineering companies in the state of California, yet the GSA was forced to go out of state to find a firm who would do their dirty work. The GSA finally hired MKA from Arizona to perform the new design. Hiring a design company from Arizona would more than double the cost for the redesign, but the GSA did not care. Money was no object. They wanted someone who could be controlled. MKA was hired about a year after we were ordered off the job.

MKA prepared recommendations as to what would be required on the job. Later, they were hired to provide a new set of plans and specs for bid purposes. At some point MKA submitted new drawings for review by the GSA. The drawings were at the 50% design phase. The drawing was going to change very little from the installed work. The GSA ordered MKA to redesign the drawing and went against the written recommendation of the MKA report in a big way.

The GSA wanted this job to cost a lot more than the MKA drawings would have required, and so they ordered major and unnecessary changes incorporated into the new design. Huge amounts of perfectly good ductwork would be removed and new ducts installed in order to make the job more expensive. Specifications would be modified to add huge costs to the project. None of the GSA engineers who were involved in the project had any experience in major VAV design, yet they dictated the terms of the new design and fired those who disagreed with them. Government at its best! They didn't give a shit about the taxpayer, as long as they got their egos satisfied, as well as having their incompetence protected and covered up.

As Mr. Robnet, who did the design for MKA as a subcontractor, stated in his deposition later, GSA was the boss and he did what they asked him to do. He did not ask the motives behind these matters. Robnet felt that San-Val should have had the opportunity to finish the job. He also stated that the GSA should have sat down with San-Val to discuss the allegations and San-Val should have been allowed to correct any allegation of defective workmanship before being terminated. But those self-serving GSA bastards ignored MKA's professional recommendation, just like they had ignored the advice of others. Was the total destruction of San-Val the primary goal, instead of getting the building fixed? The GSA wanted to shift the blame away from themselves, and we were an easy target.

More than two years later the Hawthorne Federal Building job was out for bids with a new design. The redesign and the new contract documents by MKA were quite different from the original job we did at the Hawthorne Federal Building.

The new design was far superior to the Brockmeier design, and work was to be done during normal working hours (not at night as we were required to do under the old design). Every floor would be vacant and all furniture would be removed (no more working above desks, file cabinets, conference tables, and so on).

The entire ceiling would be removed and after installation of new ductwork, a new ceiling would be installed (we had to do our work above the ceiling between the T-bar grids).

The project required a full time project coordinator, and a full time mechanical/electrical coordinator who was a professional engineer (neither were required under our contract). Critical path method scheduling, and photographs monthly and final, were also now called for. Drawings called for the removal of all existing lath and plaster ceiling in all areas affected by the mechanical work. After completion of work, a new ceiling would be installed. (We were required to cut a small opening to get above it and crawl above the existing plastered ceiling to do our work.)

A multitude of other aspects had been added to the contract: new condensate drains at cooling and heating coils; repairing existing damper frames; new beltguards for A/C units; new pulleys for fans and A/C units; the list went on and on.

In addition to the new work, the specifications were much more defined, and now were spelled out in a professional manner.

I decided to bid the project, and spent more than four weeks estimating it myself. At bid-time we were the low bidders. A few days later our bid was rejected because the GSA claimed that San-Val was not qualified. What a bunch of lying bastards! There were few others who could do the job better than San-Val. The GSA had other reasons why they did not want us on the job. That became evident a few weeks later. The new contract was awarded to Comm-Air, who had never installed a system like this before.

Comm-Air was in the service and control business, and not in the HVAC construction business. Under the terms of the contract, the prime contractor had to perform, with his or her own work force, a certain percentage of the work. Comm-Air subcontracted out over 95% of the work! That was clearly in violation of the contract. However, the GSA never enforced the contract requirement.

Shortly after the new contract was awarded to Comm-Air in late 1991, and soon after the job started, Comm-Air made a recommendation. They advised MKA and GSA that if they installed the cooling coils and an Andower control system, everything else would work and the GSA could save several million dollars. We had told the GSA years before that we needed a new cooling coil and additional controls, but they had ignored our recommendations. Again the GSA said forget it. They rejected Comm-Air's recommendation, and ordered all the work to be performed as shown on the drawings. For less than $70,000 Comm-Air could have made the system function properly. The GSA would not agree to this, after spending hundreds of thousands of dollars and more than eighteen months in investigations.

After the job was completed by Comm-Air, the GSA found that Comm-Air had deviated from the design (a major design change to AC-2 & AC-3) without a change order. Comm-Air had made changes to the design, just like we had, to make things work, but they were not penalized like we were.

A few months after the contract was let to Comm-Air, on September 18, 1991, the US Government filed a multi-million dollar lawsuit against San-Val, PAE, Fairmont Insurance Company (our bonding company), and me. I could not believe it! My first reaction was, "They can't do that!" When the lawsuit hit me I was totally unprepared.

26

David Against Goliath

The lawsuit claims zeroed in on our treatment of the ductwork, the fan damage, and the asbestos removal. It also claimed we hadn't replaced some of the vibration isolators on the roof. Overall, they claimed we had overbilled. The GSA also alleged that PAE had had no authority to make changes on the job.

Regarding the ductwork, we had resized it as per our shop drawing, which was approved by Victor Tablante himself. The ductwork was sized for the designed CFMs, according to ASHRAE Standard, which is the bible of the HVAC industry. The new design by MKA was in most cases the same size as ours, and in some cases smaller, and only in a very few places larger. How could our ductwork be undersized?

We had made changes to the ductwork on the roof because the design was wrong and AC-2 and AC-3 could not be installed as was shown on the drawing. We had received approval for these changes in the field from the offices of PAE. We had not replaced 90% of the last pieces of flexible ducts going to the grills because the contract did not call for it. We did replace the 10% of these that were defective. The claim that some ductwork was poorly installed was possible because we had to work above the existing ceiling in very tight conditions. However, we were never shown which ducts were not installed properly; had they showed them to us, we would have fixed them.

San-Val did perform some work above hard-to-reach areas as well as could be done under those conditions — conditions that might not have been as good as they should have been. The ceilings in those areas should have been removed to provide good access, but the GSA didn't want to pay the extra money.

The GSA blamed us for the damage to the fan, saying we should have known that the fan could not take the higher RPMs. The fact was that the GSA and PAE came up with the brilliant idea for installing the new larger motors in the first place. We were never asked for engineering help in this matter.

As for the asbestos, an independent testing lab hired by the GSA did the testing, and the report went directly to the GSA. The GSA issued a change order and ordered us to remove it. Everybody knew we had asbestos on the job.

Not all the vibration isolators had been installed, because the job had been stopped. All vibration isolators were already purchased and were on the job and on the roof. Why would we pay several hundred dollars for each set of vibration isolators, and have them on the job if we did not intend to install them?

Overall, as commonly occurs in construction projects, field conditions sometimes differed from the plans. San-Val faced a difficult situation, because the HVAC system had to be on line and functioning each morning. This meant making rapid decisions in the field in consultation with PAE. After agreeing on a course of action, San-Val proceeded with the work.

PAE was the private company hired by the GSA as the construction inspector for the project, and was responsible for inspecting and recommending approval of San-Val's work. There was no one else present nightly to make decisions that had to be made in a hurry. We had no contact with the GSA in San Francisco other than getting the submittals approved by them. To my knowledge, they never came down to look at the job until we had a problem with the fan almost two years into the job.

In forty-five years of business San-Val was never involved in double-checking a project engineer's selection of equipment for capacity and other qualities on any job. We had helped other engineers if our help was requested, but the GSA had never asked. They simply wanted to blame us for their incompetence.

Prior to the start of the project, as required by contract documents, a floor-by-floor, section-by-section fully itemized segregation of costs was submitted to GSA and was approved. The monthly billing was reviewed according to that breakdown and was approved by the inspector and Broadrick. That is how we got paid monthly. We had never failed to complete the thousands of contracts we did in our forty-five years in business. Every job we did was finished to the satisfaction of the owner. We would have completed this job too, if the GSA had not ordered us off the job.

As depositions were taken, it became clear that the GSA had wanted us off the job. They wanted to redesign the system then force us to pay for it. They also decided to make it extremely expensive in order to bankrupt us and force us out of business. A bankrupt contractor can't fight back. The GSA forced gold-plated extra work into the project that wasn't required, just to make it look like San-Val's work cost the taxpayers millions and must be punished.

We had undertaken a project that was flawed, ill conceived, and poorly designed, and then we were blamed for it.

In October 1991, I called my insurance company, Maryland Casualty, to defend us under our business insurance, but they rejected our claim. We had paid huge insurance premiums for 30 to 35 years, but when we needed their help, they denied our request. Time was of the essence and I had no choice but to hire my own attorneys. I hired the Law Offices of Crawford, Bacon, Bangs and Briesemeister because they were my attorneys when I sued Wayne McNulty years earlier. It was only much later that I pursued the matter with Maryland Casualty.

The paperwork and the volume of requests for documents were overwhelming for our small office staff. The deadlines they gave us to produce documents interfered with running jobs that were already in progress, and with bidding on new work. One of the big problems was that we had just moved into our new facilities in Los Angeles, and had already downsized. We had spent a lot of money getting our building ready. Had I known that the GSA was going to file a lawsuit against us, I never would have moved and would have used that money to fight back.

As the lawsuit ran its course, our legal bills ran into the hundreds of thousands of dollars. The lawsuit was to go on for years. Some of the work that the GSA listed as defective in the lawsuit belonged to my subcontractors. I did not want the piping, electrical, control or insulation contractors to have to hire their own lawyers and also take a financial hit. We never asked a penny from any of our subs to kick in to help San-Val fight the lawsuit. They were honest contractors who also did a good job under very difficult conditions. The allegations against them were completely false. I wanted to save them from the agony I was experiencing, as they had done nothing wrong. I saved several of my subs hundreds of thousands of dollars, by keeping them out of the lawsuit, which would surely have bankrupted them.

At times I wanted to kill Victor Tablante for what he was doing to me and to my family. Why did he do this? Why the vendetta? Were we just a convenient target that didn't have the financial means to fight back? I believe he didn't want to take the fall himself for a poorly designed system and shifted blame on to San-Val in order to cover up his own incompetence.

Through deposition after deposition the picture became clear. During the investigations and redesign, the GSA was ruthless to those who disagreed with them. They went out of their way at all costs to have their way, and fired anybody that didn't play their game.

The fact of the matter was that Victor Tablante, design engineer for the GSA, had no idea as to what he was looking at or what needed to be done to the system. Lacking knowledge, he ordered other engineers to modify their reports and drawings to his liking. His lack of knowledge created the Hawthorne fiasco and cost the taxpayers millions.

The depositions clearly showed that Tablante was totally confused. He didn't know what a VAV box and a sound attenuator were on the drawing. He didn't know how to size high-velocity ductwork. Looking at a simple VAV box layout, he couldn't tell if the static pressure of the system was less than one inch of static pressure, when anybody with only a little engineering experience would have known that it was under one-quarter of an inch.

He made statements regarding what he saw on the job that were contradicted by every other government witness.

Another witness who weakened under pressure was Richard Broadrick, who had walked the job and told us the scope of the work from the very beginning.

As PAE inspector, he never told us that PAE didn't have the authority to approve no-cost changes. That was unusual, because that is the purpose of the inspector on the job when there is no money involved.

During the GSA's investigations after we were kicked off the job, they had never consulted Broadrick as to how we had performed. During the investigations, he retained the U.S. Attorney General's office to represent him. Why did he need a lawyer? To his credit, he had stated that San-Val should be allowed to finish the job, but of course this advice was ignored by his superiors.

During his deposition, Broadrick conveniently lost his memory. At first he claimed that he was not at the job walk. When confronted by the sign-in sheet, he admitted that he probably was there, but didn't remember what was discussed. To me, it was obvious that he didn't want to say anything that would have further angered the GSA in San Francisco. He saw what was done to PAE and us and wanted to protect himself, so he kept silent.

Shortly after the lawsuit started, the insurance company for PAE negotiated a settlement with the GSA and was dropped from the lawsuit. PAE did not want to spend a fortune on legal fees and felt it was the best for them.

Now looking back, I think that I made big mistakes in our defense and tactics. I had never been in that position before and I did not know what to do. I was waiting for the government to realize that this was just a big mistake and to drop the charges. However, the government did not care about an early resolution to the case and ordered deposition after deposition from people whose knowledge in the case was zero.

My costs of flying all over the place and retaining two attorneys soared and soon reached the half million-dollar fee. That did not include the hundreds of thousands of dollars of other costs we incurred, or the cost for the legal fees for the bonding company for which we were also liable.

When we deposed some key people, especially Victor Tablante, I wanted our attorneys to nail his ass to the wall. We should have exposed his lack of knowledge in that conference room and should not have held back. However, I was advised against that and told by my attorneys that the case should not be won in a deposition; we should not tip our hand but save all that for trial. That was a big mistake. Had we really gone after him, it would have showed the GSA's attorney that their case was false and the case might have been settled months earlier.

Right at the start we should have taken a strong offense. I should have dictated the terms of our tactics, just as I did against Wayne McNulty. I was dead wrong in allowing my attorneys to run their game plan, and should have insisted on doing it my way, especially when it was my money that was running down the drain. I was a good contractor, but did not understand the law, and depended on the advice of others. By the time I realized what was happening, it was too late to change course.

First, I would not have allowed my attorneys to show up at any of the depositions and would have saved all my money for the trial. I would have let the government depose anybody they wanted without any of us being present. Boy, I wish I had done that! What good is it to save your evidence for trial if you go broke before you get into the courtroom?

Second, I would have then read the depositions and prepared my point-by-point defense.

Third, I would have demanded a trial by a jury and torn apart all the lies on the witness stand.

Fourth, I would have brought in expert witnesses to destroy the credibility of Victor Tablante and his lackeys.

Last, I would have sent a letter or taken out ads, publicizing this fiasco in every major newspaper and on every TV station. All of this would have been a much better use of my money.

I was working an unbelievable amount of hours a week and went without sleep many nights. When you are pressured in so many directions, you lose focus. You try to do too much, while anger within you builds and further complicates matters. It was very difficult for me to vent my anger, which didn't help matters at all. I wasn't going to take it out on my kids or my wife, and I did not take it out on my employees. I kept it all inside and suffered with that agony for years. That anger still haunts me more than ten years later.

We requested help from elected public officials and several government agencies, but it was a waste of time. Low-level aides answered our calls and our letters to elected officials. I received nothing but form letters back from my senators and congressman, the White House, the governor, the Department of Justice, the Treasury, the Department of Labor, the Department of the Interior and other agencies. My only crime was that I lacked the financial resources to fight the mighty power of the U.S. Government. Small businesses make this country what it is, yet they ignored us time and time again.

I even traveled to Washington to try to meet with my representatives, but it was no help. Because I was not a big campaign contributor, my chances to see them were slim to none. I did meet with Congressman Carlos J. Moorhead and he was very understanding, but he told me that once a lawsuit was filed, he could not get involved. We talked for 15 minutes and at least he listened. He told me to keep fighting the "bastards" and not to give up hope. He wished me well and gave me a hug before I left. I was pretty desperate by then. By that time, I had walked the floors of Congress for two frustrating days, only to be ignored and turned away. The only other meeting I could set up had been a very short meeting with Congressman Xavier Becerra, who told me that his office in L.A. would look into the matter and get back to me. Days later we were told that they also could not get involved.

While I was dumping my own money into the business in early 1993, others came to help me. On February 10, 1993, my good friend Joe Volkmar dropped off a check for $60,000. Joe was talking with our John Watson, who told Joe the financial drain San-Val was experiencing. That Joe is something else! A couple of days later John Watson came into my office and put three checks on my table. One was from him for $6,000, one was from his two kids for $2,000 and one was from one of our employees, Roy Cunningham, for $30,000. They gave me the money to help our financially hurting company. Without my knowledge John had asked them to help. That John has the heart of a lion! I was shocked and could not believe it. They risked their own money without knowing if San-Val and Steve could ever repay them. Thanks guys!

Later in the year my daughter Amy Joy also sent me a check for $40,000 to help, and told me that I could have all her money that was in a special trust account for her. I cried when I got her check and the offer she made.

I refinanced my buildings to the maximum and used the extra money to repay all the loans given to me and for the defense of San-Val. I would also borrow from my bank and my other companies, Crown Heating and ASSI (my engineering company).

While I was hurting financially, I made sure that all employees, suppliers and subcontractors were paid on time. I would never screw them, and that is why they were so loyal to me. My word was always good and I never went back on it.

I did became very bitter when one former employee betrayed me and lied in order to get back at me. It was because his services had been terminated by San-Val a few years before. The Inspector General's office interviewed most, if not all, current and former employees and subcontractors. I heard horror stories how they tried to coerce them into giving false information. My ex-employee Rich Richardson had not had a job since he was let go by San-Val. In his declaration he provided the interviewing Inspector General's people with whatever they told him they needed.

When we received a copy of the declaration a few weeks later, I hit the roof. It was all lies! I showed it to my employees and they could not believe what they read. We tried to depose him, but he refused to be served by the sheriff's department time after time. Rich and his wife didn't leave their ranch for days so that they could not be served. What a rotten bastard! I gave him a job, I paid him well, and I gave him end-of-year bonuses. When I let him go, I gave him one of our computers because he wanted one.

In Rich's declaration he claimed that he went to the job numerous times and saw poor workmanship. But Rich was not a project manager and nobody had asked him to go to the job. He also claimed that he put into the bid the cost for replacing all the flexible ducts. He said that he was the one who put together the bid for the job; a total lie. He had estimated only some of the work, which was then used by me in putting together our price. Each estimator gave me their worksheets and I took all or part of that information and incorporated it into my bids. I used my expertise to change, modify, add or deduct hours or money. The ultimate bids were put together by me and no other.

As the case dragged on, I learned that if we won the case we would clear our name but would not be reimbursed for costs incurred in defending the case. That was a shock. We had no option to file a counter-suit to recover our costs.

Near the end of the depositions, on March 12, 1993, our bonding company, Fairmont Insurance Company, had enough of this never-ending lawsuit and bailed out of the lawsuit. They settled their portion of the case with the GSA. That got me very angry because their settlement and their legal costs were my responsibility, as I had a "hold harmless" agreement with the bonding company. In other words, whatever they settled for I had to pay the bonding company back, plus all their legal costs. They did it without any consultation with us and I had no say in the matter. That broke our back, as now I owed Fairmont $700,000, besides the over $500,000 I had already spent for legal fees. We were just about ready for trial when the rug was pulled out from under me. I was devastated and angry at the world.

A short time later the Justice Department offered a deal to end the case, and within a few weeks settlement was reached, whereby San-Val would pay the government $200,000 and the case would be closed. Had I not settled, we might have gone broke due to mounting legal fees.

When it all ended, the total cost out-of-pocket was over $1.45 million. The work of a lifetime had gone down the drain in a hurry. San-Val was on the verge of bankruptcy. If we shut down because we were out of money, the bonding company would have been forced to take over more than 14 million of San-Val's work in progress. I would have also been liable for any and all losses they might incur. Having the bonding company take over our jobs would have cost me millions more because they knew nothing of the jobs and they had no idea how to do school remodeling.

Shortly into the lawsuit, the health of my wife Elaine had become worse. At first, I tried to shield her from the Hawthorne agony because I did not want her to worry. But my mood and my actions at home alarmed my wife. I was on edge and I was not myself. My wife started to ask questions. I lied and told her that we had aggravation from one of our jobs, but not to worry about it. I told her very little because it would not do her any good and there was nothing she could do to help me. I tried to leave my troubles at work, as I had done for more than thirty years previously. It was getting harder by the day as I was getting squeezed more and more by the government, and it was taking a toll on me.

Soon Elaine realized that there was more to what I was telling her and she asked more questions. Before long she understood that we were in deep trouble — she confronted me. What in hell was going on at work? I could not hide our problems from her any more. She had the right to know that we might be financially wiped out if the government won the full lawsuit. I told her everything, including what might happen if we lost the case.

She was devastated. At first she just could not believe it. The government of the United States would not do that to a man like me! She was in no shape to help bear my agony and she felt helpless. She just kept things to herself, which did not help. She watched me being crucified by the system I had trusted and her nervous system reacted by taking a terrible toll on her body.

My faith in our government almost cost my family and me our lives and my business. I was too stupid to realize that living in this country does not always protect you against evil people who are hiding behind their power and who are out to get you, at any cost, to cover up their mistakes and shift the blame onto others.

Part VII

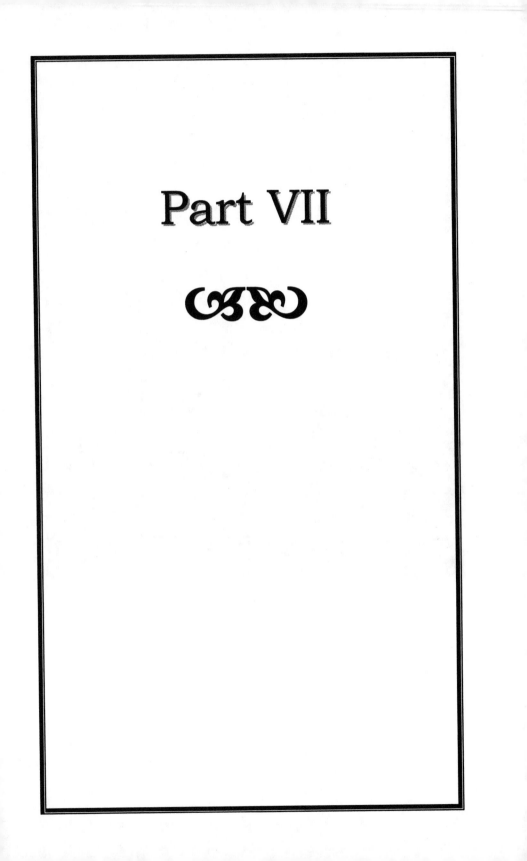

Some of our closest friends from Boston.

27

The CSULB Fight

Problems were all around me. While fighting for my life at Hawthorne, I was also fighting on a second front with California State University, Long Beach (CSULB). I had to be on top of every job because we were at a very critical point, and any wrong step could have thrown us into bankruptcy. The financial drain on the company, my sick wife, and the illegal tactics used by the GSA were overwhelming. I was forced to sell stocks I owned and put the money into the business. It also did not help when I stopped bidding on new work — it was all too much to handle simultaneously.

In late February 1991, I had started a bid for a major project at CSULB. The project was to renovate their chemistry labs and was budgeted at about 4.8 million dollars. After contacting the Physical Planning Department at CSULB, we found out that only those contractors with a B license and an asbestos license would be allowed to bid the project. The bid date for the project was April 9, 1991.

We paid a deposit and picked up the plans for the job, but couldn't get a bid form because we didn't have the second required license. I didn't understand the logic behind it, because we used licensed asbestos contractors, so why would the general contractor also need to have an asbestos license? But I decided to go for it — I decided to take a crash course and try to get my asbestos license prior to bid date, which was five weeks away.

I went to night school and studied into the early hours every evening, while making arrangements to take my test just a few days prior to bid time. I was determined to bid this job because it was 85% mechanical. Right up our alley! As a general contractor, we had used asbestos contractors many times and were familiar with procedures and legal requirements, but turned out to be much more to being a certified licensed asbestos contractor. I did well at school, to the surprise of my instructor, with so much to learn in such a short time, but I put a lot of effort into it.

Finally, I flew to Sacramento for the test because nothing closer was available before April 9th, the bid date. The test was hard, but I was well prepared and focused. I completed the computerized test more than an hour before the allotted time. I even had time to review my answers; I decided to leave them as they were and clicked on "finished." There were about 15 of us taking the test, and I finished in the shortest time. I got up, went to an instructor and told her that I was finished. I was allowed to leave, but wanted to know when I would find out whether I had passed. She told me that it would only take a few minutes. Everything was computerized and I could wait for the result.

Nervously I waited, because there was a lot riding on it. I was estimating a major job that would be open to bids in only a few days. I already spent several thousand dollars estimating the project, not knowing if I would pass the test and get my license prior to bid time. I gambled because it was worth the risk and I was confident in my ability. In just a short time my name was called and I was told that I had passed, with lots of room to spare! At this time I gave out a big sigh of relief. I did it! Now I asked how I could go about getting a temporary license. I was bidding in a couple of days and had to have my asbestos license number. I was told that the computer had already assigned my number and the awarding agency could get verification the following day, just by calling.

With a lot of smiles I thanked the instructor for her cooperation and left for the airport, hoping to get an earlier flight back to Burbank. I was able to get a flight out in less than thirty minutes. Prior to boarding the plane, I called my office and told them that I had passed and got my license. I told them to call the bonding company and tell them to drop the bid bond off the following day. I had already informed the bonding company about the job and gotten their approval to bid it.

This was a major project. We needed the work badly, and I felt that we had a good chance of getting it. Our competition would be larger and better contractors who were also mostly union contractors, but we had a better than 40% chance to get the job, which was good. Finally, the day prior to bidding the job I went to CSULB to pick up the bid documents. I had my B license with me as well as a temporary license for the asbestos. They did call the State Contractors License Board, which verified that we had both licenses. In less than fifteen minutes I was on my way back to the office with the required bid forms. What a relief!

I took extra time bidding the job because it was by far the largest project we had ever bid. I had to be sure that we covered everything and that nothing was overlooked. Finally it was time. I was nervous, but felt good about the job and with my estimate. Five or six minutes before bid time I gave the price to our employee and nervously waited for the bid results. Twenty minutes past the hour we received the news. We were the low bidder.

On May 13, 1991, San-Val was awarded the contract in the amount of $4,646,360, with a 450-day completion schedule and a $1,600 per day penalty if the job was not completed on time. After signing the contract and submitting our performance and payment bonds, we issued our subcontracts and requested submittals from our suppliers as soon as possible. A "Notice To Proceed" was issued for June 17, 1991 and a completion date of September 10, 1992 was set.

Soon after the job started we found a lot of problems with the plans and sent RFIs (Requests for Information) to JAC Engineers, Inc., the A/E on the job, with copies to Kaly Trezos, the construction officer for CSULB. The plans were poorly drawn and incomplete, and in less than ten weeks we submitted over 140 RFIs, which led to numerous change orders. There were numerous RFIs for which we didn't get responses. We sent follow-up letters, but it was like pulling teeth. We had a short completion date and we needed answers, but we got very few, which resulted in additional follow-up letters, which were also ignored.

It became a constant fight between Jim Hancock, our project manager, and John McGlynn of JAC Engineers. JAC did not want to spend much time responding to RFIs or doing additional engineering work, and blamed us for delaying the job. The lack of help from the A/E was also frustrating for our subcontractors. By October things were going downhill, and major design flaws were brought to the attention of the contracting officer. For some reason they refused to bring in another engineer to investigate these allegations. Kaly Trezos agreed with the A/E on everything, yet she did not have the expertise to make those decisions without help from others.

After several months of frustration, I decided to take matters into my own hands. Having not been very involved with the day-to-day running of the job, I had been relying on our staff to make sure that everything went smoothly. Busy fighting with the GSA, I had not spent much time at CSULB, once we bid the job and let out all subcontracts. I had heard of some problems, but that was nothing unusual on a job of this size. I had confidence in Jim Hancock and our crews to make sure the contract was executed in the proper manner. But, after hearing of the many problems, the numerous change orders, and the code violations, it was time for me to get involved. I could not let this get out of hand. I did not want another Hawthorne on my hands. We could not afford to waste what could amount to a great sum of money, all caused by delays by the A/E and the school.

I took the drawings home and studied them into the night. The design had a return air system! I was horrified and shocked, and could not believe it! I checked the drawings over and over again, but there it was. This was a nightmare beyond belief! It is illegal to use a return air system in the HVAC system in a chemistry building, such as the one we were working on.

The design, in my opinion, had to have a 100% exhaust and make-up air design. I was so sure of my findings that the following morning I called JAC and told them that we had a major problem with the duct design — it was illegal to use a return air system. The reply was, "Leave the design to us, and install the system in accordance with the drawing you bid on." I had hoped JAC would come out with a design change on their own, without the owners finding out that it was I who had discovered the problem. This had happened many times in the past. If we found a problem, we notified the A/E by phone, and they would come out with a revision; nobody ever knew that it was our finding. We did not need the glory. We were a team player and did not want to make anybody look bad. However, my help was now ignored and instead, I was lambasted by JAC.

I then sent a strongly worded letter to the A/E, with a copy to the contracting officer and the school. I explained why a system like that should not be installed. When you have numerous classrooms with fume hoods and you are using hazardous chemicals, there has to be 100% exhaust from every classroom. If there is an accident in a classroom, such as someone spilling hazardous chemicals, the students there could hold their breath while they exited the classroom. But if you had a recirculating system, the hazardous chemicals could spread to every classroom in the building in just seconds, and nobody would know that their lives were in danger. You could injure or kill many because they would not be able to react in time. We had done many buildings like that for JPL, UC Irvine, USC, and others, and had never seen a recirculating system. It's against the law! It does not take much brainpower to realize why.

Days and weeks went by with no response. When I called Kaly Trezos, she told me that they agreed with the A/E and I should stop trying to get change orders and get on with the job. At that point we were threatened with being kicked off the job and having our contract terminated. That was all I needed now! I had enough headaches with the GSA, and the last thing I wanted was another fiasco. In order to protect San-Val, I decided to get a second opinion from a good friend, Joe Nishimura of CEDG, a mechanical engineer in Burbank. I took the plans to him and asked for his professional opinion. After he looked over the design, he could not believe it himself and agreed with me all the way. I was in hot water. If I installed the system as designed and then there was an accident, then I would be sued along with the school and the A/E. That was the last thing I wanted. I did not want anybody to get hurt, and I was not going to let it pass without fighting for the students and teachers who used that building. I could never live with myself. In my opinion, it was the only honest thing to do.

Because of the numerous outstanding RFIs, work was going at a snail's pace anyway. I was frustrated with the lack of progress on the job and the ignorance of CSULB and the A/E. After making many calls to friends within CSULB, I found the names of important people to whom I could send my next letters. I sent a registered letter to the Office of the Chancellor at California State University (CSU) and key personnel at CSU Physical Planning and Development. I informed them that the system we were installing was against code and it would endanger the life of every student who attended classes in that building. Besides that, there were numerous other code violations. I also stated that the entire project was poorly designed. I advised them that we would shut the job down and not install any more return air ductwork until we were directed in writing that CSU would take full liability. This would hold San-Val and our subcontractors harmless for any problems that might arise due to the illegal installation. Because this endangered the life of every student, we were ready to go to the state Attorney General if this matter was not resolved at once. I was in no mood to play games — the lives of innocent people were at stake.

I decided to cut back manpower at the site and wait for a reply. I intended to wait one week and then go to the state Attorney General. I even contemplated going to the news media. I was not in the mood to fuck around any more with these idiots. I had also demanded a meeting and told them that they would be well advised to hire an expert consulting engineer to advise them. Less than forty-eight hours later I received a call and was told that there would be a meeting at a given time to hear our case. The quick response and the date for a meeting pleased me and I accepted. As usual, I prepared for the meeting, which was to be held on December 10, 1991, at CSULB.

I took three of our people with me and got there fifteen minutes early. Right on time a large group of people representing CSU came into the meeting, including the A/E, the Contracting Officer, and John Stopforth, S.E. Chief Construction Management from CSU Physical Planning and Development. Others present from that office were Edward C. Knipe, P.E., and J. Patrick Drohan. There were a few others representing Physical Plant and some other staff members. When Ed Knipe came into the room, we recognized each other; he also belonged to ASHRAE and I had seen him there several times prior to this project. "What are you doing here?" he asked. I told him that I was the one who was causing all the trouble on the project. He just laughed and took his seat.

The contracting officer, Kaly Trezos, started the meeting and planned to run it, but I interrupted her and told her that this was my show. I had called for the meeting, and it would be my agenda. She was taken aback and looked at John Stopforth, who advised her that it *was* my show. I turned on my tape recorder, but was asked by John

Stopforth not to record the meeting, so I put the recorder back into my briefcase. I gave out seven three-ring binders full of documents, each with an index and tabs numbered from one to ten.

I started the meeting by stating that we had bid this project in full compliance of plans and specs and were issued a contract for the renovation of the chemistry building. I told them that in my opinion, the plans were poorly drawn and incomplete. In fewer than ten weeks we had submitted over 140 RFIs that had led to numerous change orders. I then stated how we hadn't gotten answers, for months, on numerous other RFIs. I made it clear that this was inexcusable and unacceptable to San-Val. We had a 450-day completion schedule and a $1,600 per day penalty if the job was not completed on time.

To make things worse, I stated that the system was full of design flaws and endangered the life of every student and teacher that attended classes or worked there. I explained how I had called the A/E and had been given the brush-off. We had given the A/E a chance to fix their mistake without anybody knowing our role. Instead of getting a big thank you, I had gotten blasted by the A/E.

Now it was time to really make my case. I directed them to the tab section containing a copy of all the unanswered follow-up letters that I had sent to the A/E and the contracting officer after my courtesy phone call was ignored. All we had gotten were threats that we would be thrown off the job for not performing. My voice was firm and at times full of anger. This would all have to stop because we would not take any more bullshit from anyone.

"We are not your enemy," I stated, "but we are being treated as one and we can get very nasty if that is what it takes, but we hope that CSULB will come to their senses and bring in a consulting engineer to review the plans and specs." I stated further that if I was wrong and the A/E was right, then San-Val would pay the fees for the services of the consulting engineer. CSULB had nothing to lose and millions to gain.

I then started to go into the numerous code violations on the job, but was stopped short by Ed Knipe. He interrupted me and asked the A/E to produce the response letter to the return air problem. The A/E, after pausing for several seconds, replied that San-Val had sent them so many RFIs, RFPs and change orders that they had been simply overwhelmed by the paperwork. Ed then asked whether two months was enough time to produce a reply. There was silence. He then asked the A/E to reply to the allegation that return air systems were not allowed in buildings like this. To that the A/E replied that they had done this on many other jobs, and nobody other than San-Val had ever questioned their design.

At that point Ed asked for responses to other San-Val allegations, reading the RFIs page by page, only to get the same answer. Ed was started to get irritated. I, on the other hand, started to feel real good, and just eased back in my chair. Going into the meeting I felt comfortable with my accusations, but being right doesn't necessarily mean that you will win. Anything can happen, as was the case at Hawthorne, but I had learned my lesson. You have to fight with all your might and not let anything stop you. You should use every means at your disposal.

Shortly after Edward Knipe had asked the A/E six or eight questions without getting satisfactory responses, he whispered something to John Stopforth, at which time John asked for a break in the proceedings. I was told to remain in the conference room while a few of them stepped outside to confer.

After five minutes they came back and John advised me that the meeting was over, and we would be contacted in a few weeks as to what CSULB would do regarding the project. They asked if they could keep the three-ring binders, to which I replied, "Of course." He thanked me for my professional presentation and left the meeting with his staff and the A/E. I was left alone in the room with only my staff, at which time I told our people to go back to their jobs. Jim Hancock and I headed back to the office. Jim thought that the meeting had gone very well and so did I. We were wondering what would happen next.

28

A Difficult Job Turns Out Well

The holiday season slowed down the decision process for California State University, Long Beach (CSULB), but not by very much. As we had left it, they were deciding what to do about the bad design work that I'd advised them was not only illegal, but dangerous for students and faculty. It was a refreshing change that while they were making their decisions, we were kept updated as to their progress. We were not being ignored any longer. After getting good advice from their consultants, a decision was made.

In order for the CSULB project to be redesigned, the trustees of the California State University decided to shut down the existing work. San-Val was directed to shut down the project as of Friday, February 21, 1992, and to submit a final accounting for the work done and any and all claims associated with the project. What a goddamn mess! It looked like Hawthorne all over again!

It was decided that the best option was to stop all work, negotiate a contract settlement with all parties, file a Notice of Completion, and call it Phase I. We were told that once Phase I was finalized, the project would be redesigned and Phase II would proceed. We understood that JAC Engineers, Inc. had been fired and CSU was looking for another A/E.

I finally negotiated a settlement, but it was not easy. Some of the subcontractors wanted to screw CSULB, especially the temperature control contractor. When I received the prices from all my subs for the termination of their contracts, I got furious with a few of them. I was not about to go to CSULB with those ridiculous prices because there was not going to be any money left over to do Phase II. At my next weekly meeting, CSULB asked me how the costs were coming in on the termination of the contract, and I was afraid to show them the prices.

I showed them the costs I had up to that day and told them that I was embarrassed with some of the preliminary numbers, but I was after the subs to revise their prices. We were anticipating their new numbers in a few days, and we would save a lot of money. I also told the school that one of the subcontractors, the control contractor, was really screwing the district. If we allowed this contractor to get away with it, then it would not be fair to the other 22 subcontractors who had given us an honest terminating price. Some, who had not started their work, had even given the full contract amount back to us, much to my surprise. I thanked them for their honesty and told them that they would be doing Phase II for me.

The following day I made some more calls to the subs and got cooperation from most of them, except for the control contractor, who was determined to get more than 70% of their full contract of $795,000. This contractor had delivered some of the controls to the job and had done submittals, as well as a few other things. I explained that if we didn't settle fairly with CSULB, the school could hold up the money until they got a fair price. I did not want subs to lose money because it was not their fault that the design was messed up, but I wanted them to be fair to CSULB. My reputation with those subs went a long way. Only this control sub gave me fits, at which time I offered 20% of their contract. It was take it or leave it, and they would have to sue the school for the rest of the money.

Nobody from the school wanted to make these calls; they asked me to be the one who did the entire calling and deal-making. I had to do some arm-twisting, but in the end I saved CSULB over $506,000, and that saved Phase II. All subs signed on the dotted line. Thanks, guys!

Shortly after we negotiated the closeout and settlement on Phase I, I got a call from CSU that made me almost fall out of my chair. They told me how impressed they were with the way I had negotiated with my subs and how grateful they were for the money we'd saved them. Then came the big surprise. They asked if San-Val could provide them with a design-built job for Phase II. Normally, they would have hired another engineer or architect.

They already knew that we were experts in school construction and had a lot of engineering knowledge in fume hood exhaust systems and HVAC installations. They now completely agreed with me that the original design was flawed. CSU needed my help. Everyone had advised them to hire San-Val to redesign the project in order to save time and money. Could we do it? Yes, but it would require the cooperation of CSU and a new project manager. CSU agreed and thanked me for accepting the new assignment and pledged their full support. What a difference a few months made! I was relieved, as finally I was assured that another potential disaster was avoided.

After several meetings, I told them that the best way was for CSULB to prepare the scope of work that they wanted done, and based on that we would give them a price. I sent CSU ideas as to what they should and shouldn't be doing, and why. I knew that we could do the complex design that was required. I also felt that we could save the school a lot of money because we knew what costs were associated with every aspect of the job. We would also save them a lot of time.

Kent Peterson, Chief Mechanical Engineer of PSI Engineers, was hired by CSULB to evaluate the problem, review my design and recommendations, and draft a scope of work, with the help of CSULB staff. On May 7, 1992, CSULB formally requested a proposal to provide a design-built installation for Phase II, per the scope of work prepared by PSI Engineers, Inc. This procedure was very involved for me, because there were no plans to bid by; it would only be a guess.

On June 25th I submitted a detailed engineering proposal to Mr. John Stopforth, Chief of Construction Management at Physical Planning & Development at CSULB. The proposal was only for the engineering, because without plans and specs we had no way to estimate the rest of the work. I told them that it would be unfair to just give them a price, because it would be very high in order to protect our ass. By doing it this way we could save the school a lot of money and more work could be done on the project. Because of my honesty and hard work on Phase I, they agreed. They gave me an order to proceed with the design work.

Once the design was completed and reviewed by the owner, we prepared a proposal for Phase II. Mike Clevenger was brought in as a consultant to oversee the award of the new contract. Most of the negotiations were with him, Scott Charmack, and Lane Koluvek, while Gary Yeo became the new project manager.

I had met several times with Dr. Robert L. Loeschen, a professor who was in charge of the Chemistry and Biochemistry Department, and his staff. I wanted to know firsthand what they wanted, in order of importance. They knew more about their buildings than anyone else. Their needs were great, but we had a fixed budget. It would have taken several million dollars more to do everything, and tough decisions had to be made as to what was essential.

The problem on most jobs is that A/Es sometime fail to confer with people who will be using the facilities, but this input is crucial. After doing a preliminary design and cost estimates, I gave CSULB a very detailed eight-page proposal and an itemized scope of work. The proposal included a base bid, which had to be done, and I also included fifteen alternate bids to add or remove additional work. Some of the alternate bids were for only a few thousand dollars, but one was $267,921, for re-roofing the building. I wanted CSULB to have many options, with a price for each option and a chance to decide among themselves what would be best for the school. My proposal allowed them to work within their budget. I felt that some of the work items were not as critical as others, and I gave my opinion when asked, but it was their decision, their money, and their building.

Once the drawings were completed, they were sent to Kent Peterson at PSI for approval. We were already doing some preliminary work prior to the approval of the plans, to get a little ahead on the job.

Now that JAC Engineers, Inc. was off the job, the job meetings were very productive, because it was a team effort to provide the best system possible with the limited funds that we had to work with. I can honestly say that there were never any angry words spoken after Phase I was shut down. The job progressed at a rapid pace. When there is harmony and cooperation on all sides, the project benefits.

I handpicked the redesign team. I wanted team players and I hired Martinez Architects, Inc. to do the architectural design and CEDG to do the mechanical design. I did the preliminary design for all the work, which was then put on paper by the A/Es.

Finally, the redesign proposal was approved on December 9, 1992, by CSULB and work was started within forty-eight hours, after the state and the fire marshal approved plans in plan-check. We were issued a new contract on December 14, 1992 in the amount of $2,547,215, with a 460-day completion time. A separate contract was also issued for the roofing work in the amount of $165,000.

On February 8, 1993 CSULB filed a Notice of Completion on Phase I. That part of the job and the many fights at the job meetings were now completely behind us.

The last plan-check approval came on May 10th when the office of the state fire marshal approved our plans and specs. The job was going so well that most job meetings lasted only 20 minutes or less. We kept updating everybody on the progress of the job and there were smiles all round. Everyone knew the project was on schedule; near the end, it was ahead of schedule. Because I did the design and knew every part of the job, I was the one who went to the job meetings. On all other jobs I had had Jim Hancock attend, but because of the serious problem we had had on Phase I, I took over the job fully and decided to stay with it to the end.

Near the end of the job, CSULB added some of the alternate bids that were part of my proposal into our contract, because they now knew how much money was left. They were thrilled that important work could still be added into the project. The extra work was completed without a hitch, and the project was finished two months ahead of schedule, to the delight of CSULB. Notice of completion was filed by CSULB on May 20, 1994. A very difficult job that started out almost a disaster turned out quite well. It was too bad that JAC Engineers and CSULB hadn't listened to us earlier. We could have used the extra money that was wasted on Phase I.

Here was a job that came while the GSA was crucifying us on the Hawthorne job. I could have really screwed CSULB and made a lot more money, but I didn't have that in me. San-Val did not operate like that. We were fair to CSU and they appreciated it. That meant more to me than the extra money I could have made. Disaster at the CSULB project was avoided, but there was still another fight to wage.

Celebrating Elaine's 50th birthday in 1992.
Elaine's Mom standing above me, Robert, Amy, Elaine and my Mom.

29

A Hard-Won Insurance Settlement

Soon after the General Services Administration filed a multi-million dollar lawsuit against San-Val in late October 1991, I had called Ray Infantino, our insurance agent, for help. I felt that my insurance covered the problem at hand, and I followed up with a written request. I wanted Maryland Casualty, our business insurance company, to defend me against the GSA lawsuit under our policy. Ray Infantino forwarded my request to the main offices of Maryland, but at first, my request was ignored. After several follow-up letters, my request was denied again. I was forced to hire our own attorneys and pay for them out of pocket. This killed us in more ways than I first realized. After the GSA Hawthorne settlement was signed it was time to go after Maryland Casualty.

On April 13, 1993, I hired the firm of Scott C. Turner out of Pasadena on contingency to go after Maryland, who had had our insurance business for many years. I was looking for attorneys who had worked against insurance companies successfully in the past, and Scott C. Turner was one of the firms recommended to me. I had no choice but to go after Maryland. I owed Fairmont Insurance Company $700,000. I had just paid the Justice Department $200,000 and spent over $500,000 in legal fees and other costs. On top of that, I owed over $500,000 on our line-of-credit with Union Bank. We also incurred over $155,000 in in-house costs. Talk about a big mess. I was in deep shit and something had to be done to save San-Val and me from financial ruin!

Maryland Casualty at first played hardball and refused to budge from their earlier position. Months went by and a new strategy was devised. In late December 1993, Scott Turner suggested that we bring in a co-counsel. We needed the help of a bigger firm to provide help with research and to shoulder part of the legal costs. Scott could not do the research alone, nor could he bear the costs alone, as the case dragged on for many more months. On January 4, 1994, the firm of Jon-Marc Dobrin out of San Francisco was hired as co-counsel at Scott's recommendation. An all-out attack took shape.

After several months of research, it was found that there was a similar case and decision, "Overland Mechanical v. Maryland Casualty." We focused on that case. We did not want that case to be cited in our court case because it would have weakened our position. Within a couple of weeks, a decision was made by our attorneys to send a letter to the Supreme Court urging depublication of the Overland decision. Depublishing that court case would benefit us because the opposing attorney could not use it as a precedent, and it couldn't be cited before a court. Depublishing has to be done before the case is certified.

Things now got very interesting and there was a flurry of activities on both sides. Maryland's attorneys filed an opposition brief to the depublication of the Overland Mechanical opinion. Our insurance agent Ray Infantino was also named as a defendant in our lawsuit. Finally, Maryland Casualty started to rethink their position, and their defense was not as strong as it was six months earlier. June was a great month for us. It was a turning point in our case. We started to penetrate their armor.

Finally, Maryland offered a hint of a settlement offer. Their first offer came the second week in June and was firmly rejected by me. Had I taken it, I would have had to close down San-Val before our jobs were finished. That would have forced San-Val and me into bankruptcy. That was not an option. I was ready to fight to the very end even if we lost our case. I was very determined and instructed our legal team to press forward. We made it clear to Maryland that before they came to offer a settlement to us, they needed to settle with our bonding company first. I wanted Maryland to pay off the outstanding amount we owed to Fairmont. Until then, we had nothing to discuss with them.

By the end of June, a much better offer was received, but it was also rejected. We went back and forth with counter-offers. An early July settlement offer had the blessing of our attorneys, but I rejected it. Maryland's action in 1991, when they denied legal defense for us, had nearly bankrupted me, which nearly killed my wife. I wanted them to pay for their actions and their proposal was not good enough.

Besides the money I'd spent over the years defending San-Val in the lawsuit, I had lost much more. I lost my drive and my motivation; the stress had taken its toll. I did not have the will to go on much longer. My long-range plans for San-Val were destroyed. Our beautiful new building, which I had built just a couple of years earlier, was no longer important. Nothing mattered anymore. I was bitter and very badly hurt. I no longer wanted to stay in business once our jobs were completed. My wife was very ill and in agony. I was at a loss to help her, as were dozens of her doctors. I could not bear to watch her suffer like that.

I wanted to settle as soon as possible, but not at any cost. I did not want to lose a lifetime of accomplishment. My wife would surely not survive that. I went against the advice of my attorneys and directed them to go forward with the suit.

In July there were signs that we had taken the right course. We settled with Ray Infantino, our insurance agent, and released him from the lawsuit. Suing him had been the brainstorm of our attorneys — I did not even think of that. The settlement was not for much but every little bit helped. Our settlement negotiations against Maryland were enhanced by the Supreme Court's September 11, 1994 order depublishing the Overland Mechanical decision. After some more hassles, on September 13, 1994 we received an offer from Maryland that I gave my blessing to. Finally, this nightmare was also over! It was not all that I wanted, but our attorneys felt that we had reached the maximum settlement amount. I still was not completely sure. To help me get closer to the amount I was looking for, my attorneys cut their fees. At that point, I felt it was time to close the case. Scott and Jon were good, and worked hard to make our case. They felt badly for Elaine. Thanks, guys! Years of lawsuits were finally behind me, but the cost was mind-blowing!

Amy gets her bachelors degree from CSULB, June 1993.

30

Plans to Retire

Because I was preparing to retire from the construction business before the end of 1994, I took on very few new jobs, and I was selective in the jobs we did undertake. It was no longer fun to go to work. I set my timetable for retirement and wanted all jobs to end before September 30, 1994. I was only 53 years old, but I was burned out. I loved the construction business, but as agonizing and difficult as the decision to close down San-Val was, it was the right decision.

In late January of 1993, San-Val was the low bidder on the Columbia School project. It was a nice $ 1.67 million dollar contract with the city of El Monte. The job went over budget, but with the alternate bids that were part of the bid document, the city was able to fund the project. We were awarded the contract and worked with the city and the architect to put important work back into the contract and take less important items out.

We all worked as a team, which culminated in a great project that was completed on time. We had lots of change orders, but because everybody did their work in a professional manner, the project was a success. A similar job with LAUSD would have taken two to three times as long.

We did have one problem on the job when our flooring contractor walked away from the job. We had carried Miltex Flooring in our bid. After receiving their bid we realized that it was very low compared to the other bids we already had. A half-hour before we bid the job, I called Miltex and told them that their bid was very low and asked them to check their numbers and pull their bid if they had made a mistake. Their bid was $56,646, which was more than $23,000 lower than the next bidder. We already had three other flooring bids to compare theirs with, and I felt that Miltex had made a very big mistake. They called back a short time later and told us that their bid was good and to use it. We carried their bid and listed them as our flooring subcontractor.

San-Val issued Miltex a contract in the amount of $56,646 for the carpeting section of the contract. They never signed or returned the contract, but they did send us their insurance papers. When it was time to make their submittals, they submitted a much lower quality carpet. The architect then rejected the submitted carpet because it did not meet plans and specifications. Miltex refused to resubmit and refused to use the higher-grade carpet that was specified, and walked away from the job. I told them if they refused to do the job we would sue them, but they ignored my warning. Miltex figured that they had no legal responsibility to us because they hadn't signed the contract. We would prove them wrong on that at a later date.

We were stuck because we had to use another contractor whose price was $79,000. In addition, we had another problem! We had wasted six months in trying to get Miltex to do the job. Before you can replace a contractor on a public works project you have to follow strict guidelines. You also need to get approval from the owner. To replace a contractor on a job takes many months and lots of paperwork. You have to prove beyond a doubt that the contractor does not want to perform. After doing all the required paperwork and getting approval from the owner, I replaced them.

Shortly after terminating their contract, I decided to sue Miltex for the extra cost. It was clear we had a contract, because Miltex had submitted insurance papers as required by the contract and had then submitted the carpet for approval. They thought they were smart. When the submitted carpet was rejected, then they would walk away from the job because they did not sign the contract, and they would lose nothing. How wrong they were!

We filed a lawsuit against Miltex in August 1993 for breach of contract. It took some time, but we won. Miltex kept replacing their lawyers, which delayed the trial. It was frustrating, but I would not let them get away with it. This is what happens time and time again when you have residential contractors like Miltex bid on school projects.

They are out of their league. They did not even try to bid on a small project first. They jumped right into a major project with special requirements, ignoring specifications and our warnings. It is frustrating and costly to all general contractors when inexperienced contractors bid jobs they shouldn't.

While doing the Columbia School project, I was bidding a few other smaller jobs to fill in where we had voids in our backlog. I wanted to keep our few remaining workers busy as the two major jobs were winding down. One of the last projects San-Val did was for the Burbank Unified School District (BSUD). This was only fitting for several reasons. Burbank is my hometown, and we had a great relationship with BUSD. Over a forty-year period, we worked with over fifty different school districts, and BUSD was in the top five. Their staff was great to work with and never knowingly tried to screw the contractor. We had many fun experiences with BUSD.

One of my first jobs with BUSD, after Dave Gott took over the construction department, was a job at Burbank High School. This job required the removal of a large gas-fired hot-water boiler and the installation of a close to three million BTU gas-fired boiler. Some pipes had to be modified and changes were made to the control system also. After we received our contract, I called the engineer and voiced my concerns about the design. In my opinion, the specified boiler was wrong for the application. It was very expensive to maintain and required yearly Air Quality Management District (AQMD) approval to operate, plus a yearly fee that AQMD charged. I also knew that BUSD did not have trained mechanics to service the specified boiler. Most importantly, it was much more expensive than a design I had in mind.

It was standard procedure to call the engineers and let them come out with the change and make it look like they were trying to save money for the district. The owner never knew that it was our idea. But my many telephone calls were not returned, and after finally getting hold of the engineer several days later, he told me to mind my own business and just install the job as it was designed. I was upset by the manner in which he spoke to me and realized that he had very little, if any, experience in hot-water boiler design. I felt that BUSD was getting shafted and it was my duty to go direct to them with my concerns. This was the first and only job this man designed for BUSD and he was used only because he was a local mechanical engineer.

I mailed a letter to Dave Gott and pointed out to him the problems with the design we bid on. I told him that there was a better way to design this job and the district could save over $12,000 and over $1,000 every year in AQMD permit fees. I further stated that my design would save more energy and the boilers would be easy to maintain, while the specified boiler would require a specialist, which they did not have. My design called for using two smaller hot-water boilers, which did not require yearly AQMD permits. Under light usage, only one boiler would be used and this would eliminate the risk of losing hot water in the building if the big boiler broke down.

In less than 10 days, we received a go-ahead for the installation of my design. A week or so later I found out that Dave Gott had called the engineer and asked why he had used a single boiler instead of two smaller boilers, which would have saved BUSD a lot of money. It made sense to Dave, but he wanted professional confirmation of my allegations. Dave was not familiar with AQMD requirements on larger boilers. He called the engineer but was not satisfied with the answers he received.

At that point Dave called another mechanical engineer, John Denton and Associates, and asked them to review the original design and my recommendations. When Dave gave Denton my proposal, he cut off my letterhead and the signature on the bottom of the letter. After reviewing the proposal, John Denton asked Dave if it was Steve Veres who made this proposal. Dave said yes and asked John how he knew. John told him that over the years, San-Val had done a lot of work with their office, and this was a typical Steve Veres proposal. He also told Dave that they had gotten one of the best and most honest contractors around. It was no surprise that John Denton sided with me, but instead of the $12,000 in credits that we offered, Denton felt it should have been only around $9,5000. (Dave told me all this after we finished the project.) BUSD was thankful for the savings because it came out of the maintenance budget. The savings we gave them back were used on other school repairs. The job came out real well for BUSD and for us, and they thanked me for my help many times over.

This is how San-Val operated; we were always there to help the owner. If we saw something wrong, we brought it to the attention of the architect or engineer. In most cases they thanked us for saving their ass, and made the changes. That is why engineers liked to work with us. We were a team player.

One of our funniest experiences happened with BUSD in 1992. We were doing a fairly large size noise abatement project at Luther Burbank Middle School. Six weeks after we started the project, we received our first progress payment from the Burbank Airport Authority. They funded 90% of the reconstruction costs. To our surprise, a week or so later we received another check, this time from the BUSD, for the same amount. My bookkeeper came to me and told me what had happened, and asked what we should do. I told her that I would take care of it and took the check from her.

I wrote a very nice letter to Dave thanking BUSD for the very generous bonus. I told them that we were going to put the money to good use — I was taking my entire office staff to Europe for three weeks. We would stay at the best hotels and eat at the finest restaurants. When we came back, I would then take the entire staff of Dave's office for three weeks also, all expenses paid. I further stated that if we received another bonus like we had this month, we would take an around-the-world trip the next time with both staffs. I thanked them for their generosity and told them it was about time we got rewarded for our exceptional work performance.

They got a big kick out of the letter. It was passed around the office and was forwarded to the purchasing department. Later, some of the school board members also heard about it, but I don't know what their reaction was! Needless to say, we returned the check to BUSD. The staff at Dave's office would always ask when we were leaving on the trip.

The last project we did for BUSD, and San-Val's last also, was another noise abatement project at Luther Burbank Middle School. This job was smaller, just over $828,000. San-Val employed fewer than seven, including our field crews, by the time we finished this job. The project was completed on time, in December 1994. Now it was time to let our staff go and close down our operation. It had been a very challenging 31 years. Along the way I fought many battles. I lost a few but won most. Many persons would have given up a long time before, but I was too stubborn and had too much pride. I loved what I did and believed in my ability. I had my strengths and weaknesses but above all, I had my integrity, and no one can take that away from me. I can hold my head up high in knowing that I accomplished more in 31 years than many others.

By the time we settled with Maryland, we were finishing most of our outstanding work. Once I decided to shut down my business, I laid out a plan for the shutdown. The plan took into consideration the outstanding work and what was required to complete those jobs in the shortest possible time. I called for a meeting with my staff and key field personnel. I advised them of my decision and my plan to close down San-Val. Most understood my decision and the reasons behind it. There was not a dry eye in the room. I loved and respected my staff. I gave them several months' notice before their employment would be terminated and told them that I would understand if they left me before they finished the entire period. I thanked them for the work they had done for me in years past and for their support during some very difficult times.

I had to plan the shutdown very carefully. It was important to expedite the ongoing projects and bid a few smaller jobs in order to minimize our losses. Shutting down a construction business is very difficult and expensive. Now was not the time to miscalculate and add to the financial losses. A few months after I notified my staff that San-Val was shutting down, I laid off my estimators because we no longer were bidding new large jobs. The few short completion jobs that we planned to bid were going to be bid by me alone. I set the shutdown date for September 1994. In late July I had already put a For Rent sign on the building. It was a sad day!

Not one of my superintendents left me before their projects were 100% completed. They pushed the jobs and stayed to the last day, yet they knew that they had no other jobs waiting for them. That is loyalty! I paid them well and treated them with respect and they stood by me to the very end. My special thanks goes to John Watson, who I'm sure had a lot to do with that. Thanks, John! Thanks, guys! My special thanks also went to my office staff for their dedication and loyalty. I was blessed with a great office staff. We did a lot of work with a small staff. That was possible because we utilized cutting-edge technology and high tech equipment. We had come in on the ground level of computers and used it to our advantage.

In December 1993, I started to sell off equipment we no longer needed. As jobs finished, we would sell equipment coming off that job. Assets were sold every month. I did not want to do a fire sale the last day. By mid July 1994, we had cut our employees to less than fifteen and sold most of our equipment.

I could have sold the business but I was not about to finance the buyer, or co-sign with the bonding company and bank. A good friend of mine had done that when he sold his HVAC business a few years before. He financed buyers who did not know how to run the business, and in three years the new owners went bankrupt. My friend lost most of his life's savings. I wanted no part of that. I wanted to get out and go on with life, and take care of my wife and family.

I decided to bid only smaller jobs and turned down several larger jobs. I refused to bid on any work that would take me past the estimated shutdown time. I at first planned to do consulting work once I closed San-Val, but the timing was wrong. I needed to take time off and do less stressful work.

After closing down San-Val I did try some consulting work, but my heart was not in it. I had been mistaken when I thought my anger would just go away once I shut down San-Val. That was not the case; if anything, it hurt even more. I had planned to have San-Val for a very long time and that is why I had built our new facilities. My long-range plans had been thwarted. It took a long time afterwards to vent my anger and frustration. I don't think I'll ever get over it. I'm sure that I'll never forget.

My friends from CEDG surprised Elaine and me with this beatifull Geisha
Doll in 1994. Joe Nishimura and his son Chris in the middle.

31

Celebration, and a Visit to my Homeland

Marrying Elaine was the best decision I ever made. No husband could have asked for a more supportive and loving wife. She stood by me in very difficult times and never doubted my abilities. She gave me two beautiful and loving children, Robert and Amy, who made my life complete. The three of them made me the happiest man on earth. Elaine and I have been in love for more than thirty-seven years now and our love gets stronger each year. That is how we were able to survive our many agonizing ordeals. We laughed and we cried together. We raised our family in that loving environment.

One of our favorite songs is, "Through the Years" by Kenny Rogers. While dancing to the song, Elaine and I get a little emotional while listening to the words. One of my other favorite songs is by the late Frank Sinatra, it's "My Way." Paul Anka did a wonderful job writing that song. "My Way" speaks for the way I lived my life. I had my ups and downs, but never gave up. I did it my way! I learned as I went along and tried to be the best. Be proud of what you are doing and try to excel in the profession you choose.

During the early years of our marriage I worked crazy hours. I hardly saw Elaine and the kids other than late evenings and some Sundays. My business was started on a shoestring budget, so that is the way it had to be. We hardly ever took vacations until our kids were much older. Even if we went away, it was only for two or three days. We were very close with our friends, which helped Elaine cope. Early on we lived close to our best friends, Rita and Stan Spiegelman in

Brockton, Massachusetts. Their kids were almost the same age as ours, which was great. Having so many good friends in the Boston area made our move to the West Coast that much harder. It was a business decision and Elaine understood, but she was miserable for the first few years. We lived in Glendale for a year, since then in Burbank. She missed her family and her lifelong friends. It was not the same for me — I was so busy working that I did not have time to miss my friends. To cheer Elaine up, I decided to put on a very special fortieth birthday party for her in 1982. It was such a hit that for months after, it was the only thing our friends talked about.

A week before the party I was at the White House in Washington attending a briefing on national security matters. For several years I had been a very active member in the nationwide organization, Peace Through Strength. In 1981 and 1982, I was the chairman of the Southern California Chapter, with a membership of thousands. More than half of the US Congress also belonged to this organization. It's a very powerful lobby, which worked for a strong US defense to counter the Soviet threat. Our organization persuaded many members of congress to vote for higher defense spending to build up our military. I feel that our organization contributed, even if only in a small way, to the collapse of the Iron Curtain. I, along with some twenty-five other members of our organization from all over the country, were briefed at this particular meeting by President Reagan's National Security advisor Bud McFarlane, as well as by representatives of the Pentagon and the CIA. I was seated in the front row of the room and was impressed by the more than one-hour briefing. All of this while I was organizing my wife's party!

I had noticed how lonely Elaine was in California. It was time to do something very special for her and do it in a very creative way. First, I rented the function hall at a local restaurant for 75 friends and relatives. It was to be sit-down dinner with a live band for dancing. I decided to fly her entire family from Boston, as well as four of our closest friends: Rita and Stan Spiegelman, and Estelle and Mike Davis. I also got Doris and Larry Siders to come down from Northern California. These three gals were Elaine's closest friends. Nobody knew about my plans, not even my kids or our local relatives. In the past when someone had a birthday, we would get together for a birthday dinner with our friends Irv and Lil Levin and Jim and Judy

Hancock. I rented several rooms at the Burbank Holiday Inn for our out-of-town guests and when the day came, I rented a twelve-passenger van to taxi my guests around town. I made several trips to LAX to pick them up — each came on different flights and at different times of the day. Needless to say it was a very busy day. The birthday party was set for 6:30 p.m.

The day before the party I had told Elaine about a "problem" I was having on a job in Orange County about an hour's drive from us in Burbank. This was just a set-up for the following day. The day of the party, I had my secretary Georgia call Elaine around 5:00 p.m. and tell her that I was still stuck at the meeting in Orange County. Georgia told Elaine that I had asked Jim Hancock to pick her up and take her to the restaurant. I would get there as soon as I could, depending on traffic. There was nothing unusual about this, as I worked crazy hours all my life. My plan had to be a total surprise, and I had to be at the restaurant before 6:30 to make the plan work.

There was a side room next to the function hall and I would use it as a holding room for my out-of-town guests. I sneaked all ten of them into the room without anybody knowing about it and we locked ourselves in there. I made arrangements with Jim to call me at the restaurant just before he picked Elaine up. That gave me a ten-minute warning. I then ushered all the guests into the hall.

We had a table reserved in the back of the restaurant at the entrance of the hall. The waiter would show Elaine and the others to our table, but would go through the door into the hall. Normally, when we had dinner with Irv and Lil, they would be there before us, and would wait for us near the front entrance. We worked it the same way and so there was no reason for Elaine to be suspicious of anything. A few minutes before Elaine arrived, I had the lights shut off. When Elaine entered we screamed, "SURPRISE" and turned on the light. She was shocked, but that was nothing compared to what was to follow a short time later.

For the next ten minutes she was hugging our friends and relatives, which included my mom and my brother Zoli. Now it was time to start the show. I stepped to the microphone and welcomed our guests to Elaine's fortieth birthday party. I told our friends that because I had to be at the White House in Washington I had had to move the party back a week. I then asked Elaine to join me at the mike. I told her and the

Surprise 40th birthday party for Elaine in October, 1982.

Here I'm making my speech and ready for the introductions.

Elaine's Mom and Dad after they were brought into the room. Robert is behind them

Elaines closest friends were flown in from Boston and Northern California.

audience that while I was in Washington I thought that it would be neat if I could have Ron and Nancy Reagan join us for this happy occasion. But, unfortunately the President couldn't make it, so, I had gotten the next best thing. While I paused for a moment we heard someone at the front tables say, "Steve got the Vice President?" People were on the edges of their seats. Who did Steve have? Than I told her, "Heeeeere are your parents, Mom and Dad!"

Wow! What a moment! When her parents walked out of the side room the scene went wild, but the show had only just begun. In a "This is Your Life" fashion I brought out her sister Elanor, and Elanor's husband Kevin. At that point I told the audience that I had given the party because Elaine was still homesick; she missed her family and her close girlfriends. Her girlfriends were more than just friends, they were like family. Then I brought them out, one couple at a time. The first ones were Rita and Stan Spiegelman, then came Estelle and Mike Davis, and finally Doris and Larry Siders. Elaine was in tears, as were most in attendance. Great food and entertainment followed, including a five-piece dance band I had hired. People could not believe what I had done and no one had had a clue, other than Irv and Lil, and Jim Hancock. It was a spectacular event that we'll never forget. Thanks, everyone!

For the next week I drove our out-of-town family and friends all over Southern California. Elaine's parents had such a good time that they decided to move out here and live in Burbank only a few blocks from us. A few years later her sister and her family also moved to Burbank. It was my fault! I showed them such a good time that they fell in love with California! I screwed up!

Once Elaine's family moved to Burbank, it was a little easier for her. Elaine was not one to watch TV all day long or do a lot of shopping, so finding the volunteer work that she did for many years was the best medicine for her. She started to meet new friends, too, but we still treasure our friends in Boston. That is why we go back to Boston almost every year for a visit. Elaine is happiest when she visits with Rita and our many other friends. To us, our family and our friends are very important.

Elaine and I live a very simple life. We don't get in over our heads, and we do not buy things we can't afford. We are very conservative and try to save a little for rainy days. Elaine, and Amy too, are very responsible with their money and are great bargain shoppers.

After saving for years, in 1985 I purchased a 28-foot Bayliner Cabin Cruiser powerboat. We named our new boat "FREEDOM," a name with a lot of meaning for me. We kept the boat at Huntington Harbor, which was a 50 minute ride from our home. (We wanted to keep the boat moored in Marina del Rey, but there were no empty slips available there at the time.) The boat I purchased had a single engine, which made parking the boat much harder. It took me some time to master it, but with the help of other fellow boaters, I finally learned it. We loved boating; it took me away from the pressures of my business, and it was also good for Elaine.

Exactly a year later we traded the 28-foot Bayliner in for a 38-foot with twin engines. What a difference the two engines make! I became an expert in less than 10 minutes. I was able to park my boat now without breaking into a cold sweat. We had that boat, the FREEDOM II, for more than two years, when I started to look for a wider boat with more comfort. For one thing, the Bayliner had small sleeping quarters. We slept on the boat on Saturday nights, but we were not very comfortable in its V-berth bed.

We really enjoyed our boats, especially the third one, a 36-foot Carver. We would have friends and relatives join us and let everyone drive the boat. When they had kids with them, I would also let the kids drive. Eventually, I got very busy in my son Rob's business, which I tell about in a later chapter. FREEDOM III was sitting idle, so I decided to sell it.

In 1991 we had hoped to take a trip to Europe. I was going to take Elaine to France to visit Amy, then the three of us would go to Hungary, and visit my birthplace. Even though Elaine was not feeling that great, I felt that the trip might help her. However, we had to cancel our plans because of the Gulf War and the threats against Americans around the world. Our plans were then put on hold for a while. Elaine was very sick, and was in no condition to travel for a very long time. Doctors and specialists were no help. Some just gave up because they could do nothing for her. No one could put a finger on her illness. That was the worst part of it.

However, in early 1998, Elaine began feeling better, and so we took the opportunity to make plans for our long-awaited trip. I wanted to go to France, Austria, and Hungary. We also planned our trip to include attending a wedding of the son of one of our best friends in Boston, Mass. On May 23, 1998, we were off to Boston. Because of that wedding, we missed Amy's graduation from college, but Amy understood.

On the 26th we took off for Paris, France. Elaine had studied French in school, but that was not the help I hoped it would be. We stayed at a hotel close to the historical monuments. We visited Notre Dame Cathedral, the Eiffel Tower, Arc de Triomphe, Champ Elysées and more. We had a great time except for one night when we decided to go to a French restaurant near our hotel for dinner.

To our surprise, nobody at the restaurant spoke English. The waiter brought some bread, water, and a menu to our table. We looked over the menu, but it was all in French. The only thing we saw that we understood was "spaghetti." We ordered what we believed was some kind of pasta dinner, but boy, were we surprised! The waiter put two plates of cooked plain pasta on our table. There was no sauce of any kind on it. We looked at each other and tried to ask the waiter to bring something to put on it, but to no avail. There were very few customers in the restaurant and none of them spoke English. We were hungry and ate the plain pasta. Later on we laughed over the incident; it reminded me of when I first came to the USA.

From Paris we took the high-speed train to Nice, in Southern France. We went sightseeing in Monaco and gambled in Monte Carlo, and also took a nice car trip to the Italian coastline. Lots of fun and wonderful memories. It was now time to visit a very special city in a different country.

A few months before we went to Europe, I had e-mailed one of our customers, Alfred Meguscher, who lived in Vienna, Austria. I asked Alfred if he could get me the phone number of the mayor's office in Korneuburg. I told him that I had been a refugee there in 1957, and would like to visit the city in June with my wife. I wanted to visit Korneuburg and thank the mayor for what they did for the Hungarian refugees and my family. Alfred did better than getting me a phone number. He set up a meeting for me with Wolfgang Peterl, Mayor of

In 1998, Elaine and I visited with the Mayor of Korneuburg Wolfgang Peter!

The city's historical diary was butchered by the Communist
while the city was under occupation after WW II.

Korneuburg. I was shocked and surprised; again I found people going out of their way to help.

We arrived in Vienna on the 1st of June and I rented a car, which allowed us to get to the many places I wanted to see. The following day we left our hotel for Korneuburg and our 10 a.m. meeting with the mayor. Thankfully we did not get lost — it was about a 25km trip from Vienna. The mayor greeted us warmly. He had a reporter in his office and they had been discussing local politics. He asked the reporter to stay for a while. To my relief, he spoke English, which made it a great visit. I expressed my thanks to him and the people of the city for their generosity and help after the Hungarian revolt. How thankful we were for the chance for my family, and thousands of others, to start a new life in freedom.

Mayor Peterl was very impressed by our visit. He told me that I was the first Hungarian to come back for a visit! We then talked about the city, and how their country fared while under Communist occupation after WW II. The city hall was used by the Soviet military as their headquarters. The mayor brought out a big book, a historical diary for their city, filled with important documents dating back to 1895. He told Elaine and me that while the Soviet Union occupied their city, they tore every page out of the book that mentioned freedom or liberty. Some very smart people recovered those pages and hid them. After the Soviet troops left the city in 1950, the people at City Hall carefully taped the torn-out sheets together and put them back into the book. They are very proud people. When I told him that I planned to take Elaine to the refugee camp where we had stayed in 1957, he offered to have a staff member take us there.

What a wonderful meeting and history lesson! We learned a lot, but were not surprised by what the Soviets did. I had lived under the rule of the same bastards. Before we left, I gave Wolfgang Peterl a donation, and asked him to give it to a charity in the city that helps the youth. He told me that it would be put to good use. He then gave me a beautiful book of the history of Korneuburg and autographed it. We hugged each other and said our good-byes. The old refugee camp was only six blocks from City Hall, so we decided to walk it. The staff person spoke English well and pointed out important buildings along the way. She was a doll! It was a beautiful day. As we walked towards the camp, I saw the back of a building that looked very familiar, about

I stand front of the building where I lived in early 1957 as a
Hungarian Refugge 41 years earlier.

In 1998, I was standing at the Hungarian/Austrian border near the
place where we almost got captured and had to cross in a
small boat was a very emotional moment.

three blocks away. I stopped, stared at the building, and nearly started to cry.

Pointing at the brick building in the distance, I told Elaine that that was where we had been housed 41 years before. Our guide started to laugh, and kept saying over and over that she couldn't believe it. After all these years, I still remembered. As we walked towards the building I explained to Elaine that there had been four other buildings like that one, but this was ours. I'd kept it in my memory — the building that turned our lives around. The complex was now under renovation. It was a small, closed military base and was now being converted into apartments. Three of the buildings were already converted and looked very nice. It felt great to walk the grounds again. What a difference 41 years made! I never thought that I would ever return, but I'm glad I did. I could hardly hold back the tears.

The following day, we decided to drive into Hungary. I wanted to take Elaine to the place on the border where we had crossed into Austria. It was a two-hour drive from our hotel. As we got close, my heart started to beat faster. I was nervous and excited. After all this time, I was finally able to show Elaine where I came from. Armed border guards checked our papers and asked questions. After only a minute or two we were on our way. We had good maps and had no problem finding exactly where I wanted to go. Just a few miles inside Hungary we stopped at a nice restaurant to eat. They had both Austrian and Hungarian food. They also took either currency. While in Austria, I had cashed some dollars into forints, the Hungarian currency.

We finished our lunch with some delicious (rich) dessert. We were bad! We were having fun. I then checked my map and headed to the border crossing, where more than 41 years before we were almost captured and nearly died. We drove near the lake and walked to the area where we had crossed over using a small rowboat. I pointed out to Elaine the approximate area where we'd seen the small light of the Austrian border guards. I also showed Elaine, on the map, about where we had started our crossing from the farmhouse located in the outlying area of Sopron. I was crying while Elaine was comforted me. Such memories! How lucky we were to make it out! From Sopron, I took Elaine to Lake Balaton, where we stayed overnight. The hotel had just opened up for the season and rates were cheap. Elaine had fun at a nearby open market and bought lots of goodies to bring home and give

Back to Hungary in 1998 for the 1st time since we escaped.
Visiting with my Aunt Maria and her niece.

Visiting my cousin Miklos and his family.

to family and friends. I had no problem with the language, which impressed Elaine. In fact, I impressed myself. While I had forgotten some of the words, I was able to talk around them. The visit went better than I expected.

Back in Vienna, we took a hydrofoil high-speed boat down the Danube into Budapest, a great experience. We stayed at the Erzsebet Hotel in Budapest, just two blocks from Petöfi Square. We did some sightseeing and then made a couple of phone calls. In the Budapest phone book I looked up the phone numbers of an aunt and a cousin. I had not told them that we were coming. I did not know how much I could do with Elaine, and until we were in Hungary, I could not be sure of anything. I first talked with my aunt, then I called my cousin Miklos. They were both in shock. I had not spoken to my aunt in nearly 42 years.

We went to see her the following day. She still lived in the same building where she had lived since marrying my uncle, over 60 years before. The building was in need of major repairs, but her apartment was beautiful. I pointed out a brick building across the street to Elaine, and told her it was the school I went to. It still looked the same. As a matter of fact, very little seemed changed other than the fact that the Communist control was over. We had a very nice time with my aunt and a niece of hers, who was visiting.

After we left my aunt, I took Elaine to the house in Budapest where we had lived. We went up to the 4th floor and knocked on the door. I wanted my wife to see where we lived, but the residents were not at home. The building had a three-sided courtyard, and a lady on the third floor was looking up at us. What were we doing there? I told her in Hungarian that I used to live there in the 1950s. She threw her hands to the sides of her face in disbelief and asked if I was one of the Veres boys. I said yes. She came running upstairs and hugged me. She still remembered, after 41 years!

I told her I was Pista, and introduced Elaine. She tried to tell Elaine that we were very bad boys, and had made lots of noise above her apartment, playing soccer. We sure did! She would hit the ceiling in her apartment with the end of a broomstick, signaling us to cut it out. That normally did the trick. She wanted to know if we had seen Mrs. Ungar, our next-door neighbor, and one of my mom's closest friends.

She still lived there. In Hungary it was typical for people to live in the same house or apartment for many years. Housing is hard to find, and people can't afford to move.

A couple of days later we went to visit Miklos and his wife and son. They lived in Rákoscsaba, an outlying district, about ten miles from Budapest. He still lived in the house my father had bought for his mother and sisters. My cousin Miklos had been born there and lived there all his life. He was my age, 57; the last time I had seen Miklos was about 1955. His son was a big Michael Jordan fan, with a big poster of Michael above his bed. He also collected basketball cards, and nearly fainted when I told them that my son Robert sold sportscards as a business. I told him that I would send him cards of his favorite players, like Jordan, Pippin, and a few others. (I did that weekly, after our return home, and also sent them money.) The house had become somewhat run-down and I was sad to see it in such a poor condition.

While there, I realized that life was only a little better for most Hungarians. They live a very simple life and have very little. Most just barely get by. Things are getting better but it's going to take many years. The one important thing that they have going for them is that they are free now. They can travel freely outside the country, and have a freely elected government. Hungary is progressing better than most other former Eastern Block countries. I wish them all the luck in the world. They suffered long enough and deserve a break.

The trip was a total success. I was glad that we finally were able to go. I hadn't wanted to go back to Hungary until it was a free country. I had made a promise to myself that under no condition would I go back while it was under Communist control. We had risked our lives to escape and had no plans to return. Once the Iron Curtain fell, I had no reservations about it. It was a great trip filled with wonderful memories, and was well worth the time and money. I know Elaine had a great time also.

Part VIII

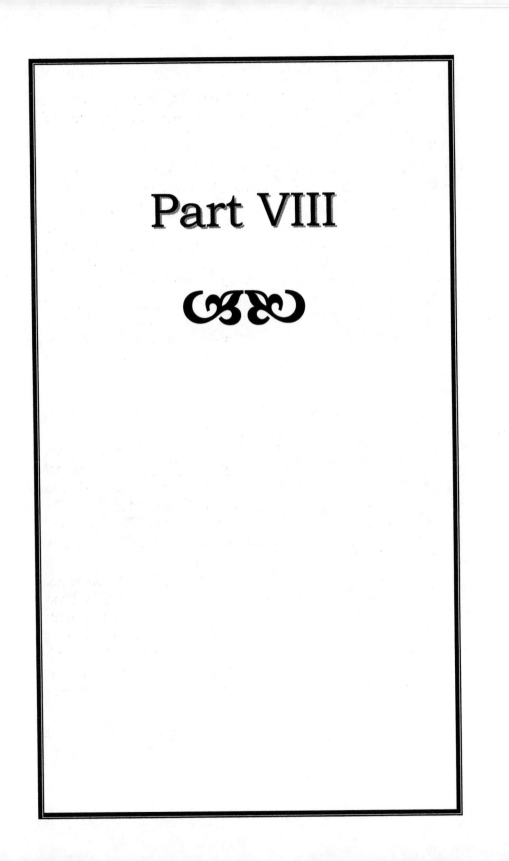

Burbank Coins & Collectibles in 1987.

Sally and Rob on their wedding day, August 4, 1991.

32

My Son Rob and our Venture Together

When Rob was born in 1966, I, like many a father, hoped that he would join me some day in my business. Although that wish was not fulfilled, I did not ever want to force him into doing something he did not want to do. I was not going to make the same mistake my father did. I wanted to give my kids an opportunity to make their own life and let them do what they wanted. I would support them and encourage them and give the best advice I could. We did insist Robert go to Hebrew school; after that he had his bar mitzvah in February 1980.

Ever since he was a young boy, Rob liked to play with coins and stamps, so it was no surprise to us that on his way home from school, he would stop by a local coin and stamp dealer on Magnolia Boulevard in Burbank. The storeowner's name was Donald Osborne. Rob would hang around Don's shop daily. One day, Don asked Rob if he would deliver advertising flyers in the neighborhood for two cents apiece. Rob agreed and Don had several hundred flyers printed up. The following two weekends, Rob delivered them on his bike.

A few days later Rob told Don to make up more flyers, because he wanted to deliver them to other areas, farther from the store. Don received quite a bit of business because of the flyers and asked Rob if he wanted to work at the store on Saturdays. Rob got very excited and asked us for permission. We said OK, even though Rob was only twelve years old. The following summer Don asked Rob if he wanted to work during summer vacation. Once again we said OK.

Soon after Rob started to work for Don, we made him open a savings account. We forced to him to put half his paycheck into his savings account. Although Rob was very upset with us, we told him that he needed to save some of his money for the future.

Don Osborne had been in business for about eighteen years and was very knowledgeable in his business. He taught Rob a lot. I did not, however, completely agree with his business philosophy. For one thing, he always had a 45-caliber pistol on him, and a shotgun on his desk. But for the most part, I got along well with Don and did not try to tell him how to run his business.

When Rob turned sixteen, he got his driver's license. Not long after that, he wanted to buy a car. Along with some of his friends he went looking at used cars. He had his eye on a used Chevy with a big V8 engine. The money from his savings account was going to be used for the purchase. He had just about enough money and was proud of the money he had saved. He was no longer upset with us for forcing him to save! I did not want him to buy a used car and I made a deal with him. We would buy a new Toyota Corolla. He would put in the amount he wanted to pay for the used car and I would pay the balance. The car never gave him any trouble and got about 26 miles to the gallon. Other than changing oil, the car never needed service for the many years he had it.

Robert was not crazy about school and after graduating from high school in June 1984, he went to a local junior college for a year. He wanted to work and make money, just like his father did, years earlier. Elaine pressured him into going to work for me and trying to learn the construction business. That did not work out very well. Rob had his mind on other things. So I fired him from San-Val, knowing he had a job back with Don Osborne. Rob was overjoyed.

A few years later Rob decided to get a bigger car. He saw a sporty used Dodge at a dealer's lot in Glendale. He told me that he was old enough to have a more powerful car than the four-cylinder Corolla. He had his heart set on it and I could not talk him out of it. I insisted that he get the extended warranty with it, and that $570 extra expense was the best purchase we made. The car had a flashy dashboard, with lots of gadgets and lights. It was built very low to the ground and it was hard for me to even get into the front seat. Soon we realized that the car was a piece of junk. Several times a week my wife would get a call from Rob to be picked up because the car had broken down again. Thank God we had the extended warranty. A few months later, Rob had enough of it. We bought another new car and traded in his Dodge. Kids!

In late 1989, Rob wanted to move out and find an apartment in Burbank. After several months, he found a nice two bedroom, two-bath condo in Burbank that was for sale. He talked his crazy Dad into buying the condo and leasing it to him for $400 less than our mortgage and association payments. I should have had my head examined!

On August 4, 1991, Rob married Sally, a wonderful girl. Sally was working as an accountant and later got her CPA. They loved the condo, but not for long. They had their sights set on a much better deal and soon the right opportunity came along.

In early February 1992, I purchased an investment property in Burbank. It was a single-family house that required a lot of work. It was not the first time I had purchased a fixer-upper. I would buy a house like that, fix it up, then sell it. Because I would do most of the work, I would make a nice profit when I sold. I was doing about $30,000 worth of improvements to that house. I would go there after dinner and work for hours most nights, and all day on weekends. I enjoyed it and the long hours did not bother me. I did the remodeling after hours, after working at San-Val during the day.

One day Rob came by the new house with Sally. While I was working in the kitchen, Rob showed his wife all the work I was going to do: put in a new kitchen, new bathroom, new roof, new HVAC system, new carpeting, re-stucco the house, new driveway, new lawn, and new copper piping. I was also going to install a new 200 amp electrical service and rewire the entire house. The house had an old swimming pool, which was defective; I was going to bury that rather than fix it. The house needed a lot of work, but it was on a very nice street, only two blocks from where I lived.

The following night, Rob came over to our house, just as I had finished dinner. I should have known he was up to something when he asked to see me in private. He told me that he and Sally liked the house and wanted to buy it from me. "Where are you going to get the money?" I asked. "Oh Dad!" he said. I knew right then that I was in big trouble! He told me that the house would be great for them and they would like to start raising a family. The condo would not be big enough. They wanted to have their own backyard and the pool would be a perfect addition. After discussing the matter, I agreed to the deal. A few more deals like that, and I would go bust!

I agreed to sell it to them for the same price I had paid for the house a month before. I would do the financing at six percent interest with no down payment. He would pay me for the house repairs, but with a catch. He wanted me to keep the pool, install a new heater, new pump, new filter, repipe the pool, replaster it, and put in a new concrete deck. When we came out of my office, Rob went to his mom, thanked her, gave her a big kiss and left in a hurry, before Elaine found out why she got the big thank-you! I told Elaine what had transpired and she nearly fell off her chair. Was I insane? I told her I probably was!

Now that the remodeling was going to be for the kids, I changed the kitchen cabinets and carpeting to a higher grade. I decided to replace all the windows and outside doors. I also installed a mantel over the fireplace and enlarged the master bedroom. The house was finished in ten weeks and it was like new! Rob and Sally were thrilled with their new home. To top it off, I also purchased all the appliances for them, which included the stove, washer and dryer, and a refrigerator. What parents don't do for their kids!

On May 9, 1995, we were blessed with a healthy grandson. His name is Ryan. Elaine and I were very happy because they lived only a couple of streets from us. On July 8, 1999, a healthy granddaughter named Samantha arrived. They are the best medicine for Elaine, and the best gift we both ever got was hearing ourselves called Grandma and Grandpa. Our grandkids are almost four years apart and they love each other. We are having such fun! In late 2000, Rob and Sally sold the house and moved into a much larger house in Burbank. They needed more room because of the two kids, and besides Sally needed an office for her work.

After Rob's short stay with San-Val, he had gone back to Don's shop. As years passed, Rob took on more responsibilities at the store, and was doing very well. When Don required surgery, Rob ran the shop with Don's wife Marsha. In 1987, Rob told Don that they should sell sportscards in the store. At that time they were selling coins, stamps, and comic books. Don wanted no part of sportscards, so Rob asked Don if he could bring them in himself. They made a deal whereby Rob could sell them in the store and Don would get 10%

from sales. Don would allot a four-foot section in the store to Rob to use for his cards.

That night Rob wanted to talk to me. He asked me if I could loan him some money to buy the sportscards he intended to sell at Don's store. He told me what he had discussed with Don that day, and also said that this would be a good opportunity for him and a great investment for me. He was so excited! After some discussion, I gave him $25,000 to buy inventory. My wife again thought I was crazy. Maybe I was, but I saw something that reminded me of a young man who had big ideas of his own, and had started an HVAC business twenty-three years before. I told Elaine that Rob was a smart kid and had a good head for business, and that we should give him a chance. It was the beginning of better things to come.

As time passed, Rob was doing very well, so Don gave him more store space to use. Rob called his business "Rob's Sportscards." We took out a business license for him and set up bookkeeping. Soon Don decided to also carry sportscards in the store. Don made arrangements with Rob as to what Rob would sell and what Don would sell. Rob was teaching Don about the sportscards business, just like Don was teaching Rob about coins and stamps. Rob loved dealing with coins, but liked sportscards better. Much of the coin inventory was on consignment in Don's store. Since 1987, I had been one of the investors and also had coins on consignment there, but only because Rob had talked me into it. I knew very little about coins and relied on Rob's knowledge and experience.

In late 1988, there was a big sportscards show in Anaheim, California. Rob decided to have a booth there. The show ran from Wednesday through Sunday and he asked me if I could come and help him. Stupid me, I said OK. I was busy at San-Val but agreed because I felt that he really needed me. Rob also asked Elaine if she could be there. Rob needed extra people to watch the merchandise because there are lots of people at a large show and he did not want his cards stolen. The convention center was 45 minutes from our house, so I decided to rent a room at the Disney Hotel because I did not want to drive home every night. We had our display cases and merchandise loaded into our two cars and headed for Anaheim early Wednesday morning. Rob would go home every night to bring more merchandise to the show or to take home some of the cards he purchased.

The show was great, we saw Rob wheeling and dealing as we had never seen him before. He bought cards from other dealers and also sold cards. He made several thousand dollars and was satisfied with the show. Elaine and I were impressed, but could not understand why people would spend thirty or forty dollars on a few cardboard sportscards. We had no clue as to the value of those cards. We have a much better understanding now.

Rob was running the business for Don and also did all the buying of coins and card collections. Rob was getting results. Don stayed mostly in the back room, doing his pricing of coins while Rob took care of the customers. Marsha, Don's wife, was also up front with Rob. Rob was very good with customers. He was a great salesman and did not let his youth get in his way. That's my boy! Things were going well for Rob. One night in early March 1989, when I came home from work, Rob told me that he needed to talk to me in my office. He was very excited and I got a little nervous. I had seen that excitement before, and it always cost me money. What was Rob up to now? I did not have to wait very long. As soon as I sat down, he dropped a bombshell on me.

"Dad," he said, "Don wants to sell his business and I want to buy it." Don wanted out and had given him the first option to buy. As could have been predicted, Rob wanted me to finance the business. Rob told me that with his brain and my money we could make it a good business. We would be partners. I asked a lot of questions, but Rob had very few answers. Don did not have a price in mind yet, which complicated things a little. Don wanted Rob to make a proposal to him and he would take it from there. I told Rob that I needed to think about it for a few days.

When I talked with Elaine she wanted no part of it. She felt that it was a very dangerous business and with all the guns around it would be very nerve-wracking for her. I told Elaine that we had to accept that Rob would never come into my business; as much as I would love to have him, it was not to be. This was what Rob loved, and with some guidance from me he could make it into a successful business. I promised her that we would not have guns out in the open, as did Don, and we would keep the store secured. The door would have a special locking system, and we would push a button to let people into the store. Elaine was still afraid, but I wanted to think about it, if we could get the business at a fair price.

Every day when I came home, Rob would find me and ask if I had made up my mind yet. He did not want somebody else to buy the business. I told Rob to relax. It's not easy to sell an existing business, I reassured him. I knew the complexities of buying and financing a business because I had learned it the hard way, with no outside help.

A few days later, against the advice of my wife, I agreed to put together a proposal for the purchase of the business from Don. Rob was jubilant. I told him that we would have to take a full inventory of the business, not including any merchandise that was on consignment, and that I would evaluate our options. I gave Rob directions as to how to take inventory at cost, and that I would figure the rest, such as fixtures, equipment, and goodwill. A few days later Rob handed me the numbers as to what he felt the net cost of the inventory was worth. He did not include merchandise that belonged to others. A few days later I went to the store to do my portion of the work. I calculated the value of the existing equipment and came up with a price for goodwill of the business. For a few days I played with the numbers and rewrote the proposal several times on my computer.

Rob was jumpy, and I had to calm him down. In that sense he was just like me. He had motivation and knew what he wanted to do, but I had to make sure that it was not at any cost. Besides, it was my money. A week later we put together a proposal for Don to consider. Rob felt that we should go in with a higher price, but I tried to explain that when you buy an existing inventory, not all of it is good and sellable. Much of it would be sitting there for years, and if we didn't buy it at the right price we could be in a lot of trouble later. Much of the inventory we had no use for, and it was important that we pay no more than what we could sell it for at wholesale. One of the things I did not want to buy was Don's bullion inventory. I did not want Rob to be involved in that part of the business. It was too risky. Rob gave Don my proposal, and a few days later Don called and asked for a meeting face to face.

We met after hours at the store. It was a good meeting and our proposal was in the ballpark. Don asked us why we did not want the bullion inventory, and I answered that Rob was too young for that portion of the business. Don seemed to accept my reasoning. I also explained some of my other concerns, and I told him that Elaine was very nervous too. With all that, it actually took us very little time to reach an agreement. By 9:00 p.m. we had agreed on terms that were fair for both sides. Rob was ecstatic. We purchased the business effective April 1st, 1989. I took a big risk, but I felt that Rob deserved this opportunity, and I was glad that I was in a position to help his dream come true. Rob was only 22 years old when we purchased the business for him. I was 22 years old when I started my HVAC business 25 years earlier, back in 1964.

33

Alarms and Earthquakes

Once we purchased the business for Rob, I had to remodel the store to our liking. The very first day after we purchased the store, I got rid of the shotgun and all the signs on the walls. At once, I started doing the construction work at night, after my work at San-Val. I would go to the shop from work around 6:00 p.m. and stay until 11:00 or later, as well as on all weekends. The dark paneling on the wall had to go first. I like a well-lit bright store, and what we had on the walls was not what I had in mind. I removed all the wall brackets and merchandise, then removed several wall panels each night. I patched the walls and painted them a Navajo White color. I only removed a few sections at a time so I could have things ready for business the next day. I also covered up the showcases and merchandise and vacuumed the floors before going home. The first few days I had Rob and Elaine help me with removing merchandise and covering up things. While doing the remodeling work at night while the store was closed I ended up having some run-ins with the law.

The store had a silent alarm system that was wired very strangely, on purpose. On the walls and inside some wall partitions Don had used old telephone lines for part of the silent alarm system wiring. It looked like old abandoned wiring, and it soon got me in trouble. The third night while I was working inside the store, I removed some of the temporary walls in the back room, not realizing that some of the walls had some of these old telephone lines. As I removed walls, I cut the old wiring; that got me into my first trouble with Burbank's finest.

Around 9:00 p.m. the telephone rang; it was our alarm company. The alarm company was supposed to call the police department if the silent alarm went off. Right after that they would call us at home and then at the store. I had just picked up the phone and had barely said a few words when they quickly asked for our code. I gave it to her and asked what was wrong. She told me that the silent alarm had been set off and she had already called the police department. They were en route. Just as she said that, I heard a knock at the front door.

I had my tool belt on and a hammer in my hand. "Oh shit," I said to Rob and Elaine. "We set off the damn silent alarm." They were working on the other side of the shop and had no idea what was going on. I told them that the police were here, and as I walked towards the front, I put down the hammer. I opened the door to see a police car with flashing blue lights, and two police officers standing there. I raised my hands. The officers had shotguns in their hands and I wanted them to stay calm. I told them that we were doing remodeling and had accidentally cut the silent alarm wires. They came in to check things out. By this time they also saw Rob and Elaine. They asked for my ID, which I took out of my wallet. Police were at our back door also. "What a great response time," I told them.

It was good to know that help had been on the way in less than a couple of minutes. Burbank has a great police and fire department. We talked with the officers a few minutes, telling them that we were the new owners, and once they realized what we were doing, they filled out a false alarm report, which we had to sign. If you get three of them a year, they fine you. That episode was over, but it was not the last episode with the alarm system.

I remodeled the showroom and the back room in just a few weeks. I also built an 8' x 10' office in the back and had just hung the new door and was nailing on the door trim. I was almost 100% finished with the remodeling. I already rewired the entire alarm system, so I knew where everything was as far as wiring, switches, and everything that belonged to the alarm system. It was almost midnight and I had only ten more minutes to go when the alarm was set off again. I was at the store alone, which was typical. While I was finishing up with nailing the molding on the door, the vibration set off the alarm without my knowledge. There was a silent alarm switch close to where I was nailing. I knew about it and was trying to be careful not to set it off, but the switch was more sensitive than I realized. The alarm company once again called the police and then called my house, according to standard procedures. My wife told them that I was at the store working alone, and then she got very nervous. She could not know what was happening at the store, and of course, she started imagining the worst.

Just as the phone rang, the cops were at the door. I motioned to them to wait a second while I answered the phone. It was the alarm company telling me that the silent alarm was set off. I gave them the code number and told them that the police were at the door. I hung up and soon the phone rang again. I let it ring and opened the door for the police, who were there with their shotguns. I told them what had happened and then picked up the phone, which was still ringing. It was my very nervous wife. I told her all was OK, and that the police were already there, and that I would be home in a half-hour. I knew one of the police officers, because he had been in our store a few weekends before. He recognized me and put away his gun, and told his partner that I was the owner. Once again I got a false alarm notice. Luckily that was the last of those.

The remodeling project came out real well and ahead of schedule. I wanted the construction to be over as soon as possible and had therefore worked long hours every night. The remodeling came in over my budget because I also installed a ducted central air conditioning and heating system. Prior to the remodeling, we had a couple of gas-fired wall heaters and a swamp cooler. In the summertime when Don owned the business the store would get up to 85 or 90 degrees, without air conditioning. According to my son who worked there, Don lost a lot of business because of that. People don't want to stay in a hot store. The next project for me at the store was to get a few new showcases and to repaint the existing showcases. I ordered light gray colored showcases with white interior; then I painted the existing showcases the same color. I used high quality epoxy paint. Once we were finished, the store looked great and we got lots of compliments from our customers.

I finished the construction in only a few weeks, without shutting down for remodeling. What a difference! In just a few weeks the store was brighter and friendlier and more comfortable. It was a good investment. A few weeks after I finished the remodeling, Don Osborne came by on a Saturday while I was at the store. He was shocked and asked what we'd done to the showcases that he'd built. He was upset that I had changed his creations from a dark brown to a bright light gray exterior, but he got over it fast.

Soon after we bought the business, Rob hired his first employee, Marco. Not long after, Elaine gave up her volunteer work at Muir Jr. High School in order to help Rob at our store. She would do bookkeeping, answer the phones and deal with some of the customers. I set up an easy-to-use bookkeeping and payroll system. Having Elaine at the store was a big help for Rob. Besides, she was not getting paid! After Elaine became very ill, she could no longer work and was confined to our home. Rob hired more help and he also hired our niece Carrie, who was looking for a job at the time. Carrie took over Elaine's duties. Carrie was the daughter of Elaine's sister Elanor.

I invested more money into the business to buy new equipment and more inventory. When I retired from San-Val I had been thinking about retiring in San Diego. I love the climate there. I was helping Rob a few hours a week and did some volunteer work on Mondays at McKinley School, a local elementary school in Burbank. I would help in math class with kids who needed math tutoring.

My plan was to help Rob for about 20 hours a week and do other things the rest of the time, like volunteering at McKinley School. I also wanted to do more traveling. But Rob soon asked me if I could give him more time. Why not? He didn't have to pay me, and besides, I took on more and more responsibilities. That allowed him to concentrate on other things. I was not one for just sitting around. I took care of customers, organized things and constantly made more shelves. We always needed to make more room for new merchandise. Not long after I came to Rob, we discontinued stamps and foreign coins. They were a very small part of our business and we needed more room for our expanding sportscards business. In 1990 we also decided to eliminate the comic books.

Soon after I came to the store, I brought one of my computers to the shop. I wanted to use it for bookkeeping and inventory work. Rob was not crazy about it, because it took up a big portion of my desk. He knew nothing about computers and did not want one in the store. I told him that computers would play a big role in our store in years to come, but he just put it down as nonsense. I kept the computer at the store and did more and more work on it. Rob soon changed his thinking. We now have12 computers in our store, including our own server.

In this business we sort and price a lot of sportscards. One day Rob pulled me aside and told me that he suspected that one of our employee was stealing cards, not just sorting them. Some of the more expensive cards were missing, and Rob wanted to know what to do. He thought that our employee was hiding some of the cards in his shirt pocket. I told Rob that he should confront him at once and ask him if he had taken any cards. I also told Rob that he should ask him to empty his pockets. At first Rob hesitated. I told Rob that this was business, and not to worry about it, just do what has to be done.

Rob went in the back room where the young man was working and told him that he suspected him of stealing. Rob told him that he had noticed many expensive cards missing from the brands he was working on. Rob then ordered him to empty all his pockets. The kid got a little nervous and started to cry. Reluctantly he emptied his pockets, and there were some of the missing cards. Rob fired him on the spot. He was mad! He had ⁓⁓pected him of stealing, but did not want to believe it.

My son had to grow up fast. Running a business requires tough decisions, but they must be made. Years later we had to fire two other employees because of stealing.

Soon I was working 40 or more hours a week. I was forced to quit my volunteer work at the school after only a few months. It felt good to work with children and help them, but my son needed me. It was actually just what the doctor ordered!

On Monday, January 17, 1994 at 4:30 a.m., a strong earthquake roughly awakened me. I woke up Elaine and had her stand under the doorway with me. The house shook like crazy for about 30 seconds. Once the shaking subsided, I put on clothes and shoes and ran around the house to check for damage. There was no visible damage and I smelled no gas. I called up Rob to check on them and told him that I was going to the shop to check things out. I told Elaine to call Amy and the rest of the family to make sure everybody was OK. I told her I would call as soon as I got to the shop.

In just a few minutes I was at the store, as was Rob. We could not believe our eyes. Our store got hit real hard, as did the rest of the stores

The mess from the January 17, 1994 earthquake. Hundreds of
thousands of sportscards were all over the floor.

on our block. In contrast, there was very little damage across the street or on the next block from us.

The Northridge earthquake had a magnitude of 6.7, and had struck a densely populated area of northern Los Angeles. Thank God there were few casualties, but economic losses were estimated at $20 billion. Sections of two of our major freeways collapsed, as did some bridges. The rebuilding of our freeways took months and created a traffic nightmare for motorists.

We lost the entire front of the store. Huge plate glass windows were shattered, and inventory had been thrown off the shelves. Hundreds of thousands of sportscards were all over the floor. We looked at each other in disbelief. Rob was on the verge of tears, as was I, but I told him that everything would be OK. We just had to get to work and clean up the mess. The store had an accordion metal gate across the full width of the shop. The shop was secured, other than the merchandise near the now shattered front windows.

I opened the locked gate and carefully went inside to check things out. I called Elaine, but did not tell her the full magnitude of the damage. I decided to get a barrel and shovel from the back room, and started to pick up the broken plate glass. That was not an easy task. The broken glass was very heavy, so we put only a small amount of glass inside the barrel, which was hard to lift. We filled our dumpster in the back with broken glass and wood. Some of our employees came by to also give us a hand. We needed all the help we could get!

Shortly after the earthquake, police cruisers came by to make sure no looting was taking place. As soon as our nearest lumberyard opened, I went and purchased plywood and 2 x 4's to board up the shop. Some of us worked on the outside, while I had some of them start the clean-up inside. We lost lots of cards because they got damaged, but it could have been much worse. We had no earthquake insurance for the damaged merchandise. The cards were housed in 3,200 count boxes. They had vibrated off the wood-shelving units. Some were completely destroyed. Mondays we were normally closed, but I was determined to open for business the following day, if only on a limited basis.

By the next day, Tuesday, the store was boarded up, but I painted on the plywood that we were open for business. The store was very dark now, due to the boarded-up windows. (Being in the construction

The property I purchased for our new store in June 1996.

Remodeling for a new showroom, July 1996.

business came in handy, and I did a good job with that.) At least the store was secure once again. We did very little business the next few weeks. It gave us time to sort all the cards that had fallen off the walls. All cards had been in year, brand and card number order. That was a monumental job, but one that had to be done.

It was the responsibility of our landlord to have the front of our store replaced. I designed a better front entrance and asked if they would do it that way. It was also cheaper. The landlord then fixed the front of our store just as I designed it. Now the store had a more modern look, and we gained 20 square feet of store space. We had a great landlord, but we were a very good tenant also. We did a lot of improvement to the building and we always paid our rent on time. Our rent was fair, but we had to do all interior improvements.

Soon after the Northridge earthquake, we started to look for a larger building. Rob's business was going well but we were limited in our growth by the size of the store. For months we looked at larger stores but we liked none of them. We wanted to stay in Burbank but the asking prices were outrageously high for a 4,000 square foot or larger building. Finally, in June 1996, I purchased a 4,100 square foot building only two blocks from our store on Magnolia Boulevard. This building had also suffered heavy damage because of the earthquake, and needed a great deal of work. The building had been closed since the quake. I was interested in the building in 1995 but the owner asked a lot more for the building than what it was worth. He also rejected an offer from me in early 1995. I made a new attempt in early 1996 to buy the building and after months of bargaining, I purchased it. I actually paid less for the building than I had offered a year earlier.

I designed the new store and worked hard between the store and the remodeling. I had to do much of the work myself in order to save money and to make sure that the work would be done right. I had sold most of my stocks to finance the purchase and the construction. The building was more than twice the size of our old store, and was modern. I acted as my own general contractor and also did a lot of the labor. I hired subcontractors for several trades but did the design for each trade myself. I also decided to make the shelving units differently. I tilted the shelf 5 degrees towards the wall. I also reduced the spacing between shelves. I did that to cut down on shelf vibration

The finished building, September 1996.

The new showroom is bright and beautifull.

and to have the boxes slide against the wall in case of an earthquake, not onto the floor.

Everything went as planned and the job came in right at our budget. The construction was first class and Rob loved the final product, as did everybody else. In less than three months, construction was completed, and we moved into our new store, without losing a day of business. We did most of the moving on Mondays when we were closed. We moved over four million sportscards. The new store was bright and comfortable.

Rob at his desk working on his card purchases.

Family partnership. Me, Elaine and Robert in 1999.

34

A Sportscard Empire

Shortly after moving into our new building in 1996, I decided to create a Web site for our business. That was new to almost everybody; very few companies had a Web site. Most people did not even know what the Internet, or "World-Wide Web" was all about. It took a few years, but as computers and technology improved, so did Web sites. I decided to stay on top of it, besides the many other things I was doing. I was into the latest in computer technology. There were no easy software programs to use and so most of the work had to be done manually in HTML (Hypertext Markup Language).

Bill Rini, a friend of my son, was very knowledgeable in Web design and helped me set up our first Web site. Thanks, Bill! We were one of the first in our industry to have a Web site and might even have been the very first. Our first site was very primitive as far as today's standards go, but I learned a lot. Today our Web site is state-of-the-art, at "burbanksportscards.com," and is being used by thousands of our customers. It has over 740,000 cards online and you can just click on an item and buy it. It has great search features and is very easy to use. I have redesigned our Web site more than 10 times since we created it. We make changes to it on a regular basis. We are never satisfied, but are constantly looking for better ways to capture new customers.

Once we were in our new building, we were able to grow. We increased inventory and purchased additional showcases. Our new computerized cash-register system had a scanner to scan products. This speeded up the checkout process. Soon we would hire additional employees. Rob was starting to be more involved in the sportscards industry and I was happy to see that. Our name and reputation in the industry was in the top few. Beckett Publications out of Texas hired Rob as a regional pricing consultant. Beckett is a great organization, and they are respected in the industry as the best in their field. We offered pricing advice to them, as did several other regional consultants in other parts of the country.

Over the years we became very close with Beckett, and were called upon for advice on many topics besides just pricing. Rob was also asked to write monthly articles for *Card Trade*, a trade publication. After writing dozens of full-page articles, he can write one in about an hour. He is great at it. Our long-term plan was working, and things were falling into place. We wanted to increase our mail-order business and become the best in the industry. I felt very comfortable with our progress, but I wanted to control our rate of growth. I did not want Rob to overextend himself.

In late 1998 and early 1999 we received several major inquiries from major players in the industry. They picked Rob's brain regarding new products or future products in the pipeline. Rob would talk on the phone with them for long periods of time. Sometimes he talked longer than was needed; he loves to talk on the phone!

Rob was also invited as a guest speaker at some of Alan Narz's seminars sponsored by Topps Company. Rob liked speaking in front of his peers. Months later he was approached by the Upper Deck Company to put on a seminar for dealers all over the country. Rob was ecstatic! What an opportunity! Not so fast, I told him. I want to see the proposal and read between the lines. Their legal department had drawn it up. I crossed out a third of the agreement, added our own notes, and negotiated a higher fee. Rembrandt, a sportscards supplies company, came on board to be a cosponsor of the seminar. It took only a few weeks to negotiate the contract.

Rob and I designed the all-day seminar. Rob wrote the text of what he was going to talk about, and I did the rest, including taking all the pictures. The seminar was going to concentrate on organization and offer solutions to sportscards shops, for the benefit of the industry. Rembrandt was going to take our text and photos and put it all into a PowerPoint presentation. They purchased a digital projector and sound system, and we were going to use my laptop computer for the show.

The first seminar was going to be in San Jose in Northern California. Eight days before the seminar, we were going to give a sneak preview test seminar to the folks at Upper Deck Company, in Carlsbad, California.

I got the PowerPoint presentation and the projector from Rembrandt two days prior to our test seminar. I had gone with Rob to run the equipment, and the presentation at Upper Deck went smoothly. Rob did well, and the people at Upper Deck were happy. We looked forward to our first "real" seminar in eight days. On our drive home I starting to think about the way the presentation had been put together by Rembrandt. I told Rob that I'd fix it up a little bit because it was dull. Rob agreed that it could use a little help.

The problem was that I had no experience with the PowerPoint software. I went to CompuServe and picked up a book on PowerPoint, then I decided to create a brand new presentation. After I was done with it, it had sound and pictures that looked alive, special effects, and much more. The day before we left for San Jose, I had Rob come over with his wife and his son. I lied, and told Rob that I had made only a few changes.

Rob's jaw dropped when the presentation started. He looked at me and could not believe what I had done. He gave me a huge hug. I'd worked on it for six days, with only a few hours of sleep per night. The hard work paid off. The first seminar was a huge success and the folks at Upper Deck and Rembrandt were elated. They just loved it, and we received praise from everybody. Things were going well but new surprises were just a few months away.

One day we received a call from a new company called Ace Sportscards (not their real name), near San Diego. They wanted to create the ultimate sportscards site on the Internet. They wanted us to provide them with an exclusive arrangement whereby we would provide sportscards to them as a third party provider. They were also lining up other providers for memorabilia, which we do not carry. Rob was jumping for joy, he was so excited! A few days later they came to our shop to check out our operation.

Their jaw dropped when they saw what we had in inventory, and the organization we had in place. Rob talked with them for about an hour while I attended to my duties. After they left, Rob told me how impressed they were with our operation and that they wanted us as their anchor. We were going to be their key supplier. This was the call Rob had been waiting for. The company had a lot of money behind them.

They also wanted to add a scan of every sportscard into their Web site, including common cards. They wanted to use our inventory for that purpose. I told Rob that before we got into any agreement, we should get it in writing — what they needed from us and what they had in mind as far as terms and compensation. Talking details is OK, but then it needs to be put in writing so that both sides can fully understand their responsibilities. I was the calm one who had to slow things down and get things from the talking phase into a detailed, written proposal.

Two days later Ace Sportscards e-mailed a proposal that did not impress us. It was all one-sided. They wanted an exclusive deal with us. They also wanted us to get rid of our Web site because it would be a conflict of interest. We said no to both. We decided we wanted to see their facilities before further negotiations, to meet with their programmers and see what they were doing. They had a beta Web site under construction.

Several days later we met with Ace Sportscards at their facility. They showed us their operation and we talked at length with their chief programmer. I listened to their grandiose plans and we looked at the Web site under construction. Rob liked the glitzy home page and the numerous photos, but I was not impressed. They had the technical knowledge to design a nice Web site, but had made theirs impractical and overbearing. It was also hard to navigate. Our suggestions were in vain. They knew what they wanted, and they only wanted our inventory, not our advice. They were the experts and we were just a supplier. That was a big mistake on their part.

On our way home I told Rob that there was no possible way this company would make it for more than a year or two. They did not know the sportscards business. Rob, on the other hand, seemed impressed with the concept and the Web site. Rob likes fancy Web sites, as do many other people. I prefer practical, easy-to-navigate sites. I felt that their concept was ill conceived.

The following day we sent Ace Sportscards our terms for a contract. We told them than under no condition would we give them or anybody else an exclusive agreement. We were already supplying hundreds of dealers and we were expanding that part of our business every year. We also told them that our Web site was online before they were in business and we would never give it up. In our counter-proposal we stated our other terms and the discounts we would give them.

A few hours after we e-mailed our proposal, Rob received a not-so-happy phone call from them. They were very angry with us and told us that they couldn't consider our terms and conditions. They were going to get another supplier. We told them to do what was right for them and wished them good luck.

For weeks they looked for a new supplier, but found none to their liking. They came back with a more reasonable proposal and still wanted us as their sportscards supplier. They had accepted almost everything in our proposal, but wanted to get a better discount. We gave them a little better discount and signed on the dotted line. The discounts we gave them were no better than the discount we gave to our other good dealers. They did not merit special treatment as far as we were concerned.

Two months after we signed, we received a call from the second highest officer at Beckett Publications, Mark Harwell, Vice President. He wanted to meet with us regarding a project they had in mind. A few days later, Mark came to our store to give us an insight as to what they were planning. Rob and I were surprised. They wanted to set up a Web site portal for about a hundred dealers. They would design the Web site with input from us, and they would charge a fee for items sold on their site. Because at the time it was confidential information, we were to keep it between the three of us until they had the portal operational. Mark told us that they already had programmers working on it. They would also hire outside consultants to help with this major undertaking. They would call it the "Beckett Marketplace" on their site. They already had a great, easy-to-use Web page for pricing and player checklists at "beckett.com."

Now we were much more interested, because Beckett has been in business for a very long time and had a great reputation. From the first meeting we had with Mark, I knew the project would be first-rate and successful. There was no "we know it all" type of attitude with the folks at Beckett. That is why they came to us. They knew of our operation and that there was nobody else who could help them as

328 / A Light In The Distance

much as we could. Besides, we already had experience in Web site sales and we were the largest sportscards shop in the world, to the best of our knowledge. Beckett wanted us to help them with testing of the Web site design prior to its going live. They needed a dealer's point of view. In return for our help, we would be the only dealer on the system until the site was fully operational. We would have a couple of months to ourselves with no competition on the Beckett portal.

Because of our confidential agreement with Ace Sportscards, we did not tell Beckett that there was another Web site in the works. We gave Mark ideas and he took lots of notes. Mark is highly educated and a brilliant guy and I love him, even when he uses words I don't know. Sometimes I had to remind him to talk at my level. Rob would laugh at some of the words Mark used because he knew that I probably did not know what Mark had just said.

Mark, Rob and I made a great team. Beckett would mail me Beta copies of the program for testing. I would evaluate and give them feedback as to what looked good and what needed improvement. Hundreds of e-mails were exchanged between Beckett and me during the design. They also flew me down to Dallas for a few days to meet with their staff and programmers in order to get everybody coordinated. It was a very successful trip to Texas.

While Ace Sportscards and Beckett were designing their new Web sites, Rob received a call from Don Jones (not his real name), the CEO of one of the largest manufacturers of sportscards. I'll call them Company A. They had something new in mind and wanted to meet with us to discuss their ideas. Rob said OK; they would set a date within a few days. When Rob told me what was going on, I was taken by surprise. Things were happening very quickly and we were right in the middle of it.

Rob was glowing and could not wait for the meeting. After thinking about it, Rob and I decided that maybe we should tell Don Jones to have Beckett at the meeting also. We talked with Beckett and Don Jones and told them of a "what if" proposition without giving anything away. Finally, Don Jones decided that Burbank Sportscards should set up a meeting at our store for the five of us: Dr. James Beckett (owner of Beckett), Mark Harwell (his vice president), Don Jones (CEO of Company A), Rob, and myself.

Our industry's most powerful people were to meet with us at our store. That showed the respect these people had for Burbank Sportscards. Don Jones laid out his plan, which was very similar to what Beckett was already working on. Don wanted us to be an exclusive supplier to them, to which I said sorry, but we can't be exclusive to anybody. "Company A" was a powerhouse in the sportscards manufacturing business. Nobody ever said no to Don Jones. Well, they would have to pay us a lot of money up front before I would say yes. Soon Mark interrupted Don. He told him about the Web portal they were ready to go online with. This was the reason we wanted Don to talk to Beckett, so they wouldn't waste a lot of money. There was no room at this time for two big sportscards portals.

It was a good meeting, and Don Jones and Dr. Beckett also had a chance to see our operation first-hand. I know they were impressed. It was not clear as to what would happen next, but I think the meeting was a setback for Company A's plans. They shelved them, at least for a while. We did not bring up the name of the other entry into the field, Ace Sportscards.

A few months later, Ace Sportscards went live with their Web site. Sure enough, their operation was flawed from the minute they went live. We supplied cards, sets, boxes, and supplies, but they were doing less than 10% of the business they had forecasted. They had big plans and big expectations, but no experience. In less than a year they were out of business, just as I had predicted.

In late October 1999, Beckett went live with the Beckett Marketplace. It was not 100% ready, but they wanted to get online experience as early as possible. I was sending numerous e-mails per day to my contact, Airey Baringer at Beckett, regarding changes that needed to be made or bugs that needed to be corrected. They worked hard and had most bugs out of the system the first few weeks. We made a great team, and the site came out fantastic! By January 2000, Beckett was signing up new dealers to their Marketplace site. It was an easy sell. If it was good enough for Burbank Sportscards, then it was good enough for them. We were a big draw. We are the largest dealer on the site and have by far the most cards, photos and supplies online.

In early November of 2001, we received a call from another wannabe sportscards portal. I'll call them Company B. They are located in the

Los Angeles area, and they have other business interests in the sportscards business. They are also sportscards show promoters. We have known them for several years, and have done business with them in the past on a small scale. They wanted to set-up a Web portal, something similar to what Beckett has done, and wanted us as their key supplier. Having us on their portal would give the site instant credibility. We would make their site legit.

They also wanted us to maintain our full inventory on their computer. I would not allow that on a major scale. To maintain inventory control on several sites is a monumental task and can't be done very easily. It was not an option for us. We decided to stop and think about this. I told Rob that before we went any further we would need to come up with a different game plan for Company B and other possible future clients.

A few months prior to receiving Company B's inquiry, I was already talking with Beckett regarding setting up a more advanced database for us. The plan was to have a separate server host the site and allow other companies to tie into it or into part of it, at our option. We would set up links for other e-commerce sites whereby their customers could pull inventory off our site without them knowing that they were on the Burbank Sportscards server.

Our server would act as a ghost server, but portals like Company B would generate the order forms. Only if we set up a system like that would I go forward with other portals. We talked with Beckett again and they agreed to do it for us for a fair price. This way we could maintain much better inventory control and eliminate a big headache. Rob liked the idea. I gave Beckett the go-ahead. From that point forward, if somebody wanted us to supply them with sportscards, they would have to link to our server — otherwise we wouldn't do business with them.

Our state-of-the-art Web site made it easier for people to purchase cards without leaving their home. A collector would have to travel to maybe a dozen stores to find what they could find on our site in just minutes. We put a great deal of work into it, and it was finally working out as we hoped it would. I do wish I knew a lot more about sportscards. It would make my job a lot easier, but I leave that portion of the business in Rob's hands. My wife at times was afraid we were buying too much inventory. I would tell her not to worry; things are going well.

Our shop is busy and we have 14 employees, many of them part-time. While we have a large store, it's already too small for what we need to do. We have new and exiting things lined up to expand our sales opportunities. We are receiving calls from major e-commerce players monthly.

As I helped Rob build his sportscards empire, I realized I had unexpectedly found a new "love" for myself. I love to watch Rob operate, and we are very proud of him.

By November 2001, we were already involved with several other e-commerce sites and were shipping nearly 200 orders a day. Some days we would ship over 250 orders. Our mail order business is more than 85% of our business. It's time to be very selective and do things on our terms, not on other's terms. We are the largest sportscards shop in the world — they need us more than we need them.

A busy pack war Saturday at Burbank Sportscards. Rob in the middle.

Major League baseball players Fred Lynn and Steve Garvey at our store.

35

Giving Back to the Community

We live in the greatest country on earth, mainly because of the generosity of its citizens, the millions who volunteer or financially support worthwhile causes. For over 35 years I have supported numerous causes, and in recent years, more than ever. I'm proud to live in this country and do my part for the benefit of others, just as others helped me in my time of need. I hope I repaid my debt many times over, but in my heart I know I need to do more. I intend to do that for the rest of my life because of what I feel for this country. I'm just glad that God gave me the opportunity and health to do so. It gives me a great feeling when I support a worthy cause.

One of the many ways I contribute is through our Burbank Kiwanis Club. I had rejoined the Burbank Kiwanis Club after I had closed San-Val. What a great organization! Kiwanis International is a worldwide organization serving the needy in our communities. Each chapter does things a little differently and supports different causes. Our chapter supports many worthwhile causes, by volunteerism or financial aid. Most of the money we raise is for the youth in our community.

Our Kiwanis Club sponsors a very active Key Club at the Burbank High School, with a membership of over 200 students in the year 2001 — a great bunch of kids, who work hard on community projects.

Our club also adopted the McKinley School. Members of the Kiwanis, along with the Burbank High School Key Club, painted the hallways inside the school, which had not been painted for about 10 years. I was in charge of that project; the club paid for all the paint and other supplies. The school really seemed to appreciate what we did for

A big Thank You note on the corridor wall at McKinley School
after our club members and our Burbank High Key Club
painted the corridor walls.

them. The hallways looked great. The kids at school made up a big thank you poster thanking our club and the Key Club for the work we did. Thanks, guys who helped with the project!

During the mid 1990s, I was asked to serve on the Board of Directors, and proudly accepted. In 1999 I became the club's president as we entered the new millennium. What a great honor! I instituted new programs, which were very successful.

Our members give so much for others, and during my term as president, I felt it was time to do something for our members. I ran a computer class for the members and friends of Kiwanis. We had over 20 people in the class. The computer course covered basic understanding of computers, Microsoft Word, Excel, and Adobe Photo Deluxe, a photo editing software. I also provided a step-by-step instruction manual.

Herb, our Kiwanis editor, took the course. After the third week of the class, our weekly Kiwanis bulletin started to look a lot better. Herb no longer glued a photo on the bulletin before making his copies. He cropped the photo, then imported it into the text at the right size to fit the space available. He would make some photos darker or lighter to improve the quality of the photo. He asked a lot of questions in class and was one of my best students. Herb proudly showed off his new skills in the bulletin. Great job, Herb!

After we completed the 8-week course, I conducted a few advanced classes for the club, but limited the class to six people. That was a hands-on learning class and required prior computer experience. My students are still showing me new things that they learned because of our computer class. It was a hit!

While we have our pet projects, we also undertake some special fundraising. One of our members, Victor Georgino, convinced our club to support a Habitat for Humanity project in Burbank. Our city has never done a project like that, but we thought it was a great idea. Victor got our Kiwanis Club and the entire community involved. We raised over $110,000 for the multi-unit project and had the city give us the land that was turned over to Habitat for Humanity. It was a very successful project. I physically worked several Saturdays on the job and ran large crews. It felt good because I knew it was for a great cause.

The finished Habitat for Humanity project in Burbank
was started by our Burbank Kiwanis Club.

It was a dream come true for eight lucky families, because of the vision of one man. Thank You, Victor!

It was my turn next to get the club involved into another major fundraiser. It all started with a newspaper article.

Late in the evening of May 14, 1997, Burbank resident Agustin Luz had cautiously answered a knock at his door. It was Sharon McPhearson, a 43-year-old widowed mother of six, whose car had ran out of gas on Glenoaks Blvd., stranding her and three of her children. She was in town looking for a job. Though it was late at night, and she was a total stranger, Agustin, himself a father of two small children, did not hesitate in coming to her aid.

He offered to go and get gas for her car, and upon his return he and Sharon started to transfer the gas into the gas tank. With the gas tank on the driver's side of the vehicle, Sharon and Agustin were forced to stand on the street-side to put the gas in. As the children watched in horror, their mother, along with the Good Samaritan who had come to the family's aid, were suddenly struck by a hit-and-run drunk driver.

Sharon McPhearson died at the scene. Severely injured, Agustin Luz was rushed to the hospital in critical condition. He was hospitalized for more than two months and required four surgeries. He had a broken neck, broken back, and a broken leg. Dozens of stainless steel pins and screws were used to repair the countless broken bones., Agustin and his family now faced an uncertain future, because Agustin was their sole provider. The tragedy was overwhelming for both families.

After Agustin was released from the hospital, on July 26, 1997, our local newspaper, *The Burbank Leader,* did an article on him. A picture showed him in a halo head brace to hold his head in place while his neck healed. He also had a body brace. The article with the heading "SOMEHOW, HE'S STILL SMILING" caught my eye as I read the paper that night.

I was on the verge of tears as I showed the article to Elaine. I told Elaine that we should help the family. She agreed. Because of the article, I knew he lived on Glenoaks Boulevard near the Burbank High School. In less than a minute I had looked up his telephone number, and the following morning I called him. I told him that I had read the article and would like to help them get on their feet. Agustin and his wife Beatriz had two daughters, Melanie, four years old, and Veronica, seven months old. I offered to buy food for them and take it to them around noon, if it was OK with them. I asked what they needed from the grocery store. They asked for only a few things, like milk for the baby, diapers, baby food, and maybe some fruit. When I asked what their daughter Melanie would like, I heard her say in the background, "Coco Puffs cereal!"

It was time to go shopping at Hughes, our local market. We filled our shopping cart with lots of goodies, including meat, vegetables, canned goods, diapers, baby food, fruits, pastries, paper goods, and other items we hoped they could use. Just before noon, Elaine and I arrived at their apartment with seven bags of groceries, not knowing what to expect as we knocked on the door. Mrs. Luz opened the door and welcomed us into their home, a small one-bedroom apartment.

After introducing ourselves, we took the seven bags into the kitchen and put them on the kitchen table and on the counter top. They were shocked when we walked in with all those bags. In just a few minutes Beatriz took us into the bedroom where her husband was lying, and introduced us. It was not a very pleasant sight. He was in that awful-looking contraption that was holding his head in the proper alignment for healing. He greeted us with a warm smile and a handshake. While we were talking, little Melanie came into the room. She was all smiles; she said "Hi" and gave Elaine and me a kiss. She thanked us for her Coco Puffs. She was a shy girl but a real darling. In that moment, her smile made it all worthwhile.

We stayed for a while and talked, and as we were leaving, I told them that we would help them with their groceries every week for months, if need be, and that I would talk to some friends of mine and see if we could help them even more. The lives of this young Mexican family deserved my help and the help of others. As we walked to our car I felt good, as did my wife. It was only the beginning.

As I checked into the details of the accident, I found that this horrible event would have been much worse, if not for the generosity of Lt. Ed Skavarna of the Burbank Police Department. Here's a guy who never saw Sharon McPhearson before in his life, yet he reached into his own pocket to buy over $1,000 worth of airline tickets for five of the dead woman's kids, ages 4 to 17, so they could be with family in Cincinnati, Ohio, during this traumatic time instead of being placed with the L.A. County Department of Children's Services, which would have split them up. Carry Brown, Sharon's oldest daughter (herself a 24-year-old mother of two) lived in Cincinnati. She did not have the money to bring the five orphaned children back for the funeral, but agreed to bring them if someone paid the airfare. Later on, when American Airlines found out what had happened, they picked up the tab. I have known Ed Skavarna for several years. He is our customer and a very good friend of ours. Great job, Ed! You have heart and compassion.

The following week we went shopping again for the Luz family, but by then I decided to make this a much larger undertaking. I was determined to help both families whose lives had been changed forever. These two families needed much more than just food. I started making calls to friends and business associates. The following week at our Kiwanis board of directors meeting, I called on our club to help me in this major undertaking and to make it a club project. I asked them to help me help both families. Before the evening was over, the Burbank Kiwanis Club had committed $5,000 as seed money for the two families. This was only the beginning.

Within a week I sent out over 150 letters to club member and friends of Kiwanis. I mailed several hundred flyers to local businesses asking for their help. I contacted the local NBC station and they did a plug for our fundraiser. One of the first offers and our largest financial help came from a local restaurant in Burbank. Mr. James Lucero, owner of the Smoke House restaurant, pledged to buy food for the Luz family for a year. Other offers poured in. Donations from $1 to hundreds of dollars were received from local citizens and businesses. Hundreds of wonderful and giving people made this project a success.

A member of our club suggested that I contact Scott Harris, a friend of his, who was a reporter at the L.A. Times. I did just that. I asked Scott to write a story about this accident and the fundraiser we were doing for both families. Scott wrote a great article. Many more donations came because of that article. Thanks, Scott!

The generosity of club members and friends of Kiwanis was more than I expected. They gave without hesitation. One of our club members, pledged $100 per month for a full year, and another member $100 every other month. Checks were arriving from club members at a rate

In 1998, about a year after the accident, the Luz family joins me and Gary Kessler (President of our club) at one of our weekly meetings.

that surpassed any other fundraiser. Besides our club members, I got help from many local businesses and service organizations. I spoke at several service club meetings and received generous donations, especially one from the Sertoma Club of Burbank, who donated a very generous $1,000 to this cause. The Burbank Fire Fighters kicked in $500, and Hydro-Aire, Inc. of Burbank a very generous $1,500, which was followed by two more checks the following two Christmases. Kids' clothing from Disney Studios was a big hit with both families. I was sending clothing to Ohio as well as money.

The first three weeks most of the support was for the Luz family, until we started to get donations, then we started to issue checks at least once a month to both families, and on many occasions twice a month. Most of the payments were $1,000 or $1,500 per check to each family.

At first I was told that the hit-and-run driver had no insurance. After the driver was caught I found out from inside sources that, at the time of the accident, he had insurance. He had made his monthly payment on the insurance policy, then he allowed the policy to lapse. At the time of the accident, he had insurance, but it was cancelled for non-payment a few days later.

I got the name of the carrier and the policy number. (It's nice to have friends in high places sometimes.) I called a friend of mine, Dean Levin, son of our good friends Irv and Lil Levin, for advice. Dean is an attorney in Woodland Hills. He told me what to do, and that I didn't need an attorney for what I had in mind. The following day I filed a claim on behalf of both families for the policy amount of $15,000. I sent copies of police reports and all other papers as requested. The claim was honored and payment of $15,000 was made to both families on May 21, 1998.

We had a trust account set up for the McPhearson kids. I also contacted several Kiwanis Clubs in the Cincinnati area as well as several local papers and asked for their help. I sent them all the details and the *Cincinnati Enquirer* did an article. We received over 20 donations because of that article. Some of the donations had letters or notes attached. One of the letters made me proud to have started this project. Susan Grote of Cincinnati saw the article and sent a $500 check, along with a wonderful letter. In that letter she wrote, "I realize money can't replace the children's mother," but she hoped the check

Proud member of the Burbank Kiwanis Club, serving the community.
My family joined me at my installation as President of the
Burbank kiwanis Club, October 1, 1999.

would help. Thank you, Susan and thank you, all who made this worthwhile undertaking an overwhelming success! This is what makes this country great!

Our Kiwanis Club supported both families for almost three years. By the time the Luz-McPhearson Relief fund was closed and the final checks were distributed on June 7, 2000, the lives of both families were quite different from the first day I had knocked on the door of the Luz household. Agustin was back at work fulltime, and an aunt, Cindy Thompson, had adopted the five orphaned McPhearson kids. The kids are happy and now live in a stable household. God bless all of you.

Before I finished with that project, I was into my second major fundraiser. This time it was for the Kosovo refugees. I was the ringleader once again and got my Kiwanis Club involved. The plight of the refugees as described in the news hit home. I knew how the refugees felt. I could not stand by and do nothing while they were starving. Our club and friends of Kiwanis showed their generosity once again. The raised monies were turned over to the Burbank Chapter of the American Red Cross Kosovo Relief Fund. Thanks, everybody!

This is what most service organizations do, all around the country. They bring help to those in need. Our club, the Kiwanis Club of Burbank, has been serving our community for over 76 years. I salute all men and women who belong to service organizations!

Surprise party for me in July 1998.
Elaine and Amy singing "My Way" their way.

The kids are eating it up, they got me good.
Sally, Shil, Amy and Rob.

36

My Wonderfull Family

I had In July of 1998, Elaine and my kids turned the tables on me. It was payback for what I did for Elaine. Every few months Rob and I go to a manufacturer's night meeting. Rob told me that the next one would be held at the Castaways Restaurant in Burbank, and if I wanted to bring Elaine it would be OK. Later that day in the store Rob asked Elaine if she would like to come to a business meeting that Sunday afternoon. Elaine told him that she would look at her calendar at home and she might come, depending on how she felt. What a set-up! They made sure I was at my desk and heard the conversation. I didn't make anything of it.

Because the meeting was held in Burbank I would go with Elaine and Rob would drive himself. Normally I would drive with Rob because most of the meetings were 30 minutes from our shop. Prior to leaving our house, Elaine asked if I wanted to put on a nice shirt and slacks, or if I wanted to go the way I was. I told her that my work outfit was fine for these meetings. She didn't make a big deal of it and said, "OK honey." As usual I had my Burbank Sportscards work shirt on. We went to the meeting on time and when I entered the room I got the shock of my life.

"SURPRISE!" everyone yelled! For a few seconds I just stood there, shell-shocked out of my socks. At that point I saw my grandson Ryan run toward me, followed by Rob and Amy. Elaine was elated. She got me good! There were my friends and my family and they were getting a big kick out of it. More than sixty people were in attendance and I got a little emotional as I picked up my grandson. My kids got the biggest kick out of it. They were just eating it up. They were laughing and kept telling me that they got me. They sure did! Great job, Elaine and kids!

Twelve out-of-town friends came in from the Boston area to join in this event. Elaine invited some of my former business associates and she also invited Agustin Luz and his wife. Joe Volkmar, John Watson, Irv Levin, Dave Gott, Joe Nishimura and their wives were also there. After I had a chance to greet everyone, we sat to down to eat. There was a DJ to provide entertainment.

After we had the main course, Elaine stepped up to the microphone and thanked everyone for being there and told her audience why she was giving me the surprise birthday party. I was always working or was helping others and it was about time that someone did something for Steve. Above the microphone on the wall, a "HAPPY BIRTHDAY PISTA!!!! sign was displayed. They had also made a big cake, which was in the form of a US flag, which was very appropriate. Elaine recalled some of my accomplishments and how involved I was with the Burbank Kiwanis Club, The Habitat for Humanity project, as well as some of the fund raising drives I did, including the Luz-McPherson relief fund. As a matter of fact, my friends from Boston donated in my name to the Habitat for Humanity organization. Thanks, guys!

Elaine then asked Amy and me to join her at the microphone. They wanted me in the middle. Then the DJ started to play the background music for one of my favorite songs "My Way," with a twist. Elaine and Amy alternated in singing lyrics Elaine had written. They called the song "Steve's Way!" I got a copy of the lyrics later and here they are:

> And now, we gather near, cause your birthday's here, and we are certain.
> You're our All-American guy, though you traveled far from the Iron Curtain.
> You worked and studied hard, you passed each test along the byway — and more, much more than this, you did it your way.

For you are a man and what you have done
but make life better for everyone.
Because you can, because you dare,
because you love, because you care.
The record will show you are our hero,
you did it your way.

Your friends are here and family too,
who care for you not in a shy way.
Oh no we love you so —
we're telling you our way.

I was so moved by their rendition of "Steve's Way!" — as were my friends and the rest of the family. Elaine and Amy did a great job and the party was a fantastic success. My thanks to my loving family and my friends who journeyed 3,000 miles to join in the festivities. What friends. We love them! Thanks, guys!

For some periods from 1997 to 1999, Elaine was doing fairly well, health-wise. She was getting back to being more like herself and she went on with her normal duties. She wasn't 100%, but was doing much better than the previous years. She was able to do many more things than before. That was a big improvement, but would soon change.

It had been more than eleven years since Elaine had become sick, but then we were hit with more bad news. In 2000, her right leg started to swell up. She was diagnosed with stage 2 lymphoma cancer. It was a terrible blow to us. Just as Elaine was getting a little better and was more like herself! She was feeling better than she had for the past ten years. We could not believe it! Just how much suffering must she endure? Why was this happening to her? She had never hurt anyone. We went to get second and third opinions, first from UCLA and then from the City of Hope Medical Center. The results were the same, but with slightly different treatment recommendations.

We were beside ourselves. One of the hardest things we had to do was to tell our children. They both took it very hard, especially Amy. Amy would go on the Internet and research Elaine's illness. We learned a lot about lymphoma. In the beginning of this, we did not tell her mother or my mother about the latest problem with Elaine. There

Robert's family December 2001:
His wife Sally, Robert, Samantha and Ryan.

was no reason to let them worry more than they already did. My mom was close to ninety now, and Elaine's mother not far behind her. We finally told them when Elaine started chemotherapy. We did not want them to find out from the rest of the family or from our friends.

We relied on our love for each other and I was there to support her in every way I could. We were going to do the best we could and depend on the advice of our doctors. Our love for each other would help us overcome, besides, we are each other's best friends. It's a great feeling to be in love and I love Elaine and my children immensely. Our friends are very supportive, and we are very blessed by that.

About a year after she was first diagnosed with cancer, Elaine received chemotherapy. Up to that point the doctors were waiting and monitoring her. That's standard procedure. After her right leg got quite enlarged, the doctor started the chemo.

In July 2001, Elaine received a summons for jury duty. She went to her cancer specialist to get a medical excuse because of her cancer and the treatment for it. The doctor advised her that she no longer had cancer, therefore there was no need to give her a medical excuse. The blood tests were good and everything looked great. What a nice surprise! Elaine was so happy her cancer was in remission. Thank God, we thought.

A month or so later, she had her regular visit with her doctor. He was leaving the practice within the next few days, so this was the last time he would see Elaine. He felt comfortable with her checkup but ordered a battery of tests, including a CAT scan to make sure that everything was OK. Elaine made the appointments and took the tests.

A few days after all the tests were completed, we received a very disturbing call from her new doctor. He wanted to see Elaine as soon as possible because there were problems revealed by the tests. The cancer was not in remission and it was spreading.

There was also a large mass of cancer pressing against her right kidney and the right kidney was not functioning. This was something new and unexpected. Elaine was at our shop when she got the call and started to cry. How could this be when she had been told only three weeks before that she no longer had cancer? We were devastated once again.

Shil designed this puzzle proposal and gave it to Amy in June 2001. Their last names are incorporated into the puzzle.

Shil and Amy in a 2001 photo.

We saw the new doctor and he explained the new situation to us. It did not look very good. We were very concerned about the cancer pressing against the right kidney. He recommended that we start radiation therapy as soon as possible to relieve the pressure on the kidney, but he was not sure if the kidney would be saved. He told us that we needed to see a radiation specialist right away. The radiologist concurred with our doctor. Within a week, Elaine started radiation treatment. Once the problem with her kidney was under control, further chemotherapy might be in order. The doctors will have to do more aggressive treatment from this point forward in order to keep the cancer in check.

We now have to do CAT scans at least twice a year to keep a closer eye on her cancer. Now she is in constant pain. Her body is burning and the doctors can't control it. We saw a skin specialist, allergist, and every other type of a doctor, but none of them are able to help her. There is no clear forecast or prescription by any of her doctors to this day. Her numerous medications are taking their toll on her. Since her body was filled with pain, strong medications were required. Sometime she can hardly walk because of all the medications. She sleeps only for a few hours a night. The itch at times was overwhelming, and the medications and creams helped very little. Some nights she would just cry in bed. I would hold her and tell her that everything would be all right.

The September 11, 2001 attack on the World Trade Center hit many very hard, and Elaine much harder than many. Her nervous system was already fragile and this event got to her in a terrible way. There was no personal connection, but because of her weak condition she also felt the pain of those who lost love ones.

I'm dumbfounded why doctors can't stop her body from burning. They believe that it's the combination of her cancer and her nervous system. They are concentrating on those two things at the present time. Sometimes she gets into a depression and that makes things much worse. I'm doing everything possible to help her and to ease her pain. I'm frustrated and heartsick over her suffering. I wish there was more I could do for her. We are praying to God that a solution to her problems will be found soon. She has suffered long enough. It's time to give her her life back, so she may enjoy the retirement years with her children and grandchildren. She more than deserves it! She has done so much for others; let her have some peace, to enjoy life and her family.

Now I'll speak of Amy, our daughter. She was born in September 1, 1970, and for a while things were hard for us, as related earlier. I took her handicap very hard and was mad at the world for a while. It did not take long for her to cheer me up. Her beautiful smile made me melt every time I looked at her. Soon, she became something very special for us. The middle name we gave her was "Joy," and she was all of that: the joy of our life. She lights up the room when she enters with her warmth and personality. She is a very outgoing girl and has not allowed her handicap to interfere with her goals.

Amy worked hard in school to get good grades. She was highly vocal about unqualified teachers. She felt that some teachers had no place in a classroom and made her opinions known. She was very active with Girl Scouts and later with dancing. Her favorite thing to do at home was jigsaw puzzles, the larger and more complicated, the better. She had patience and enjoyed that a lot. She also liked to play quiz games with Elaine. They would play for hours at the kitchen table. Scrabble was one of her favorites.

For years, we were very involved with the Variety Club to raise money for children whose parents could not afford prosthetics for their child. Amy would appear year after year on the TV telethons to raise money. Monty Hall was the MC at the telethon and show biz people would appear in order to help raise the funds. Amy had a great personality and was great in front of the camera.

When Amy was eight or nine years old, she wanted to learn a musical instrument. First she tried the harp, then the organ. She liked the organ, so we purchased a nice organ that had special features. The foot pedals were the chords and she was able to play the melody with her left hand while playing the chords with her foot. A short time later, we hired an organ teacher who lived only a few houses from us. Amy enjoyed the lessons and we were pleased with her progress. She was also taking dancing lessons and loved it very much.

In May of 1987 she performed in the "Best of Burbank" competition with another girl named Judy. They put on a great performance. Amy danced in the background while Judy sang the song "New York, New York," then they both danced and the audience loved it.

After graduating from high school in 1988, she went to college at California State University, in Long Beach (CSULB). While in college, she started to work part time. In September 1989, once again I had to dig into my pockets. I bought Amy her first new car, a red two-door Toyota Corolla. She loved the car and had it for more than ten years. Her side trip to France while still at CSULB started out as a disaster, but became a great learning experience for her. She has many close girlfriends, and they have a great time when they get together. Everybody loves Amy.

After getting her bachelor's degree, she decided to get a job and work toward her Master's Degree on a part time basis. At first Amy worked for the County of Orange part time, then in 1995 she got a job at PacifiCare in Santa Ana.

She was hired to help set up the Stop Smoking program there, the same work she had done in Orange County. PacifiCare did not have an anti-smoking program in place at that time. She worked full time and went to school for her Master's Degree after work. It was very hard, but she was determined to do it. We were very proud of her. Finally, she graduated in 1998. In spite of being busy with work and school, Amy also had a social life. Elaine was getting a little nervous as to when she would be getting married, but Amy was not quite ready. Amy was waiting for bells to ring and whistles to blow. I told her that it does not work like that. There are no guarantees in life. I jokingly told her many times that I'm still waiting for the bells to ring. We both laughed.

In early May 1999, Amy was at home and went to visit a friend with Elaine. Amy drove Elaine's new Toyota Camry. When they came home, Amy told me how much she loved mom's new car. I told her that if she liked the car so much, then take it, it's hers. She told me that her Corolla was still running well, but she thanked me for the offer.

A couple of days later she called me. She told me that she couldn't believe that she turned down a new car and wanted to know if the offer was still good. I told her that it was. I told her to select the color she wanted and I would buy it for her. She got very excited and thanked me. A couple of days later she called and she told me that she loved the Camry, but she would prefer a Honda EXL, which was about the same price. She told me that the Honda was more for younger people and she would prefer that, but she would take the Camry if that is what I bought her.

The following day, Elaine and I went to some Honda dealers near us to test drive the Honda EXL. It was a nice riding car, and the same week I bought one. Amy liked the idea that the radio controls were on the steering wheel, which would make it easier for her since she does not have a right arm. Dealing with car dealerships is my next favorite pastime after root canal! The pressure tactics and the games they play turn me off. In order to save money and aggravation, I decided to buy the car on the Internet and saved over $2,500 on the same model car we were looking for.

For the past few months we have been making arrangements for her upcoming marriage to a wonderful young man whom we like very much. His name is Shil and he is a chemist. Amy and Shil live in Concord, in northern California, not far from San Francisco. One day in June 2001, I got a call from Shil at the store. He told me that he wanted to propose to Amy and asked for my permission. He e-mailed me a picture of a puzzle that he had designed and then had made up.

The puzzle proposal was very creative and clever. Part of the puzzle was a question: "Amy will you marry me?" When he gave her the puzzle, he held back a few of the pieces. It took Amy a few hours to put together the large puzzle, but at the end she was upset. Some pieces were missing, she told Shil. He pulled the missing pieces from his pocket and gave them to her. She put the pieces into the puzzle and with a loud "YES" she put in the final piece, which was also the answer to the question. Shil was very sneaky. He had only a yes piece made up, and gave her no option to say no! Now that is how you're supposed to propose. Amy was very impressed. So were Elaine and I. Finally, she made up her mind! Hurray for Amy! Thanks, Amy! Hurray for Shil! Thanks Shil!

The day Amy and Shil got engaged, we received a call from Shil's parents, who live in Canada. They congratulated us and invited us to Canada for a July engagement party. What a great party! Elaine and I had a wonderful time. We had a chance to meet their large family and circle of friends. Shil's parents originally came from India, but have lived in Canada for many years. Shil lived in Canada also and came to the states in the 90s. He had also attended CSULB. He lived in the same complex as Amy did and they met at poolside, I believe. They were good friends before they started to date each other.

Amy still works for PacifiCare, but now out of the Concord office. She changed jobs within the company in order to be with Shil. She is doing very well and loves her job very much. She calls on doctors and medical groups, educating them as to what her company does or does not cover under certain medical procedures. PacifiCare has been very good for her. Before she moved to Concord they wanted her to become a department manager, but Amy turned down the opportunity. She likes to get along with everybody. If you are the boss it's hard to do. We are very proud of her and have a very special relationship with her.

Amy wanted a garden ceremony, with an indoor reception. When it was time to hire a banquet hall for the wedding, Amy and Elaine visited several banquet centers and finally decided on the Castaways, on the hill overlooking Burbank.

It's a beautiful place and we have been there many times before. Once the hall was reserved, a big burden was removed from Amy's shoulders. The date is set for June 22, 2002. Shil's family is also planning a big ceremony for them in Canada, in early August. They expect to have about 400 people in attendance there. We expect to have about 150 here in Burbank.

Within weeks, we hired the photographer, florist, entertainment, and video people. Soon after that, they found a wedding dress they both loved. I let them do the work while I paid the bills. Once all the arrangements were completed, the kids decided to buy a house. They went house hunting in and around Concord. I did not want to interfere, but I did talk them out of one of the homes. They were very serious about a just-completed new house with a hill behind it. I advised them to forget about it. Having a hill behind the house could complicate things in years to come.

Several weeks later, they found a beautiful new five-bedroom house in Fairfield, California. Elaine and I went to visit the kids in late October 2001, and saw the house. We were very pleased. I wanted to help them lower their monthly payments so we loaned the kids money. They just closed escrow and are moving in the first of December. Shil wanted to buy the house as an investment, whereas Amy wanted to wait until after the wedding, but Shil won the battle. This is probably the last one he will win for a while.

We were blessed with two wonderful kids and we are very proud of them. Thanks Rob and Amy!

37

Afterword – Final Thoughts

Many people made my success possible, and to each of you goes my heartfelt gratitude. A very special thanks to the HIAS organization. Without their financial help and sponsorship, we might never have come to America. To my friends, there is no word to describe the way I feel towards you. You made me a better person and your friendship I'll treasure forever. Many people share a piece of this book, because of your contribution in my life. I'll remember you for the rest of my life. To the people of this great nation, thanks for giving my family and me an opportunity to come here and to start our lives over as your friends and neighbors. You are my heroes! God Bless America!

As I look back and reflect on my life, I can't help but wonder what it would have been like if we hadn't seen the light of the Austrian border guard's flashlight. Would we have survived? What would my life have been if I still lived in Hungary? It would not have been anything like the life I lived in the United States. We took a big chance in escaping from Hungary. We risked everything just to be free. Each of us receives a helping hand and we might not even realize it. Others helped my success along the way. They were my friends, neighbors, employees and sometimes total strangers. I could not have done it without their help.

When I came to the States, I did not have the education that was necessary to get a good job. But I was not going to be a laborer for the rest of my life. I was determined to be successful and that required me to get a better education. I wanted to learn more and make a better life for myself. I sacrificed my social life in my teen years to go to school at night. That was the best decision I made in my business career. I sacrificed in my early years, which paid dividends down the road.

I regret many of the things I did in my adulthood. Long hours at work kept me away from my wife and kids. I wish I had spent more time with my kids when they grew up, especially in their early years. I regret the fights with my father, which caused my mom many sleepless nights. I'm sorry Mom! At times I was inflexible and uncompromising, which at times hurt others I love very dearly. If I could live my life over again, I know I would do many things differently. We learn as we go along and we pray that we make the right decision most of the time.

And now it's close to midnight, November 30, 2001, and I'm writing the final paragraph in this book. Finally it's finished. I did it because I wanted to share my story with my family, friends, and others. I found it an incredible journey and hope I communicated that.

This is a favorite quote. In a 1961 speech by John F. Kennedy, Kennedy was actually quoting Theodore Roosevelt ("Citizenship in a Republic," delivered at the Sorbonne, Paris, April 23, 1910):

> The credit belongs to the man who is actually in the arena — whose face is marred by dust and sweat and blood... who knows the great enthusiasms, the great devotions — and spends himself in a worthy cause — who at best if he wins knows the thrills of high achievement — and if he fails at least fails while daring greatly — so that his place will never be with those cold and timid souls who know neither victory or defeat.